The World Affairs Companion

The Essential One-Volume Guide
to Global Issues

New Edition

Gerald Segal

A TOUCHSTONE BOOK
Published by Simon & Schuster
New York   London   Toronto   Sydney   Tokyo   Singapore

SIMON & SCHUSTER/TOUCHSTONE
Simon & Schuster Building
Rockefeller Center
1230 Avenue of the Americas
New York, New York 10020

Copyright © 1991, 1988, 1987 by Gerald Segal

10 9 8 7 6 5 4 3 2 1
Pbk. 10 9 8 7 6 5 4 3 2 1

ISBN 0-671-74157-8
     0-671-74156-X Pbk.

Contents

Acknowledgements

Marrying a journalist can do serious harm to an academic's reputation, but this book is my admission that the essentials of any contemporary international issue *can* be expressed in 1,000 words. Well, more-or-less.

A special debt is owed to Nick Brealey who not only made sure we made the second edition, but persuaded me and his colleagues across the pond into producing a bigger and better third edition. Various academic colleagues, students, the staff of the Royal Institute of International Affairs, and reviewers of earlier editions have caught errors before they reached your eyes.

The author and publishers wish to thank the Stockholm International Peace Research Institute and *The Economist* Newspaper Ltd for permission to reproduce diagrams and charts. The maps were drawn by Richard Natkiel.

Gerald Segal
April 1991

Maps

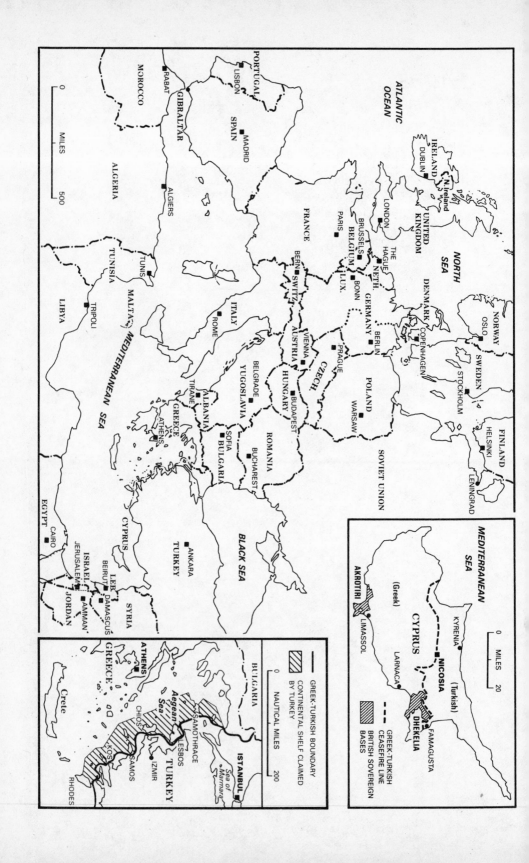

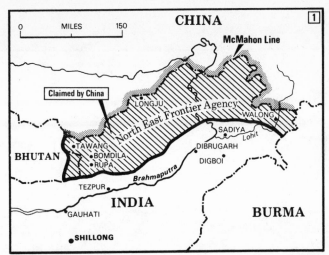

1

CHINA

0 MILES 150

McMahon Line

Claimed by China

LONGJU

North East Frontier Agency

WALONG

SADIYA

Lohit

DIBRUGARH

BHUTAN

TAWANG

BOMDILA

RUPA

DIGBOI

DIGBOI

Brahmaputra

TEZPUR

INDIA

BURMA

GAUHATI

SHILLONG

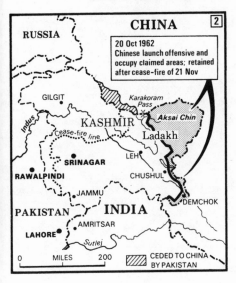

2

RUSSIA

CHINA

20 Oct 1962
Chinese launch offensive and
occupy claimed areas; retained
after cease-fire of 21 Nov

GILGIT

Karakoram
Pass

Aksai Chin

KASHMIR

Ladakh

Indus

Cease-fire line

LEH

SRINAGAR

CHUSHUL

RAWALPINDI

JAMMU

DEMCHOK

PAKISTAN

INDIA

LAHORE

AMRITSAR

Sutlej

0 MILES 200

CEDED TO CHINA
BY PAKISTAN

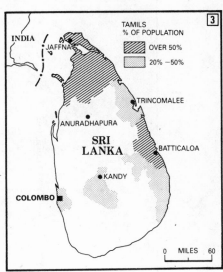

3

INDIA

JAFFNA

TAMILS
% OF POPULATION

OVER 50%

20% – 50%

TRINCOMALEE

ANURADHAPURA

SRI
LANKA

BATTICALOA

KANDY

COLOMBO

0 MILES 60

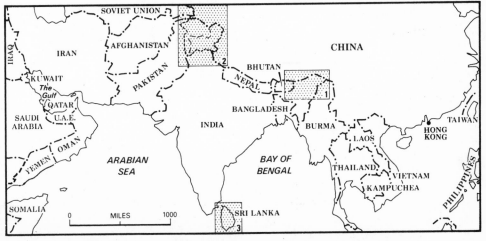

SOVIET UNION

AFGHANISTAN

2

BHUTAN

CHINA

IRAQ

IRAN

KUWAIT

The
Gulf

QATAR

PAKISTAN

NEPAL

1

SAUDI
ARABIA

U.A.E.

BANGLADESH

BURMA

TAIWAN

HONG
KONG

YEMEN

OMAN

INDIA

LAOS

ARABIAN
SEA

BAY OF
BENGAL

THAILAND

VIETNAM

SOMALIA

0 MILES 1000

SRI LANKA

3

KAMPUCHEA

PHILIPPINES

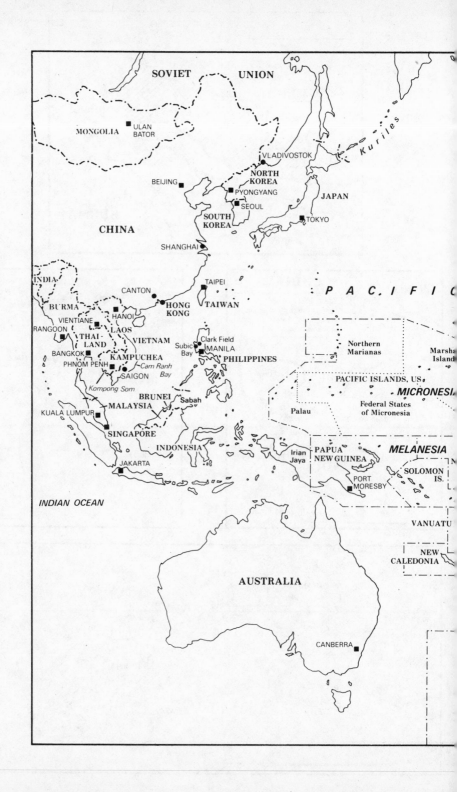

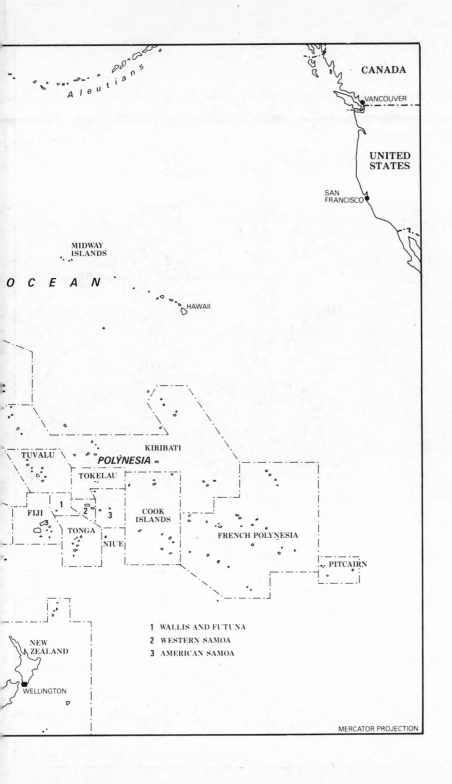

CANADA

VANCOUVER

UNITED
STATES

SAN
FRANCISCO

A l e u t i a n s

O C E A N

MIDWAY
ISLANDS

HAWAII

KIRIBATI

TUVALU   *POLYNESIA*

TOKELAU

FIJI   1

2   3

COOK
ISLANDS

TONGA   FRENCH POLYNESIA

NIUE

PITCAIRN

NEW
ZEALAND

1 WALLIS AND FUTUNA
2 WESTERN SAMOA
3 AMERICAN SAMOA

WELLINGTON

MERCATOR PROJECTION

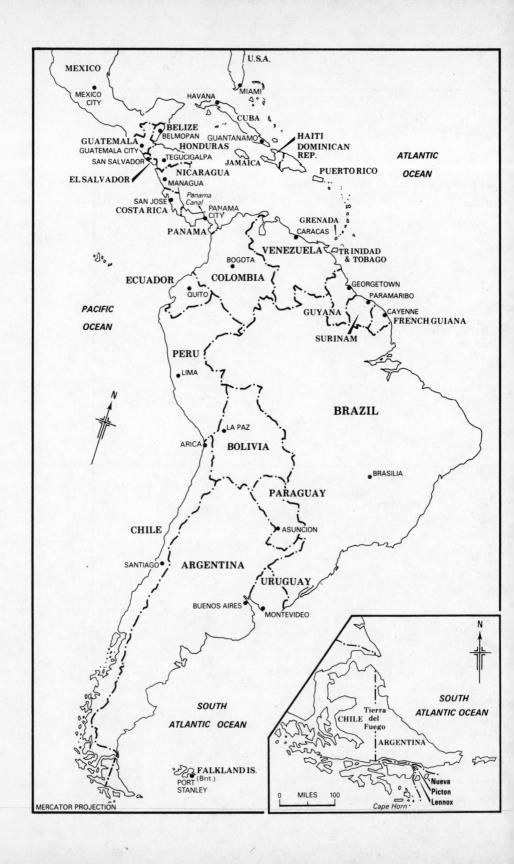

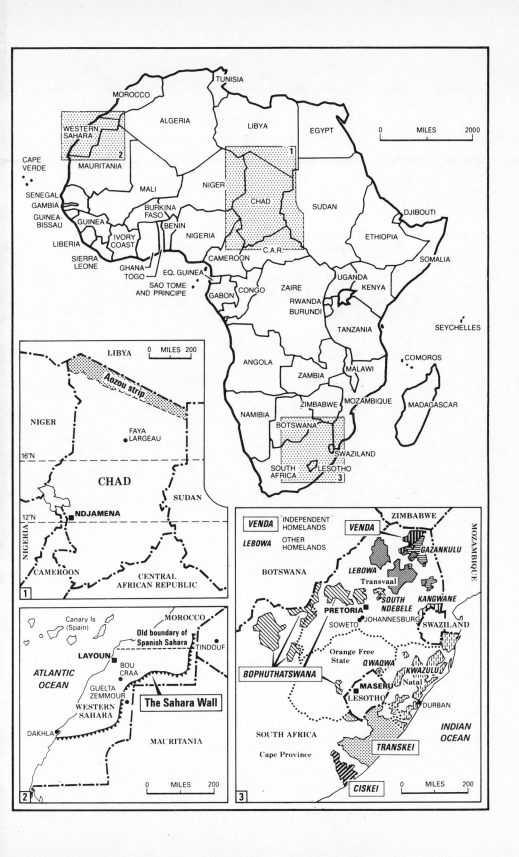

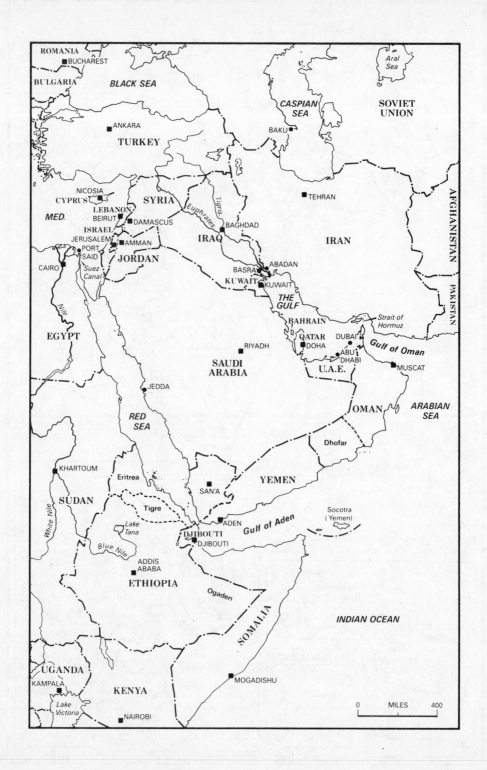

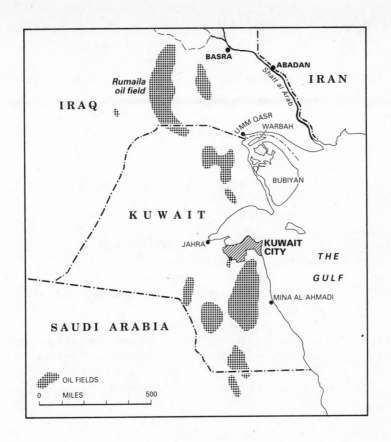

Abbreviations

ABM	Anti-ballistic missile
ADF	Arab Deterrent Force
ASA	Association of Southeast Asia
ASAT	Anti-satellite weapon
ASEAN	Association of Southeast Asian Nations
AWAC	Airborne warning and control system
BW	Biological weapons
CAP	Common Agricultural Policy
CARICOM	Caribbean Community
CENTCOM	Central Command for Southwest Asia
CENTO	Central Treaty Organization
CIA	Central Intelligence Agency
CMEA	Council for Mutual Economic Assistance (also known as COMECON)
CND	Campaign for Nuclear Disarmament
CSCE	Conference on Security and Cooperation in Europe
CW	Chemical weapons
DGSE	French Directorate of External Security
ECSC	European Coal and Steel Community
EC	European Community
EEZ	Exclusive Economic Zone
EMS	European Monetary System
END	European Nuclear Disarmament
EPLF	Eritrean People's Liberation Front
FAO	Food and Agriculture Organization
FDI	Foreign Direct Investment
FDN	Nicaraguan Democratic Front
FNLA	Angolan National Liberation Front
FROLINAT	National Liberation Front (Chad)
G7	Group of Seven (Great Powers)
GATT	General Agreement on Tariffs and Trade
GCC	Gulf Cooperation Council
GCHQ	Government Communications Headquarters
GDP	Gross Domestic Product
GDR	German Democratic Republic
GNP	Gross National Product
HIOE	High-income oil exporter
IAEA	International Atomic Energy Agency
ICAO	International Civil Aviation Organization
ICBM	Intercontinental ballistic missile

ICJ	International Court of Justice
IDA	International Development Association
INF	Intermediate-range nuclear forces
ITO	International Trade Organization
ITU	International Telegraph Union
IRA	Irish Republican Army
KGB	Committee for State Security (USSR)
LRCS	League of Red Cross and Red Crescent Societies
LRTNF	Long-range theatre nuclear force
MAD	Mutual assured destruction
MFA	Multi-fibre Agreement
MIRV	Multiple independently-targeted re-entry vehicle
MNLF	Moro National Liberation Front (Philippines)
MPLA	Angolan People's Liberation Movement
MRBM	Medium range ballistic missile
NATO	North Atlantic Treaty Organization
NIC	Newly industrialized country
NIEO	New International Economic Order
NIIO	New International Information Order
NPA	New People's Army (Philippines)
NPT	Non-proliferation Treaty
OAS	Organization of American States
OAU	Organization of African Unity
OECD	Organization for Economic Cooperation and Development
ONUC	United Nations Operations, Congo
OPEC	Organization of Petroleum Exporting Countries
PDRK	People's Democratic Republic of Korea
PDRY	People's Democratic Republic of Yemen
PLO	Palestine Liberation Organization
RDF	Rapid Deployment Force (US)
ROK	Republic of Korea
SAARC	South Asian Association for Regional Cooperation
SADCC	South Africa Development Coordinating Committee
SADR	Saharan Arab Democratic Republic
SALT	Strategic Arms Limitation Talks
SDI	Strategic Defence Initiative
SDLP	Social Democratic and Labour Party (Northern Ireland)
SDR	Special Drawing Rights
SEATO	Southeast Asian Treaty Organization
SIS	Secret Intelligence Service
SLA	South Lebanon Army
SLBM	Submarine-launched ballistic missile
SLFP	Sri Lankan Freedom Party
SPF	South Pacific Forum

START	Strategic Arms Reduction Talks
SWAPO	Southwest African People's Organization
TULF	Tamil United Liberation Front
UN	United Nations
UNCLOS	United Nations Conference on the Law of the Sea
UNCTAD	United Nations Conference on Trade and Development
UNEP	United Nations Environmental Programme
UNESCO	United Nations Educational, Scientific and Cultural Organization
UNFDAC	United Nations Fund for Drug Abuse Control
UNFICYP	United Nations Force in Cyprus
UNGA	United Nations General Assembly
UNHCR	United Nations High Commission for Refugees
UNICEF	United Nations International Children's Emergency Fund
UNIFIL	United Nations Interim Force in Lebanon
UNITA	National Union for the Total Independence of Angola
UNP	United National Party (Sri Lanka)
WEU	Western European Union
WHO	World Health Organization
WTO	Warsaw Treaty Organization
YAR	Yemen Arab Republic

Introduction

Is the Soviet empire collapsing?
Will Germany and Japan become great military powers?
Will there be more crises like the Iraqi invasion of Kuwait?
Is foreign investment a threat to our independence?

These important and intricate questions confront us daily. But because world politics today seems like such new history, it is impossible to make complete sense of the bewildering and Byzantine actions of all the players on the international board. The aim of this book is to help the newswatcher, newspaper reader, armchair strategist or student of international politics to make sense of the world by providing key facts and brief analyses of the essential issues in the international game.

The new agenda

Since the previous edition, it seems as if we have won a war or lived through a revolution. Certainly 1989, with its concern about the decline of the Superpowers, upheaval in China, and revolution in Europe, was the most important year since the end of the last world war in 1945. As a result, there is a new agenda for international relations, and certainly much that is new to understand. For example, the first flush of 'victory' for the West in the Cold War felt exhilarating, but what follows may be far more dangerous. The Iraqi invasion of Kuwait in 1990, and the subsequent war to free it mounted by the Allies under the UN banner, warns us that the post-Cold War world may be far from peaceful. It certainly suggests that there will be new alignments of friends and foes.

The main issues

The world today faces several main challenges to peace and prosperity. Foremost, of course, is the danger that we might someday use our nuclear weapons and vaporize civilization as we know it. But such weapons are unlikely to be used without there having been a dispute, and therefore it is the massive shifts in the strategic balance of power in recent years that should draw our main attention. Which powers are on the rise and which are on the decline, and what do they all want anyway? Answering such questions brings us to the challenges of the new international interdependence, for it is increasingly clear that states, especially the more developed ones, are no longer truly independent. While this is in part a matter of economic interconnections, there are also new challenges that result from what we are doing to our own habitat. Managing environmental issues relating to our fragile planet has

xxi

only recently been accepted as a matter for discussion at the world's top tables.

History and trivia

So how are we to make sense of all these issues? Deciding what to include in such a guide and what to leave out is difficult. A mass of historical detail would leave the reader without a sense of how the present derives from the past. A welter of up-to-the-minute information would lose touch with the historic roots of conflicts and negotiations. Trying to understand current world problems without appreciating their past is as short-sighted as a doctor trying to diagnose an illness without knowing the patient's medical history. What is more, books of current facts, especially nowadays, are out-of-date before they reach the bookstalls. But there is a place on the shelf, between the encyclopaedia and the quality news magazine, for a book on the world today.

Using the book

Because the book is organized around discrete international issues, some readers may prefer simply to take in those topics that are of current interest. Each entry stands on its own, but its intricacies and interconnections can best be pursued by reading the surrounding entries or by using the Index to find cross-references. Other readers may prefer to read the book in larger chunks or as a broad assessment of current world politics. The first three sections on global issues are meant to set the scene for much of the more detailed information in later sections. But all sections share certain common themes.

The shrinking globe

First, the main players of world politics are strange creations called states. It is a fast-fading truism that states are sovereign – i.e., they control their own fate and therefore are independent actors. But despite official genuflection to this notion, sovereignty is increasingly viewed as merely a Victorian value that is less and less useful to the people of richer states. Of course, much of current world politics concerns states, but decisions and effects are usually far more interdependent.

Unequal players

Moreover, these states are not equal. World politics is often a vicious business where the strong pick on the weak, but it is also a fickle game because states are constantly changing position, with even great powers rising and falling. It used to be said (even in the previous editions of this book) that the Superpowers dominate the globe, but this is now far less true as other powers, such as Japan and the states of Europe, rise to take some of their power and responsibility. Europeans are especially conscious of how they once dominated the world, then faded in the 20th century, and now may be on their way back to greater influence.

East–West, North–South

It is an equally important theme of this book that seemingly intractable conflicts can end with little warning, and new ones emerge just as quickly. The pace of change has never seemed so swift as the last decade of the 20th century. Old certainties about empires which prosper and collapse in double-quick time are replaced by new uncertainties. It used to be true that the Cold War between a capitalist West and a Communist East affected nearly every conflict in the world. This is no longer so, and as a result the old ideologies are hard to find. Similarly, the regular rumblings of the North–South struggle dividing rich and poor barely now appear on the international agenda. Wealthy and starving peoples alike are beginning to accept that an open trading system with easy movement of money is a key to prosperity, even though it means a loss of sovereignty and independence. Indeed, the new interdependence means new challenges to rich and poor.

Finally, the bulk of this book is concerned with conflicts around the globe, few of which are fading just because the Superpowers are. The recent revolutions in the balance of power do not mean that local conflicts will not continue for good or bad local reasons. While there is no single theme that helps us understand these tensions, it is probably true that all essentially depend on the parties involved sorting out their own squabbles. Outsiders can help, and no doubt may have ulterior motives in doing so, but especially at such a time of major strategic shifts, now is the moment *not* to be passive.

Local wars, local solutions

Needless to say, the selection and analysis of world issues cannot be free of all bias. The future may be certain but the past is unpredictable. An attempt is made to present the evidence as understood by the parties but limitations of space preclude a more complete analysis. In any case, no author can hope fully to escape his or her own bias or particular interests. In international politics, where you stand on the issues does often depend on how the globe looks from where you live. Europe and Britain are on the distant northern fringe of an Asian's globe.

Global bias

The selection of topics is not encyclopaedic. Issues that are overwhelmingly domestic (such as Basque terrorism) are left out. Domestic unrest that has important international implications (such as in the Lebanon) is included. An attempt is also made to pinpoint some future trends (such as the Pacific century) while some more-or-less resolved conflicts are omitted. Because the world spins on, some major post-war conflicts, such as the East–West confrontation in Vietnam, have been largely resolved. The issue now rates only passing mention in another section covering more recent Southeast Asian conflict. Certain less pressing issues, for example the points of conflict in Chile–Argentine relations, are included under broader topics. Some issues, such as spies or disaster relief, are not intended to be catalogues of cases but rather to provide perspective for current events, in the hope that what is important and what is trivial in the news will become clearer. Of course, because world affairs are constantly changing,

Perspectives for current events

the most recent events will always be a bit blurred. Even the clearest picture of a fuzzy object will be fuzzy. I hope this book will help to sharpen the focus.

General reading   Suggested reading is provided at the end of each section to help guide those interested in further details and other points of view. Basic facts and the history of international relations are available from a broad range of books. But some of the most useful general compilations include the three Keesing's publications, *Treaties and Alliances* (1990), *Territorial Disputes* (1982) and *Political Dissent* (1983). See also G. Evans and J. Newnham, *The Dictionary of World Politics* (London: Harvester, 1990), A. Palmer, *The Penguin Dictionary of Twentieth Century History* (London: Penguin, 1979), Patrick Brogan, *World Conflicts* (London: I.B. Tauris, 1989), Andrew Boyd, *An Atlas of World Affairs* (London: Methuen, 1987) and Guiseppe Schiavonne, *International Organizations* (London: Macmillan, 1981). On economic issues, of special value is data collected in the United Nations' annual *Statistical Yearbook* and the World Bank's *World Development Report*. On individual regions see the series of *Yearbooks* published by Europa and on the Asian region see the annual *Yearbook of the Far Eastern Economic Review*. Military issues are covered annually in *Strategic Survey* published by the International Institute for Strategic Studies and the Stockholm International Peace Research Institute's *Yearbook*. Current military data comes from the SIPRI annual as well as the *Military Balance* of the IISS. For those interested in current news with access to online computer services, useful sources include *World Reporter*. See also *Keesing's Contemporary Archives* or *Facts on File*. There is of course no substitute for a good batch of daily newspapers and the quality weekly press.

1

THE POWER OF
POLITICS

Shaping the World Today

Why are world affairs organized as they are? Why are there strange units called states when they are rarely homogeneous? Indeed, why are these states of such different sizes and how can you change your status? In the last decade of the 20th century, much like after a great war, there is an opportunity to reshape the world today. But first we need to know how we put ourselves in this unusual position in the first place.

Global snapshots

In fact, it is only in the most recent years of human existence that we have had a world of regular contacts between different states – what we call international politics. Exploration of most of the planet has been accomplished only in the past three hundred years, detailed mapping is less than one hundred years old and we never saw the entire planet until the 1960s, when the missions to outer space sent back the first memorable snapshots. We now know that world affairs take place in a finite space: but since that space is in fact a globe there are no 'edges' to the world nor is there a 'right side up' (unlike a board game).

Who lives where?

The roughly spherical 'board' of international relations is mostly (70%) water. The other 30% is not densely populated either. Eleven per cent is arable or under cultivation, 24% is pasture, 31% is forest and 33% is occupied by buildings, roads or not used at all. Nearly all this land is now divided into two parts (the Americas and Eurasia/Africa) but both can in turn be sensibly divided into two further sub-sections (North and South America; Eurasia and Africa). Although these huge 'islands' move imperceptibly, they can be regarded as permanent features on the board. The land is inhabited by some 5,000 million people, 32% of whom live in South Asia, 25% in East Asia, 15% in Europe, 13% in the Americas and 11% in Africa. The people playing the game have divided the land into over two hundred organized political units, most of which are under one government and called states.

Manipulating maps

Different representations, or maps, of this international board can be drawn. The only one that roughly represents the physical realities is a globe. But like trying to press orange peel flat on a page, there are inevitable distortions in any attempt to compress three dimensions into two. Maps can also be drawn to show relative sizes of population, gross national product, ideologies, military power, percentage of world trade or resources. Depending on which aspect of the world is being discussed, any one map, or a combination of maps, may be more relevant. And to complicate matters further, some states have joined in alliance or union with others, forming regional, ideological or military blocks that represent common interests. But this is getting ahead of the story. We need to step back and understand how the present political map became today's unequal patchwork.

The rise of European power in the 15th century marks the start of world politics as we know it. Before then three-quarters of the world was inhabited by people essentially minding their own business, gathering food, herding animals and cultivating the land by hand in splendid isolation from most other people except their immediate neighbours. Three-quarters of the world's population lived in areas (mostly Eurasia) where more effective cultivation by plough had evolved. Yet most of these people also existed in isolation, albeit isolated civilizations instead of isolated villages. The break in this pattern and the transition to more regular and extensive contacts between civilizations only came with European expansion. *The origins of world politics*

In the 15th century the European kingdoms found their trade routes to the south and east blocked by powerful, hostile empires. Armed with modern firearms and bold enough to attempt hazardous, long-distance sea ventures, first the Spanish and Portuguese and later the north Europeans set out in search of new trade routes and new opportunities. Sea routes rather than land routes formed the first avenues of this new international contact. Of course some, notably the Russians, began expanding on land eastward, but most sailed west to 'discover' and conquer the Americas. By the 18th century, the basic structure of the modern international political system was established. Only East and South West Asia escaped. By the 19th century, Africa had become the focus of European colonial attention, while the older colonies of the Americas were gaining their independence. *European expansion*

Colonial rule rarely lasted for more than a few hundred years. In some cases it merely added a layer of somebody else's experience to a political order that was already established. European colonialism was certainly not the first experience of imperialism, or responsible for bringing conflict to previously peaceful areas. The spread of European power brought new political and religious ideas in its wake and closer international relationships in trade, including foodstuffs. The interchange of plants helped create a boom in food production which spawned uncontrolled growth in population. More people meant, in turn, a greater demand for trade and hence multiplied the clash of interests between states. What had previously been merely trade in luxury items now encompassed trade in food and people (slaves). *Colonial power*

This exchange of ideas and goods where interests clashed, led to wars over power and wealth. There was also a new desire for *New world politics*

a trading currency of exchange, to replace the old barter system.
This creation of money also helped create new mercantile classes
which began to challenge hereditary rulers or military leaders for
power. In the United States and France especially, new political
orders were established in the 18th century which provided for
more popular rule. The impact of these ideas of individualism
shook the political order of Europe and hence changed the way
states dealt with each other in the wider world.

Industrial
revolution
Along with these new politics came new power. Europe's first
industrial revolution in coal and iron, coupled with new commercial inventions, vastly increased the region's power. This was
swiftly followed by a second industrial revolution, in steel and
electricity, which soon spread to the rapidly expanding empires
of Russia and the United States. However, unlike Western Europe
and the United States, Russian power was built on a much more
fragile domestic political base. The Russian Revolution of 1917 not
only laid the groundwork for the Superpower status of the Soviet
Union today but also introduced a new idea in international politics – the alliance of people on the basis of class rather than
nationality, religion or culture. By claiming to cut across state
boundaries, this notion at first challenged the state system. But
the Soviet Union, as much out of weakness as anything, soon
came to accept the existing international order in the short term,
while it developed its strength at home.

The rise of
Superpowers
The collapse of the old Russian empire and its replacement by
the Soviet Union, following the First World War, took place as the
old empires of China and the Ottomans were being dismembered.
New power centres also grew up in the United States and Japan.
Certainly the Soviet and American powers offered the appeal of
new, popular diplomacy opposed to the bankrupt balance-of-
power principles of fading European empires. The seeds were
sown for a new great power confrontation – the conflict of Soviet
and American political idealism.

In the Second World War the United States triumphed in Asia,
and, with its allies, in Europe. After the war, the most powerful
land power was the Soviet Union. As it swept through Eastern
Europe, the Soviet Union planted friendly, communist-led régimes
and, in its wake, challenged the political order in Western Europe.
The old empires of the European powers were shattered and the
board was reset.

Unequal states
The post-war world was no more equal than that before 1939.
In fact, the international balance of power was dominated by two
great powers and a few aspiring or fading lesser powers. The six
largest accounted for nearly 50% of the total land area (Soviet
Union 14.8%, Canada 6.6%, China 6.4%, United States 6.2%,
Brazil 5.6%, Australia 5.2%). The four most populous accounted

for about half the world's population (China 23%, India 16%, Soviet Union 6%, United States 5%). By the 1980s, the four most productive were to account for about half the world's Gross National Product (United States 22%, Soviet Union 11%, Japan 10%, West Germany 7%).

Fifty-one states formed the United Nations in 1945 but it was already clear that not all the states were equally important. Two powers, the Soviet Union and United States, clearly dominated all the others (the term Superpower was coined in 1944). However, the locus of world power had not entirely shifted from Europe. The continent was effectively divided into East and West and the Superpowers split the Europeans into the key alliances that formed the basis of their global contest for power. But although the European allies were important to Moscow and Washington, the decline of the European age of international relations was already apparent.

East versus West

The basically East–West pattern of the international game was undone to some extent by the second major feature of the post-1945 world, decolonization and the granting of independence to many developing states. Although this process tripled the number of international players, it did not change the essential pattern of international power or wealth. These new states may have accounted for large swathes of the world's surface and huge segments of its population but they lacked power to alter the essential East–West balance.

New states divided

The new states might have had a greater impact if they had formed a coherent group, but they were deeply divided by ideology, wealth, location, size, culture and type of colonial legacy. The conflict which had the most significance on the East–West pattern was the Sino–Soviet split in the early 1960s. China, the third largest power, slid out of the Soviet embrace and drifted towards greater independence. But neither China, nor any other grouping of states, was able to form an effective third force to challenge the Superpowers. International relations were more complex with an independent China and an assortment of 'non-aligned' states, but the Superpowers had little need to take their eyes off the fundamental East–West balance.

The centrality of East–West relations also depended on the third great change in the post-1945 world – the development of nuclear weapons. These devastating weapons for the first time gave humankind the ability to destroy life on the planet. World leaders now held the fate of the planet in their hands; national security became, in part, global security. This nuclear revolution, coupled with the third industrial revolution in electronics and communications, made the world a smaller and, at the same time, more dangerous place.

Nuclear revolution

War dead   Although the nuclear threat hung most ominously over the northern hemisphere, it is in the south that most people have died in wars since 1945. Of the total of more than 21 million, East Asia led the way with 6 million civilian and 3.4 million military dead. Africa suffered 4 million civilian and 1.4 million military deaths, and South Asia had 2.5 million civilian and 0.6 million military dead. The Middle East 'only' had 0.7 million civilian and 1.3 million military deaths, while Latin America had a 'mere' 0.4 million civilian and 0.2 million military dead. The nuclear age was still an era of carnage in conventional warfare.

Yet just as European politics seemed to be getting boring and while there seemed to be no end to the conflicts in the developing world, the balance of power lurched again. In the past, most shifts were manifest during war, but in the late 1980s the nuclear threat helped ensure peaceful change. The United States was gradually coming to terms with its declining influence, even though many in the United States were reluctant to accept this view – especially in the light of the United States' leading role in the Iraq-Kuwait crisis. But it was the rapid reforms in the Soviet Union that took the world by surprise. Mikhail Gorbachev pulled back Soviet forces from distant engagements and above all, allowed the East Europeans to abandon Communism. The breaching of the Berlin Wall on 9 November 1989 marked the end of the Cold War, and perhaps a new European renaissance. Not since 1945 had the balance of power been so uncertain.

Reading

P. Kennedy, *The Rise and Fall of the Great Powers* (London: Unwin/Hyman, 1988).

W. McNeill, *The Pursuit of Power* (Oxford: Basil Blackwell, 1982).

J.M. Roberts, *The Pelican History of the World* (London: Pelican, 1980).

L.S. Stavrianos, *The World Since 1500* (London: Prentice-Hall, 1982).

Fading Superpowers and New Great Powers

The rise and fall of great powers, not to mention their consequent rivalry, is the greatest of games in the world today. For a brief few decades since 1945, there emerged two so-called Superpowers who had the nuclear weapons capable of destroying all of civilization in a nuclear holocaust, alongside the awesome ability to deploy military forces around the globe. But by 1990, the confidence of the Superpowers in managing international affairs was clearly slipping. The world was gradually reverting to the more familiar, yet more complex, scramble of great power politics.

The Superpower age emerged as the United States and Soviet Union dominated the post Second World War world. Each led one of the two most powerful military alliances and both controlled more nuclear weapons than any other state. They each espoused political programmes hostile to the other and struggled to win friends and influence in distant parts of the globe.

Although the Russians and Americans had worked together to defeat Germany and Japan, they could not agree on the shape of the post-war world. Europe was divided along the lines of military control agreed during the war. It certainly was unnatural that central Europe should be ruthlessly divided by what Churchill called an 'iron curtain', but until a clear dividing line was drawn, crises were commonplace. The demarcation of spheres of influence became a feature of the Cold War – a conflict in which it was too dangerous for two nuclear powers to fight directly, but which allowed their rivalry to be played out by proxy or in a war of words and sabre-rattling. *Hanging the Iron Curtain*

Europe was sufficiently stabilized by the Cold War that the main instabilities soon emerged in the regions more distant from the direct interests of the Superpowers. The Korean War of 1950–3, was followed by a series of crises in Asia and the Middle East as Superpower conflict was 'displaced' from Europe and parts of the developing world sought independence from the old European great powers. But the most dangerous conflict of all – over Cuba in 1962 – involved the Soviet deployment of nuclear missiles in the American backyard. The two Superpowers were sufficiently scared by how close they came to nuclear war to establish new systems for managing crisis and sign the first major arms control agreement – the Partial Test Ban pact of 1963. *Developing détente*

As the Superpowers recognized that their nuclear arsenals were not useful instruments of policy, they also began to realize *Learning the limits of power* the real limits to their super status and the risks they should run as rivals. Strategic Arms Limitation Talks (SALT) agreements were reached in 1972 and in 1975 measures for East-West détente in Europe were signed in Helsinki. But as far as both Superpowers were concerned, the limits that such agreements placed on their rivalry, did not mean the end of their competition.

Renting the Third World

The Soviet Union was bound to win some new friends in the developing world in the 1960s and 1970s as, unlike the former colonial powers, it started from almost no base of influence. As states were given their freedom and suffered subsequent bouts of instability, the United States and its allies were bound to suffer some reversals. Egypt, Syria, Ghana and North Vietnam were among some of the earliest developing states to take Soviet aid. But during the 1970s it became increasingly clear to the Superpowers that while they thought they could buy the friendship of developing states, they could in fact only rent it for a day.

The China card

The United States attempted to shift the balance in its favour by improving relations with the second most powerful Communist country, China. The Sino–Soviet split was the single most important alteration in the strategic balance since 1945 and for a time China seemed prepared to co-operate with the United States in a quasi-alliance against the Soviet Union. But by the early 1980s China realized that its own priority, domestic economic development, was hampered by its obsession with the 'Soviet threat'. China's more independent foreign policy left the Superpowers to face the decline of their power more starkly.

The new Cold War

By 1980, the Superpowers seemed to be trying to deal with their frustrations by descending into what was called a 'new Cold War'. The Soviet invasion of Afghanistan in late 1979 and the election of the conservative Reagan administration in the United States in 1980 led to a heightened tension, mostly manifest in rougher rhetoric about competition. But in most spheres, the reality was far less dangerous. The Polish crisis of 1980–1 lasted far longer than the Czech crisis of 1968, but at no time did the United States seriously challenge the Soviet sphere of influence in Eastern Europe. The Iran-Iraq War raged from 1980, with oil tankers regularly being sunk, yet both Superpowers showed immense restraint. And by increasing the size of their nuclear arsenals without upsetting the stability of deterrence, the Superpowers could merely threaten to make the rubble bounce higher.

Cutting the Superpowers down to size

The impotence of nuclear weapons and the inability of the Superpowers to gain by conflict in the developing world encouraged a rethink of what it meant to be a Superpower. As the United States and the Soviet Union lost confidence, China, Japan and the European Community began to assert their claim to take some of the 'super' out of Superpower. The United States recognized that it no longer dominated the international economy and had to treat Japan and Western Europe in particular with much greater care. Yet it was the Soviet Union that was in the deepest trouble, as its economy failed. Both Superpowers were in the mood for a deal, if only to salvage something from their once-exalted status.

The selection of Mikhail Gorbachev as leader of the Soviet Union in 1985 led to the adoption of major reforms in Moscow's domestic and foreign policies. But it was the belief that a breathing space was needed from a tense international atmosphere that led to the decision in 1989 to allow the Soviet allies in Eastern Europe to cast off Communist government and become independent states. Yet this defeat for Soviet power was not a simple gain for the United States. The real winners were the West Europeans who soon found various East Europeans knocking on the door of the European Community. *Ending the Cold War*

The lifting of the overlay of Superpower relations was uneven. On nuclear weapons issues, the Superpowers still dominated. But in Europe there was an emerging five-power framework comprising the Superpowers along with Germany, France and Britain, and in Asia, Japan, China and India were all experimenting with their own versions of multipolarity. In the Middle East, the Iraqi invasion of Kuwait was met by an American-led response from the international community in which the Soviet Union and other great powers played a constructive part. The defeat of Iraq in 1991 would not have been possible had the United States had to act alone. As the euphoria over the ending of the Cold War faded, it gradually became clear that the new multipolar world might be even more dangerous. *New great power politics*

Reading

M. Bowker and P. Williams, *Superpower Détente* (London: Sage, 1988).

R. Garthoff, *Détente and Confrontation* (Washington: Brookings, 1985).

F. Halliday, *The Making of the Second Cold War* (London: Verso, 1983).

P. Kennedy, *The Rise and Fall of the Great Powers* (London: Unwin/Hyman, 1988).

M. McGwire, *Military Objectives in Soviet Foreign Policy* (Washington: Brookings, 1987).

J. Nye, *Bound to Lead* (New York: Basic Books, 1990).

How Empires Die

It usually takes centuries for empires to fade, and war is usually the handmaiden. The great empires of antiquity, whether in China, Rome or Mesopotamia certainly died due to a lethal combination of 'imperial overstretch' and internal decay. Even in the 20th century, European empires faded under similar circumstances. But in the nuclear age, the thought that nuclear-powered empires might die in the same fashion would be enough to turn most people into supporters of colonialism. Thankfully, there seems to be new and more peaceful ways of coping with the end of empires.

From Turkey to Britain
The grand Ottoman Empire of Turkey collapsed in the traditional way – under threat of external attack and due to internal decay. The resulting instability was so severe that unrest in its former holdings in the Balkans provided the spark that lit the First World War in 1914. By contrast, Britain may have won the Second World War, but the cost was so heavy that it too surrendered its empire on which the sun never set. But the post-1945 decolonization of European empires was a far more peaceful process, if only because there was a stand-off between the two new Superpowers of the Soviet Union and the United States. Most of the bloodshed was confined to regional conflict.

An American empire
In the good old days of empires, the Superpowers might have been expected simply to snap up the pieces that fell off older powers. But empire-building in the late 20th century had to be less formal because of the risk of nuclear war. So the United States held on to its power by concentrating on economic influence, and by only using its military punch as the last resort. In Vietnam, that brute force was useless, but closer to home in Latin America it proved more effective. In any case, the American empire was rarely as formal or as powerful as that of the old European empires. To be sure, there were formal alliances with Europeans, Asians and states in the developing world, but especially in the more developed world, the United States was rarely able to enforce its will as was common in the heyday of European colonialism.

The Russian empire
The other Superpower – the Soviet Union – was quite a different matter. Most of its empire was acquired at the time of European colonialism. But as a continental power, Russia merely extended its borders and did not depend on long lines of communication by sea as did Britain and France. When all other European empires had retreated, Russia (and China) remained the only

two formal empires still in control, and Russia even extended its grasp to include Eastern Europe. But the iron law of empires could not be ignored.

Internal decay, and pressure from the outside world and the occupied people, were key forces driving Mikhail Gorbachev to reform Russia by abandoning the outer-empire. Although he willingly surrendered Eastern Europe, by 1990 he was at least trying to fight for control of the inner empire of the Soviet Union. So far the decolonization has been remarkably swift and peaceful. Most of the bloodshed inside the inner empire has been one minority killing another and the troops seemingly under Moscow's control have merely been trying to maintain law and order. But as factionalism was mixed with nationalism, as in the Caucasus and Central Asia, the strains of imperial overstretch became painful. Moldavia wanted to join Romania, the Baltic republics wanted independence, and even Armenia, Georgia and parts of the Ukraine wanted to go it alone.

Russia's empire shrivels

Europe held its breath as the air leaked, sometimes violently, out of the balloon that was the Russian empire. The shrivelled remains, Russia, still looked like being the largest country in either Asia or Europe, but it was shaping up as a far less impressive power. As Russia rapidly sought inspiration from other imperial collapses, there was even talk of learning something from the French or British experience.

Managing Russia's retreat

Only Britain and France have retained any kind of coherent relationship with their former colonies. But France, unlike Britain, has only recently begun to try to organize a Gallic commonwealth. A pioneer summit was held on 17–19 February 1986 (in Paris, of course) and was attended by more than forty representatives, from Canada to Vietnam. Algeria, who fought a bloody war of independence, was a notable absentee. Plans for an earlier summit were always ruined by the 'Canada question' – Ottawa's objection to independence for its French-speaking province of Quebec.

The Gallic commontalk

This Gallic commontalk is so far only focused on encouraging the protection of the French language and culture. It has a long way to go to catch up that other great gathering of colonies – the Commonwealth. This grouping of forty-eight states, including the United Kingdom, represents one billion people – a quarter of the world's population – in countries from Canada to Tonga. Although the Commonwealth lacks any constitutional or federal authority, none of the other former colonial powers maintains such cordial relations with the vast majority of its former colonies. Unlike other organizations set up to promote Third World interests, the Commonwealth includes some developed states. Discussions on aid and a new international economic order can take place in a more manageable and practical forum.

God save the
British
monarch   The foundation of the Commonwealth was laid by the creation of Canada as a Dominion of Britain in 1867, Australia in 1900, and New Zealand in 1907. At the imperial conference of 1926, the United Kingdom and the Dominions were defined as autonomous and this principle was enshrined in the Statute of Westminster in 1931. The British monarch remained the titular head of state for many Commonwealth members, and was nominally the head of the Commonwealth. In 1946, the Canadians passed a citizenship act which made their people Canadian citizens first, and British subjects second. Other Commonwealth states followed suit.

Decolonization   In 1947, independence was granted to India, Pakistan, Ceylon and Burma, and the ensuing decades saw a flood of colonies given their freedom. In 1949 the Irish Republic withdrew from the Commonwealth but when India became a republic, in the same year, it chose to remain in the group. The growing concern of developing states with racism forced South Africa to leave the Commonwealth in 1961. Pakistan quit in 1972 because Bangladesh, formerly a part of Pakistan, was about to be recognized by Britain and other Commonwealth members. Tiny Fiji took itself out of the organization when a coup in 1987 led to the formation of a Republic and discrimination against the largest section of the population, citizens of Indian origin. India and the white-Commonwealth were opposed to these racist policies, but other Pacific island states kept the Commonwealth from taking action as was urged in the case of South Africa.

Commonwealth
principles   Membership in the Commonwealth requires the unanimous consent of all members. Meetings are held every two years, with decisions taken by consensus. The January 1971 meeting in Singapore issued a Declaration of Commonwealth Principles which focused on racial prejudice. The August 1973 conference was concerned with the implications, especially in trade, of Britain joining the EC. Britain had previously seen its Commonwealth links as a reason for not joining the European Community, and both Britain and its Commonwealth friends were unsure whether the move to Europe would spell the end of the Commonwealth. In fact, although Britain's trade did become more orientated to Europe, the links to the Commonwealth barely suffered.

Taking on
apartheid   The June 1977 meeting in London produced the Gleneagles Agreement on restricting sporting contacts with apartheid régimes such as South Africa. It was agreed that governments would not support such relations and would 'take every practical step to discourage' sporting contacts. Although the agreement was vague, and not legally binding, it has served as a focus for efforts to restrict links with South Africa. The August 1979 meeting in Lusaka approved the British-arranged Zimbabwe settlement and again focused on racism in general. Britain finally agreed to mild

measures, despite previous firm insistence by the Conservative government that sanctions would be counter-productive.

The 1983 New Delhi meeting discussed calls for a new economic order and the debt problem in the Third World. Like many Third World forums discussing such questions, it had little practical impact. But, including as it did states such as Britain, Canada and Australia, the conference was able to discuss these issues and above all come to compromises with leaders of the developed world. The experience was no doubt good for both groups.

Realistic North–South relations

Whether Russia can convince enough of its former colonies that they will be wealthier working seems far more doubtful. At least some republics, such as the Christian ones in Georgia or Armenia, might in the end prefer the protection of Russia against threats from Muslim neighbours. Even some of the Muslim republics might seek Russian aid in their rivalries with other Muslims, for example in Central Asia. Certainly many West Europeans would be happier to see a quick and peaceful exit for the Baltic states, followed by a relatively stable evolution to a new Russian commonwealth. But whatever the case, even a shrunken Russia will remain the world's largest state and in its leaner form, it may also be fitter.

Saving the Russian empire

Reading

J. Chadwick, *The Unofficial Commonwealth* (London: 1982).

B. Gwertzman and M. T. Kaufman (eds), *The Collapse of Communism* (New York: 1990).

P. Kennedy, *The Rise and Fall of the Great Powers* (London: Unwin/Hyman, 1988).

N. Mansbergh, *The Commonwealth Experience* (London: 1982).

A. Smith and C. Sanger, *Stitches in Time* (New York: 1983).

The Sometimes United Nations

It has been easy to ridicule the United Nations (UN). As the Israeli joke put it, there are four sides to every issue: your side, my side, the right side and the United Nations' side. To be sure there is much that is very wrong with the UN. It has often been out of touch with reality, unwieldy and run by incompetents. But as the most universal of the proliferating international organizations (in 1989 there were one hundred and fifty nine members) it continues to serve useful, if mostly mundane functions. In most cases it remains a mirror of the world it is meant to help and, despite the adverse publicity the UN earned, the cracks in the mirror are no larger than they ever were. As the post-Cold War world faced its first crisis – the Iraqi invasion of Kuwait – the UN was used by the great powers, led by the United States, to sanction tough measures against the aggressor. Could it be that the UN would finally fulfil its original promise?

Collective security

The ritual incantations of support for the UN have their roots in the odd mixture of idealism and realism that existed when the organization was created. The idealism was rooted in the horror of the Second World War and the carnage that followed the failure of the previous world organization, the League of Nations, to confront the aggression of Japan, Italy and Germany. The UN was supposed to overcome these failings by operating a system of collective security where aggression would be repelled by the common action of a concerned world. What is more, to help prevent conflict breaking out at all, the UN would take an active role in furthering economic and social progress.

Great power carve up

These twin, idealistic principles were qualified by the realities of power politics – the great power concert. The UN would give greater power to five great powers who would be able to veto any action they disliked. In addition, the UN would be barred from becoming involved in the domestic affairs of states, even though a number of threats to international stability came from the breakdown of government inside states.

So long as the United States and its Western allies retained a majority in the United Nations, Western states placed greater stress on the idealism than on the realism. In the early years of the UN, the large number of Commonwealth and pro-United States Latin American states ensured that the West remained in charge. The Soviet Union (which was given three votes to help make up for its isolation) and its allies, were prepared to tolerate this unequal state of affairs because they felt the UN would not be effective and, in any case, the Soviet Union, as one of the five great powers, could veto what it disliked.

The balance of realism and idealism was worked out in the details of the founding Charter of the UN, drawn up at the Dumbarton Oaks Conference of August–September 1944. At the Yalta Conference in February 1945, Roosevelt, Churchill and Stalin agreed the procedures that ensured the great power dominance of the UN. The founding conference of the UN took place in San Francisco in April–June 1945. The Charter was signed on 26 June by fifty-one members, twenty of them from Latin America, eleven from Asia and only three from Africa.

The UN Charter

The UN placed its headquarters in New York, partly in recognition of the United States' leading role in formulating the Charter. The official languages are now Arabic, Chinese, English, French, Russian and Spanish, symbolizing the genuinely international character of the organization. But by far the most important balancing act of the UN was evident in the types of institutions it set up. There were, and still are, three main bodies.

The most powerful is the Security Council (UNSC) which has responsibility for 'maintaining peace and security'. Its fifteen members are dominated by five permanent members (Britain, China, France, Soviet Union, United States) with the right to veto any non-procedural matter. (The Chinese seat was occupied by Nationalist China until 1971.) The veto is the vivid evidence of the 'power' in the term 'great power'. The other ten UNSC members are elected for two-year terms by the UN's second main body, the General Assembly (UNGA).

The Security Council

In the UNGA all UN members are notionally equal – each with one vote. The UNGA meets regularly each year in September and has seven main committees which deal with a range of issues. The UNGA can discuss any subject, but a two-thirds majority is required before an 'important question' can be passed. However, the UNGA merely has the power to recommend, unlike the UNSC which can 'enforce' observance.

The General Assembly

The third UN institution is the Secretariat headed by the Secretary General, who is elected for a five-year term. President Roosevelt had visions of the Secretary-General as a 'world moderator' but the reality has been an increasingly powerless figurehead whose good offices are regularly by-passed. Early Secretary-Generals, like Trygvye Lie or Dag Hammarskjold, have been succeeded by the ineffective U Thant, the over-cautious Kurt Waldheim and the nondescript Peres de Cuellar.

The Secretariat

There are obviously organizational reasons why the UN has been so ineffective. But the real problems are the more general international political disputes that have caused so much blood-

East–West conflict

shed since 1945. The first, and still most debilitating, conflict was
that between East and West. In the early days of the UN, the
United States used the organization to help pressure the Soviet
Union to pull out of Iran and to cease support for subversives in
Greece. In 1950, when the Soviet-supported North Koreans
attacked South Korea, the United States obtained support from
the UNGA in the 'uniting for peace' resolution for the despatch of
UN troops under American command after the UNSC was no longer
amenable. Strictly speaking, this was a circumvention of the
UNSC's powers but the United States had the UNGA votes to carry
the motion.

Washington's advantage began to fade by the early 1960s when
more decolonized states were admitted. In 1960, sixteen new African members were seated and, despite United States opposition,
Communist China replaced the Chiang Kai-shek régime in the
Chinese chair in October 1971. By the 1980s the organization had
become genuinely universal, with thirty-one members from
Europe, thirty from the Americas, fifty-one from Africa and forty
from Asia and the Middle East. Taiwan, the two Koreas and
Switzerland are notable non-members.

North–South   This rapid increase in members not only wrested the control
relations   of the UN from the United States; it also raised the second major
issue for the organization – North–South relations. The UN had
been an early participant in the decolonization process, helping
the Netherlands out of Indonesia and the British out of Palestine.
UN 'peacekeeping' forces in the Congo (1960–4) were engaged in
combat and helped manage the fiasco of Belgium's withdrawal
from this colony. But when North–South relations moved beyond
the broadly popular issue of ending colonial rule, the UN became
the setting for the damaging, extremist rhetoric of North–South
relations. The South demanded various 'new orders', meaning the
transfer of resources from North to South. The South, encouraged
by the Soviet Union and funded by OPEC dollars, sponsored absurd
attacks on Israel and in 1975 the UNGA declared Zionism to be 'a
form of racism'. The picture of gun-toting Yasir Arafat of the
Palestine Liberation Organization (PLO) addressing the General
Assembly made a mockery of the high idealism of the UN. It was
no wonder that the United States (by far the largest banker of the
UN) responded by cutting back its funding and began decrying the
one-state-one-vote principle in the UNGA that had given it so much
power back in the 1950s.

Peacekeeping   But, for all its obvious excesses, the UN has its good points.
First, its various types of peacekeeping have been useful. By now
we are familiar with the strange mixed-race, multi-lingual, blue-
helmeted soldiers, lightly armed and operating in squalid or
remote places under bewildering acronyms like UNFICYP, UNIFIL,

or ONUC. They have to carry out difficult, if not impossible, tasks because the UN itself is rarely sure about what it is doing and does not give its forces much authority. These soldiers have been described as 'false teeth' or as an umbrella taken away the moment it rains. Nevertheless, enough states have seen fit to make use of UN troops in a wide range of passive and active roles.

United Nations forces performed a sedative role in the 1949 and 1965 India-Pakistan conflicts over Kashmir. They helped mediate in Indonesia in 1962–3 and between Cambodia and Thailand in 1962. The UN sent observers to various parts of the Arab-Israeli conflicts and they have been in Cyprus for over twenty years. Although the UN has failed in its primary role as the enforcer of collective security, basically because the great powers refused to reach agreement, in the recent era of great power détente, there are signs of a more active UN role. Assisted by an increased enthusiasm for informal meetings, the Security Council has organized a way to stop the Iran-Iraq war, to send a peacekeeping force to Namibia, and to help restore peace in Central America.

Peaceful troops

Following the Iraqi invasion of Kuwait in August 1990, the great powers managed a dozen tough Security Council resolutions, culminating in one sanctioning the use of force by a United States-led coalition of mainly NATO and Arab states. As impressive as the new activism appeared, it was still short of the kind of collective security action first envisaged for the UN. It remained evident that without leadership by the United States, the UN would have failed to take any significant action against Iraqi aggression.

Second, UN-organized international co-operation has also been evident in the various moves, only some of which were effective, to impose sanctions on Rhodesia (later Zimbabwe) and latterly on South Africa. Third, the UN serves a passive role as a venue for traditional diplomacy. In the more obscure, smoky corridors or small back rooms, enemies can meet, signals can be sent and talks can begin. Even in a shrinking world of modern communications, there is still a need for face-to-face contacts.

Back-room diplomacy

Fourth, the UN has established a wide range of specialized agencies and associated organizations that are of practical use. The World Bank and the International Monetary Fund (IMF) are perhaps two of the best-known suppliers of funds to states in economic need. The UN International Children's Emergency Fund (UNICEF) and the High Commission for Refugees (UNHCR) provide essential help for individuals in need. The International Telegraph Union (ITU) and International Civil Aviation Organization (ICAO) assist modern means of communication, although the latter has been lamentably ineffective against the threat of aircraft hijacking.

Specialized agencies

Finally, the UN is simply a place where the poor and weak, in a world so dominated by great powers and the developed states, can feel they are being heard. To be sure, this has too often deteriorated into absurd and outrageous proposals, childish antics and shrill speeches. The impotent may feel better for upbraiding the powerful but their actions only undermine the ability of the UN to act effectively.

In the more multipolar world of the 1990s, there is much speculation that the UN will finally be able to fulfil its promise. Although it is likely that reforms will take place – greater payment of debts by great powers like the Soviet Union and the United States, and perhaps even a seat on the Security Council for Japan – there is little sign that the UN could manage effective collective security. Clearly the organization is doing better, but there is so much more that might be expected of genuinely united nations. Although there are reasons to deride or ignore the organization, if the UN did not already exist it would certainly have to be invented.

Reading

C. Archer, *International Organizations* (London: Allen and Unwin, 1983).
D. Armstrong, *The Rise of International Organizations* (London: Macmillan, 1982).
S. Bailey, *The United Nations* (London: Macmillan, 1989).
E. Luard, *The United Nations* (London: Macmillan, 1979).
A. Verrier, *International Peacekeeping* (London: Penguin, 1981).
D. Williams, *The Specialized Agencies and the United Nations* (London: Hurst, 1987).

North–South Relations

Now that the confrontation between East and West is over, it is time to take a hard look at the so-called North-South demarcation between the rich North and the poor South. According to the Brandt Report (the Independent Commission on International Development Issues), the South includes all of Asia except Japan, Australia and New Zealand, all of Africa, the Middle East, Central and South America. However, there are many ways to define poverty, and in all cases it seems that many countries in the South have more in common with the developed rather than the developing world.

There are booming states such as the newly industrialized countries (NICS), including South Korea and Taiwan. There are middle-income oil exporters such as Venezuela, Algeria, Iran or Malaysia. There are even high-income oil exporters such as Saudi Arabia or Libya. These 'middle class' states suggest any real index of human development (see chart) is impossible to calculate with confidence. And now that we know so many East European states – once considered to be developed states – are really very poor, it is nonsensical to talk of a global division between North and South. *The middle class*

Nevertheless, there have been a number of attempts to shape solidarity in the South. The Non-Aligned Movement (NAM) was founded at a twenty-five-nation conference in Belgrade in 1961 and in its regular series of meetings rapidly became a symbol of the achievements and failures of Third World diplomacy. At a time when European decolonization encouraged optimism in the developing world, the NAM stood as a hopeful third way between the frigid paths of the Superpowers in the Cold War. But with great power détente, the natural rivalries within the NAM were revealed as the main reason why such a third way could not be found. *The non-aligned movement*

Another assortment of states identifying themselves as the South have claimed that they are treated unequally by, and are dependent on, the developed economies of the North. In 1964 the Group of Seventy-seven was formed to articulate these states' desires (this group now comprises one hundred and twenty six states). At the United Nations General Assembly in 1974, a similar collection of states demanded a New International Economic Order – one that would require developed states to transfer wealth to the less-developed South. The South's main hope, and therefore *The new economic order* main target, was the Northwest (meaning the market economies) rather than the Northeast (the centrally planned economies). Not surprisingly, the North could see little point in transferring resources to states, many of which had faster growth rates than they had, while at the same time being insulted and blamed for a colonial legacy of ills. The South's demand was based on a mixture of motives; a request for (1) charity and (2) guilt money; (3) a socialist belief in justice through equality; (4) an appeal to the self-interest of trading states anxious about the collapse of international trade if the South were too poor to buy the imports and (5) most recently, a concern that if the economies of the South collapsed, they would default on their debts to Western banks and cause an economic crisis in the developed world. With the price of a new nuclear submarine equivalent to the education budget of twenty-three developing countries with 160 million school children, there was a case to answer.

Aiding the South   The appeal for justice was usually dismissed on the basis of the diversity of the South, ideological opposition to socialism, and problems in the economics of developed states. Claims on the basis of guilt and charity resulted in total aid from OECD states of $48 billion in 1988. But by the time of the revolutions in Eastern Europe, it became clear that much Western investment and aid would be moved from the seemingly bottomless holes of the developing world to the more promising states in Europe. As a percentage of GNP, the largest donors to the poor South were the likes of Netherland (1%) and the Scandinavian countries. The United States remained the largest single donor in absolute terms ($10.1 billion) until 1989 when Japan surged past (although still only 0.3% of GNP).

Trade and Debt   There was certainly little practical reason for the developed world to be worried about the state of the poor South. These poorest states account for some 0.3% of total world trade and therefore have no impact on the prosperity of the most developed states. It is true that some states of the South might default on their debt, but then this is only an acute problem for some of the middle-income states, not the real South.

The problem of investment   In the long term it was investment more than aid that could provide new technology and the efficiency that the real South needed. Unfortunately many NIEO states and members of the Group of Seventy-seven were hostile to the terms of foreign investment, in some cases rejecting it entirely as a 'neo-colonialist means of exploitation'. The coming of multinational corporations was often viewed as 'economic and cultural imperialism', even if it did bring growth far more swiftly and permanently than bulk aid. In any case, the developed states are not queuing up to invest in the real South. They obtain far more growth at home by investment

Human Development Index

	Life expectancy at birth (years) '87	Adult literacy rate (%) '85	Real GDP per head (PPP-adj'd) '87, $	HDI	Rank by GNP per head	Rank by HDI
Niger	45	14	452	0.116	20	1
Mali	45	17	543	0.143	15	2
Burkina Faso	48	14	500	0.150	13	3
Sierra Leone	42	30	480	0.150	27	4
Chad	46	26	400	0.157	4	5
Guinea	43	29	500	0.162	31	6
Somalia	46	12	1,000	0.200	23	7
Mauritania	47	17	840	0.208	40	8
Afghanistan	42	24	1,000	0.212	17	9
Benin	47	27	665	0.224	28	10
Burundi	50	35	450	0.235	18	11
Bhutan	49	25	700	0.236	3	12
Mozambique	47	39	500	0.239	10	13
Malawi	48	42	476	0.250	7	14
Sudan	51	23	750	0.255	32	15
Central African Republic	46	41	591	0.258	29	16
Nepal	52	26	722	0.273	8	17
Senegal	47	28	1,068	0.274	43	18
Ethiopia	42	66	454	0.282	1	19
Zaire	53	62	220	0.294	5	20
Rwanda	49	47	571	0.304	26	21
Angola	45	41	1,000	0.304	58	22
Bangladesh	52	33	883	0.318	6	23
Nigeria	51	43	668	0.322	36	24
Yemen Arab Rep.	52	25	1,250	0.328	47	25
Liberia	55	35	696	0.333	42	26
Togo	54	41	670	0.337	24	27
Uganda	52	58	511	0.354	21	28
Haiti	55	38	775	0.356	34	29
Ghana	55	54	481	0.360	37	30
Yemen, PDR	52	42	1,000	0.369	39	31
Côte d'Ivoire	53	42	1,123	0.393	52	32
Congo	49	63	756	0.395	59	33
Namibia	56	30	1,500	0.404	60	34
Tanzania	54	75	405	0.413	12	35
Pakistan	58	30	1.585	0.423	33	36
India	59	43	1,053	0.439	25	37
Madagascar	54	68	634	0.440	14	38
Papua New Guinea	55	45	1,843	0.471	50	39
Kampuchea, Dem.	49	75	1,000	0.471	2	40
Cameroon	52	61	1.381	0.474	64	41
Kenya	59	60	794	0.481	30	42
Zambia	54	76	717	0.481	19	43
Morocco	62	34	1,761	0.489	48	44
Egypt	62	45	1,357	0.501	49	45
Laos	49	84	1,000	0.506	9	46
Gabon	52	62	2,068	0.525	93	47
Oman	57	30	7,750	0.535	104	48
Bolivia	54	75	1,380	0.548	44	49

	Life expectancy at birth (years) '87	Adult literacy rate (%) '85	Real GDP per head (PPP-adj'd) '87, $	HDI	Rank by GNP per head	Rank by HDI
Burma	61	79	752	0.561	11	50
Honduras	65	59	1,119	0.563	53	51
Zimbabwe	59	74	1,184	0.576	45	52
Lesotho	57	73	1,585	0.580	35	53
Indonesia	57	74	1,660	0.591	41	54
Guatemala	63	55	1,957	0.592	63	55
Vietnam	62	80	1,000	0.608	16	56
Algeria	63	50	2,633	0.609	91	57
Botswana	59	71	2,496	0.646	69	58
El Salvador	64	72	1,733	0.651	56	59
Tunisia	66	55	2,741	0.657	70	60
Iran	66	51	3,300	0.660	97	61
Syria	66	60	3,250	0.691	79	62
Dominican Rep.	67	78	1,750	0.699	51	63
Saudi Arabia	64	55	8,320	0.702	107	64
Philippines	64	86	1,878	0.714	46	65
China	70	69	2,124	0.716	22	66
Libya	62	66	7,250	0.719	103	67
South Africa	61	70	4,981	0.731	82	68
Lebanon	68	78	2,250	0.735	78	69
Mongolia	64	90	2,000	0.737	57	70
Nicaragua	64	88	2,209	0.743	54	71
Turkey	65	74	3,781	0.751	71	72
Jordan	67	75	3,161	0.752	76	73
Peru	63	85	3,129	0.753	74	74
Ecuador	66	83	2,687	0.758	68	75
Iraq	65	89	2,400	0.759	96	76
United Arab Emirates	71	60	12,191	0.782	127	77
Thailand	66	91	2,576	0.783	55	78
Paraguay	67	88	2,603	0.784	65	79
Brazil	65	78	4,307	0.784	85	80
Mauritius	69	83	2,617	0.788	75	81
North Korea	70	90	2,000	0.789	67	82
Sri Lanka	71	87	2,053	0.789	38	83
Albania	72	85	2,000	0.790	61	84
Malaysia	70	74	3,849	0.800	80	85
Colombia	65	88	3,524	0.801	72	86
Jamaica	74	82	2,506	0.824	62	87
Kuwait	73	70	13,843	0.839	122	88
Venezuela	70	87	4,306	0.861	95	89
Romania	71	96	3,000	0.863	84	90
Mexico	69	90	4,624	0.876	81	91
Cuba	74	96	2,500	0.877	66	92
Panama	72	89	4,009	0.883	88	93
Trinidad and Tobago	71	96	3,664	0.885	100	94
Portugal	74	85	5,597	0.899	94	95
Singapore	73	86	12,790	0.899	110	96
South Korea	70	95	4,832	0.903	92	97
Poland	72	98	4,000	0.910	83	98
Argentina	71	96	4,647	0.910	89	99
Yugoslavia	72	92	5,000	0.913	90	100
Hungary	71	98	4,500	0.915	87	101

	Life expectancy at birth (years) '87	Adult literacy rate (%) '85	Real GDP per head (PPP-adj'd) '87, $	HDI	Rank by GNP per head	Rank by HDI
Uruguay	71	95	5,063	0.916	86	102
Costa Rica	75	93	3,760	0.916	77	103
Bulgaria	72	93	4,750	0.918	99	104
USSR	70	99	6,000	0.920	101	105
Czechoslovakia	72	98	7,750	0.931	102	106
Chile	72	98	4,862	0.931	73	107
Hongkong	76	88	13,906	0.936	111	108
Greece	76	93	5,500	0.949	98	109
East Germany	74	99	8,000	0.953	115	110
Israel	76	95	9,182	0.957	108	111
USA	76	96	17,615	0.961	129	112
Austria	74	99	12,386	0.961	118	113
Ireland	74	99	8,566	0.961	106	114
Spain	77	95	8,989	0.965	105	115
Belgium	75	99	13,140	0.966	116	116
Italy	76	97	10,682	0.966	112	117
New Zealand	75	99	10,541	0.966	109	118
West Germany	75	99	14,730	0.967	120	119
Finland	75	99	12,795	0.967	121	120
Britain	76	99	12,270	0.970	113	121
Denmark	76	99	15,119	0.971	123	122
France	76	99	13,961	0.974	119	123
Australia	76	99	11,782	0.978	114	124
Norway	77	99	15,940	0.983	128	125
Canada	77	99	16,375	0.983	124	126
Holland	77	99	12,661	0.984	117	127
Switzerland	77	99	15,403	0.986	130	128
Sweden	77	99	13,780	0.987	125	129
Japan	78	99	13,135	0.996	126	130

The table ranks the countries in ascending order of their score on the human-development index. The UNDP's researchers combined the first three columns in each part of the table – showing life expectancy, adult literacy and purchasing power – to deduce the index shown in the fourth column. For each indicator, a 'minimum' value and a 'desirable' value had to be specified. Minimum values were set equal to the lowest actually observed in 1987: 42 years for life expectancy (as in Afghanistan, Ethiopia and Sierra Leone), 12% for adult literacy (as in Somalia) and $220 for purchasing power (as in Zaire). Desirable values were set at 78 years for life expectancy (as in Japan), 100% for adult literacy, and $4,861 for purchasing power (this is the average official poverty line for nine industrial countries, adjusted for purchasing-power parity). One further complication: to reflect 'diminishing returns in the conversion of income into the fulfilment of human needs', logarithms rather than absolute values of purchasing power were used. With these minimum desirable values fixing the end-points, and with the interval between them set equal to one, the countries could be located on each scale. A simple average of the three readings then yields the HDI. The last two columns in each part of the table show the ranking by unadjusted GNP per person and the ranking by HDI, respectively.

Source: The Economist, May 26 1990

in the developed world, or in the NICS and HIOES where they are welcome and encouraged. In essence then, there is little self-interest for the North in meeting the demands of the poorest parts of the South, no matter how shrilly they are put. When faced with continuing instability and wasteful military adventures on the part of many of these states in the South, the North can find ample excuse to avoid meeting their demands. Only the threat of middle-income states to wreck the international monetary system seems to galvanize the developed world into a more cooperative attitude.

South-South cooperation   Cooperation among states in the South is one possible way to halt the widening gap beween developed and under-developed states. For example, some OPEC states do appear willing to give aid but most states in the South prefer to look after themselves or, as in ASEAN or the OAS, to cooperate on a regional basis. Selfishness, it seems, is an attribute not confined to the North.

Failure by the rest of the real South to meet the challenge will be serious. The new technologies now revolutionizing industries in the developed world will soon render largely obsolete the real South's one advantage hitherto, cheap labour. The NICS seem best placed to exploit the new technologies and maintain their pace of development. The HIOES still have a chance, albeit dwindling, to buy in the new technologies for future development. The middle-income states of the South may well be too late for the new industrial revolution, but the developed world is beginning to understand that it has a strong self-interest in keeping these states afloat. It is the real South (except, probably, China and India) that is least likely to prosper. Sadly, these countries have been left behind not only by the North, but also by their supposed brethren in the South.

Reading

N. Harris, *The End of the Third World* (London: Penguin, 1987).

'A Survey of the Third World', *The Economist*, 23 September 1989.

The South Commission, *The Challenge to the South* (Oxford: Oxford University Press, 1990).

The World Bank, *World Development Report* (Oxford: Oxford University Press, 1990).

G. Williams, *The Third World Political Organizations* (London: Macmillan, 1987).

International Money

The problems of international economics may appear impossibly complicated, but we ignore these issues at our peril. Mistakes in international economic policy can have a devastating impact on the lives of individuals, and sensible management of the international economy can continue to give millions of people undreamt of prosperity. The world-wide depression of the 1930s was the most catastrophic example of how bad things can get. The international banking system collapsed because banks and governments lent far more money than they had and, when some debtors defaulted, the banks went bust. International investment then dried up, leading to unemployment and protectionism. And yet the complex interdependence of capitalist economies by the 1990s had provided so much wealth that its members recognized they were all dependent on each other for future prosperity.

The desire to avoid 1930s-type suffering after the Second World War focused on how to provide quick money and advice to governments which found themselves short of financial reserves. The new international monetary system was to be based mostly on fixed, but sometimes flexible, currency exchange rates. Its members were overwhelmingly the market economies of Europe and the Americas and later came to include states emerging from the grip of colonialism. The International Monetary Fund (IMF) was established by a conference at Bretton Woods (New Hampshire, USA), in July 1944 with these economic and political ends in mind. As states borrowed larger amounts, so stricter conditions would be imposed to encourage them to reduce their budget and trade deficits.

Founding the IMF

The IMF opened for currency operations on 1 March 1948. It was based in Washington, had thirty members (it now has one hundred and fifty one) with a board of governors composed of a representative from each state. Voting power primarily reflects the contributions to the Fund's financial resources and the size of a state's economy. The United States has about 20% of the vote, many others have less than 1%. The United States had begun with 31% of the vote but the OPEC states' share doubled in 1976 and developing states now have 28% of the vote (though 75% of world population). Any major change in the IMF system requires an 85% vote, so the United States retains a veto.

The initial, idealistic concept was for a multilateral, open, international economic system, with mutually convertible currencies

IMF idealism

25

and for substantial authority to be given to a genuinely international body (the IMF). But because Western economies were so
devastated after the war, an initial transition period of five years
dragged on for sixteen years. There was a heavy European
demand to borrow dollars for development, which was partially
balanced by American Marshall Aid and military expenditures in
Europe. The IMF wisely stayed out of early balance-of-payments
crises, and domestic controls and currency devaluations were
allowed to run their painful course. But since 1956 the IMF has
become more involved in supplying credits.

Gambling and   By the late 1950s the United States began to move into deficit,
the dollar crisis mostly due to its military spending, despite a surplus in the trade
of goods. By 1961 the total foreign holding of dollars was greater
than the value of the United States' gold reserves, which forced
up the price of gold. The problem was in part caused by the
increase in internationally mobile capital which was used in high-
risk currency speculation rather than being moved in response to
real economic changes. Ad hoc measures to control this 'casino
capitalism' failed and lack of confidence in the dollar and sterling
became acute.

SDRs   To staunch the flow of uncertainty, in 1968 a new currency
reserve unit was created by the IMF. Special Drawing Rights (SDRs)
produced an additional borrowing capacity. The IMF had managed
the impossible; it had created something (SDRs) out of nothing.
But because the United States dollar was still deemed to be over-
valued and the economy unstable, investment flowed out of America. The American trade deficit continued to balloon, putting yet
more pressure on the dollar. Of course, if the dollar were deva-
lued, the United States could export more and the deficit would
be cut. In August 1971, the United States effectively did devalue
its currency by abandoning the gold standard (a fixed value of
gold in dollars). Washington also slapped a surcharge of 10% on
imports. The Smithsonian Agreement at the end of 1971 realigned
currencies and the dollar's value declined by an average of 10%.
The Japanese yen and German mark were most strongly revalued.

Floating rates   Yet the tinkering was not enough. In June 1972 the value of
the pound sterling was allowed to float freely and in 1973 the
dollar and other currencies followed it out into the dangerous
waters of currency speculation. Although first seen as temporary,
the bobbing currencies were the death of the Bretton Woods
system. Of course, rates did not genuinely float free, as governments intervened to stabilize their currencies and make some kind
of economic planning possible. If currency rates were allowed to
drift completely free, governments would find it virtually impossible to know the value of their imports and exports, and hence
– a finance minister's nightmare – prices and wages would be

uncontrollable. In practice, currency rates reflected relative interest rates (higher rates draw more investment) rather than the state's true trade balance or the strength of its economy. Toward the end of the 1970s the international monetary system seemed to be in disarray. An IMF attempt to set rules for currency floats failed and the use of gold as a standard was finally abandoned.

Also in the 1970s, the sharp rise in oil prices meant a huge transfer of reserves to OPEC states, causing deficits in developed and non-oil-producing developing states. To allow states to keep imports up, the IMF and international banks lent money deposited with them by the OPEC states. Developed economies were strained by the necessary budget deficits and higher interest rates but basically adjusted to this new system. The less able developing states slipped into heavy debt. The IMF tried to ease the problem by lending money but imposing stringent plans for economic reform. Not surprisingly, this IMF medicine in turn caused serious social unrest in the developing world.

The looming debt

Perhaps the most serious long term trend was the decline of the United States as the dominant power in the international economy as Western Europe and Japan grew wealthier. The cause of the American decline was a fatal mix of declining competitiveness of the American economy, a growing defence budget and the failure of the President and Congress to cut the budget and trade deficit. In the four years from 1983, the United States plummeted from being the world's largest creditor to the world's largest debtor. In October 1987, the world's market economies lost faith in the American confidence trick and stock markets around the globe tumbled by 20% (i.e. the gains of 1987). This was more a tremor than a crash in the system, but it forced a sharp drop in the value of the dollar as the most direct way of solving the American budget fiasco.

Decline of the United States

By the late 1980s it was apparent that the capitalist economy, with its three major sectors in Europe, North America and East Asia, was thriving, but only because they were able to manage the market. Yet it was also clear that markets do not like being managed and that often once-sovereign states find themselves at the mercy of an international economic system which can only be controlled by concerted action from the leading actors. States certainly wanted more stable exchange rates (in 1981 the dollar varied in value by 40%) as floating currencies were unnecessarily influenced by short-term factors and pure speculation. Yet a return to fixed rates was unlikely, if only because of the large amount of speculative capital sloshing around international markets and the diverse interests of individual countries.

Managing market forces

Although the United States dollar still accounts for 57% of all foreign exchange reserves, compared to 7% in yen, and 53% of

New power centres

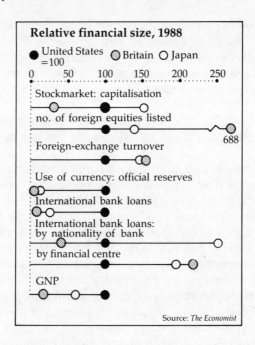

Relative financial size, 1988

● United States =100   ◎ Britain   ○ Japan

0   50   100   150   200   250

Stockmarket: capitalisation

no. of foreign equities listed

688

Foreign-exchange turnover

Use of currency: official reserves

International bank loans

International bank loans:
by nationality of bank

by financial centre

GNP

Source: *The Economist*

international bank loans are in dollars (13% in yen), the trend was clearly towards a reduction in the role of the American economy as the benignly hegemonic power in the international economy. Japan and Europe (led by Germany) were taking up the slack, inevitably complicating the question of leadership of the international market economy.

Foreign Direct Investment

Europeans had long grown used to heavy foreign investment in their home economies, and the United States was now learning that East Asians as well as Europeans could buy parts of American industry and property. East Asians were used to heavy American involvement in their economy, and now the Europeans were coming to do business. The interlocking parts of the international economy meant that individual states were rapidly losing control of their economy, and yet prosperity required states not to intervene for fear of reducing international competitiveness. As Europe marched towards 1992 with a plan to create a single market, it was clear that the new agenda for the international economy had far less room for the antics of individual states.

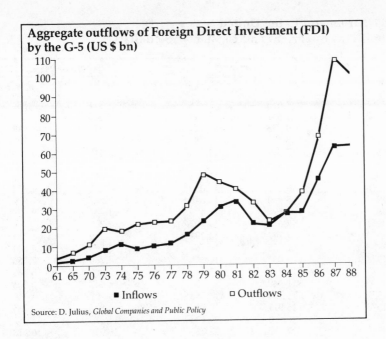

Aggregate outflows of Foreign Direct Investment (FDI) by the G-5 (US $ bn)

■ Inflows   □ Outflows

Source: D. Julius, *Global Companies and Public Policy*

FDI outflows by the G-5
(compound annual growth rates, valued in domestic currency)

	FDI flows 1983–8		FDI stock* 1988
	Nominal (%)	Real (%)	($ bn)
United States	24	20	324
United Kingdom	22	16	184
Japan	39	37	114
Germany	18	15	78
France	39	32	57

*For consistency across countries, the stock is taken to be the cumulative FDI outflow over the period 1961–88.
Source: D. Julius, *Global Companies and Public Policy* (London: Frances Pinter, 1990).

**FDI from and to the United States
(millions of current and constant-1980 dollars)**

	OUTFLOWS		INFLOWS	
	Current	*Constant*	*Current*	*Constant*
1961	2,653	7,288	311	854
1962	2,852	7,646	346	928
1963	3,483	9,214	231	611
1964	3,759	9,789	322	839
1965	5,010	12,716	415	1,053
1966	5,416	13,275	425	1,042
1967	4,807	11,473	698	1,666
1968	5,295	12,034	807	1,834
1969	5,960	12,845	1,263	2,722
1970	7,590	15,490	1,464	2,988
1971	7,618	14,707	367	708
1972	7,747	14,293	949	1,751
1973	11,435	19,784	2,800	4,844
1974	9,052	14,368	4,760	7,556
1975	14,244	20,584	2,603	3,762
1976	11,949	16,235	4,347	5,906
1977	14,254	18,158	3,728	4,749
1978	16,911	20,060	7,897	9,368
1979	26,993	29,436	11,877	12,952
1980	22,750	22,750	16,918	16,918
1981	14,509	13,238	25,195	22,988
1982	16,277	13,948	13,792	11,818
1983	5,815	4,798	11,946	9,856
1984	6,676	5,303	25,359	20,142
1985	13,860	10,621	19,022	14,576
1986	21,445	16,112	34,091	25,613
1987	41,202	30,053	46,894	34,204
1988	14,805	10,383	58,436	40,984

Source: D. Julius, *Global Companies and Public Policy* (London: Frances Pinter, 1990).

Reading

E.A. Brett, *The World Economy Since the War* (London: Macmillan, 1985).

R. Cooper *et al*, *Can Nations Agree?* (Washington: Brookings, 1989).

H. Grubel, *The International Monetary System* (London: Penguin, 1984).

C. Gwin *et al*, *The International Monetary Fund in a Multipolar World*, (New Brunswick, N.J.: Transaction Books, 1990).

H. Lever and C. Huhne, *Debt and Danger* (London: Penguin, 1985).

R. Solomon. *The International Monetary System* (New York: Harper and Row, 1977).

S. Strange, *Casino Capitalism* (Oxford: Basil Blackwell, 1986).

Managing International Debt

In the 1980s, when the risk of a nuclear apocalypse seemed so acute to many, others were concerned about the risks that the 'time-bomb' of international debt would also explode, ruining the international economy. But from the vantage point of the more optimistic 1990s, the fears seemed exaggerated. For all its seemingly shambolic shifts, the international market economy had its own ways of defusing the threat of debt.

Recent concern with the scale of international debt is a result *The oil shock* of two weighty events. First, in the 1970s the oil exporting states earned massive surpluses. Most of the windfall profits were deposited in Western banks which, in turn, lent to governments desperate for funds to finance gargantuan oil bills. Unfortunately, many of the new borrowers had unstable governments. Between 1973–9 the external debt of oil importing states tripled, with annual debt service payments (the cost of the interest on loans) up to $45 billion per year. Old loans were 'rolled over', i.e. new loans were made to pay the costs of old ones. Forty per cent of the loans were from commercial banks, up from 16% in 1970, and less easy to roll over than debts to governments. Thirty per cent of the loans were in the form of export credits and the rest were inter-government loans. The debt servicing ratio (the proportion of export earnings needed to pay the interest on the loans) averaged 12–15% and in advanced developing states, like Brazil and Mexico, reached more than 50%. By 1980 the oil-importing states had over $250 billion in medium and long term debt.

Rising oil prices hit the economies of indebted developing *The interest* states, but the second most powerful blow came from the recession *rate shock* in developed states which forced up interest rates on loans. By 1981–2, when interest rates remained high and inflation was falling, the 'real' interest rate rose even more sharply. To make matters worse, the recession in the developed world reduced the demand for the commodity exports of many developing, indebted states. Thus not only were these struggling developing states having to pay more interest on their debts, but they had less money to spend because their exports were collapsing. This was as much a 'credit crisis' as a 'debt crisis'.

Worse still, the developing states failed to devalue their cur- *Corrupt debtors* rencies, thereby making the holding of foreign assets (like a Miami apartment) especially attractive. Thus, much of the capital loaned to the developing states went straight out to the private accounts of corrupt leaders. One estimate suggests that in 1979–82, some $28 billion left Mexico, $21 billion left Venezuela and $12 billion left Argentina in this fashion. Between 1983–5, Mexico lost some $16 billion and Brazil some $5 billion as residents sought safer and higher returns abroad in bank deposits, securities and property.

The worst cases   This debilitating debt burden did not strike all states equally. Nearly half of all bank lending went to five countries, and Brazil and Mexico together took one-quarter. Eighty per cent of developing countries received under 2% of the loans while thirty to forty of the least developed states received almost nothing. By the early 1980s, the inevitable happened. A number of heavily indebted states, from Communist Poland to capitalist Brazil, demanded rescheduling of debts and threatened to default. Developed countries suddenly took seriously the danger that their banks would collapse and their modern economies would lurch into a 1930s-type depression.

The World Bank   Needless to say, such catastrophe was not supposed to loom over the post-1945 international financial system. The World Bank (more formally known as the International Bank for Reconstruction and Development) was established as a United Nations specialized agency in December 1945 to provide loans to member governments for economic development. The Bank lent at commercial rates with money raised on world money markets. It was at first as much concerned with reconstruction as development. By the mid-1950s it was only lending $500 million per year, more than half of which went to Europe and other developed regions. The less developed regions could not afford the interest rates.

As a result, a 'soft' loan affiliate was established, the International Development Association, to provide loans at lower rates. The IDA was based on the principle that human development and relief of poverty were desirable ends in themselves, even if the receiving state was otherwise economically incompetent. In the 1970s, IDA soft loans totalled about $2 billion per year and focused on development aid and smaller, mostly agricultural, projects. By the 1980s, the IDA was providing up to $12 billion per year.

America's flawed leadership   The United States clearly plays the leading role in international finance. Washington had a 39% vote on the governing executive board of the World Bank in 1950, but thirty years later the Americans had only a 21% vote. Poor states' votes rose from 12% to 32%. Nevertheless, even though most decisions are taken by consensus, the developed world continued to dominate the decisions of the Bank. For that reason it was disturbing that the United States in the 1980s was running a huge budget deficit. The Reagan administration had cut taxes but increased spending (mostly on defence) and therefore used high interest rates to draw in foreign funding to finance the American budget deficit. High American interest rates forced up those of other developed states and as a result the international debt burden for developing states rocketed. By 1987 the huge American budget deficit made the leader of the global economy the largest debtor nation.

In the last half of the 1980s a number of changes in policy were adopted which reduced the threat that the debt time-bomb would explode. With United States encouragement, the IMF offered more aid, albeit under strict terms, to the most indebted nations. The threat of a 'debtors cartel' began to fade as the richer nations made clear they recognized at least a degree of responsibility in easing the crisis. What is more, as oil surpluses began to dwindle, the major capitalist economies began a period of sustained growth which cut interest rates and provided larger markets for the exports of the developing states.

Defusing the threat

Of course, several middle-income states, notably Brazil and Mexico, remain heavily in debt. But the international economy had learned to spread the debt so that any future collapse would not hurt any single developed country (or its banks) especially hard. The revolutions in Eastern Europe in 1989 began drawing funds away from the Latin American debtors as Europeans, Americans and Japanese looked for new opportunities in Europe. The risk was that just as in earlier years, unsound investments would be made in Eastern Europe. But the opportunity was that with the demise of Communist economics, many of the states in Eastern Europe would adopt sensible strategies for growth and soon be able to repay debts.

Still looming dangers

As Mark Twain noted, 'a banker is a fellow who lends you his umbrella when the sun is shining, and wants it back when it begins to rain'. Less than a year after the revolutions in Eastern Europe, the skies have become overcast over a number of countries. With Poland taking the full brunt of the 'big bang' adjustment to a market economy and Hungary and Czechoslovakia about to do the same, the eyes of the bankers were on the climate in Europe. The weather forecast was for sunny spells with a chance of showers.

Reading

E.A. Brett, *The World Economy Since the War* (London: Macmillan, 1985).

R.J. Dale and R.P. Mattione, *Managing Global Debt* (Washington: Brookings, 1984).

E. Luard, *The Management of the World Economy* (London: Macmillan, 1983).

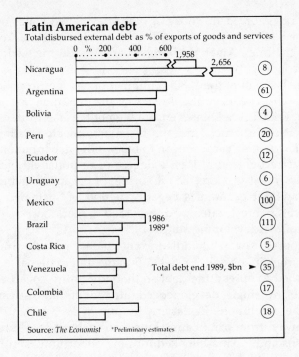

Latin American debt
Total disbursed external debt as % of exports of goods and services

	Total debt end 1989, $bn
Nicaragua	8
Argentina	61
Bolivia	4
Peru	20
Ecuador	12
Uruguay	6
Mexico	100
Brazil	111
Costa Rica	5
Venezuela	35
Colombia	17
Chile	18

Source: *The Economist*   *Preliminary estimates

J.E. Spero, *The Politics of International Economic Relations* (London: Allen & Unwin, 1985).

The World Bank, *World Development Report* (London: Oxford University Press, 1987).

The World Trading System

One of the earliest, and most important, motives for contacts between states is trade. In recent years, trade has been transformed, becoming more global and making people far more interdependent. The inhabitants of the developed world take it for granted that their main streets will be stocked with quality cameras from Japan, roses from Israel and wines from France. But a world with such sophisticated trade is also troubled by disputes over markets, tariffs and profits.

It is only in the last two hundred years that trade has become *Why trade?* essential to the economic prosperity and development of many states. In theory, states trade to obtain resources, goods or services they do not have or that others can provide more cheaply. Before the First World War, 43% of world trade was in the hands of Britain, the United States and Germany. The vast majority of trade was between these three and with white-settled, resource-rich states such as Canada or Australia. After the war, Britain was replaced by the United States as the major trading nation. By 1953 the United States accounted for 21% of world trade (though that was less than 5% of American GNP), Britain 10%, France 8% and the Netherlands 8%. North America and Europe together still accounted for some 66% of total world trade. In the twenty years from 1965, world trade more than doubled in real terms, far outpacing economic growth in industrial countries. Clearly international trade had become far more important for our prosperity.

Trade was largely bilateral but after the Second World War *GATT* multilateral attempts were made to regulate international trade. A twenty-three-nation United Nations conference on trade and employment agreed, in Geneva in October 1947, to a General Agreement on Tariffs and Trade (GATT). By 1990, ninety-six states were party to GATT, with another thirty-three *de facto* members; the Soviet Union is among the notable non-members. The unusual and bold idea behind GATT was to establish a system for tariff reductions. However, it remains unclear whether GATT has done more than merely codify what was already possible in the international market.

GATT was originally intended as an interim organization to be superceded by a UN specialized agency, the International Trade Organization (ITO). Opposition from the United States Congress killed the ITO ideal of a permanent regulating body for world trade and instead GATT has emerged as a multilateral trade agreement, not an international institution. Members meet once a year and there is also a permanent Council of Representatives with a Secretariat and Director-General based in Geneva. GATT's primary function is to run irregular conferences which allow states to engage in a series of bilateral (and slow) negotiations to reduce tariffs.

The Dillon Round

During the 1950s world trade doubled; and it more than doubled again in the 1960s. But most of this trade was between developed states. By the mid-1970s the poor countries, with four-fifths of the world population, accounted for less than 15% of world trade. Not surprisingly, therefore, various rounds of tariff negotiations through GATT concentrated on trade between developed states. As a result of the Dillon Round in 1960–2, many tariffs between the United States and the EC, and between Britain and the United States, were cut by 20%. But in general the tariff reductions were disappointing.

The Kennedy Round

The Kennedy Round, 1963–7, applied the principle of across-the-board tariff reductions on individual products. The reductions averaged 36% with forty-six countries making concessions affecting 75% of world trade. But trade growth slumped in the 1970s as oil prices shot up. The trade in primary resources (such as oil) did increase as a proportion of international trade and the Newly Industrialized Countries increased their share of the total trade. However, poorer developing countries still took little part in international trade. Their agricultural products were not wanted by developed states who were themselves taking measures to protect their own agriculture. Prices of Third World primary resources, such as sugar and tin, fluctuated wildly with the failure to agree OPEC-type cartels. Poorer producing states were also hit hard by higher oil prices and the consequent rise in the cost of western industrial products.

The Tokyo Round

The third GATT round, in Tokyo between 1973–9 dealt mostly with industrial countries who cut some tariffs by up to one third. Concessions by eight industrialized countries and the EC covered imports valued at $141 billion, of which $127 billion were industrial products. Some progress was made in resolving disputes on such distorting trade practices as subsidies, countervailing duties and dumping. But Article nineteen of the Agreement allowed states to restrain imports where they caused 'serious injury' to domestic industry.

The Uruguay Round

In Uruguay, in September 1986, the agenda was set for another GATT round. The ambition was to extend GATT's cover from one-third to two-thirds of world trade – pulling in services, investment and agriculture. Major problems included agricultural protectionism and export subsidies, liberalizing the fast-growing trade in services, and a search for better means of settling disputes. Agriculture was the key, for only by liberalizing its trade would developing states have much incentive to accept other changes. In keeping with the general decline in the solidarity of the Third World, developing states began taking a far more active role in GATT, taking advantage of the provision of Most Favoured Nation status (the right to trade with each other on the most favourable terms available).

But getting the developing states to learn to play the GATT game instead of carping from the sidelines was a prolonged process. Because of long-standing complaints in the Third World that GATT was a rich man's club, the United Nations Conference on Trade and Development (UNCTAD) was set up in 1964, as a permanent organ of the General Assembly. Yet UNCTAD has been even less successful than GATT. In a series of conferences, it has led the polemical campaign for a New International Economic Order. UNCTAD organized confrontations between the developed world and the Group of Seventy-seven developing states (which now has one hundred and twenty six members), insisting that the rich transfer more resources to the poor. The conferences, attended by thousands, seem little more than an excuse to set up an international bureaucracy. *UNCTAD*

In 1985, after ten years of lobbying, UNCTAD finally rounded up the ninety-plus signatures needed to ratify a scheme to support commodity agreements. It was hoped that a common fund to purchase buffer stocks would permanently raise primary commodity prices, improve developing states' terms of trade and enhance the NIEO. Ten years on, this is an idea whose time has long gone. The proposed funding is so tiny and the market is so much more complex than posited by the proponents of the NIEO. UNCTAD has also been a dismal failure in organizing increased trade between poor and developing states, as was evident by the sparsely attended Delhi trade conference in July 1985.

More successful have been the 'voluntary' agreements, such as the Multi-Fibre Arrangements (MFA) controlling the developed states' imports of textiles. Although many developing economies claim it limits their access to markets in developed states (which it does) the MFA has also helped manage the process of opening these markets, which might otherwise have been slammed firmly shut. *'Voluntary' agreements*

In the end, the basic rationale for trade has hardly changed and developed states cannot be forced to accept imports. Moreover, they will naturally adopt such tactics as dumping (selling goods on foreign markets at low prices merely to keep domestic factories open) and imposing 'national standards' (absurd regulations to keep out imports) so as to protect local industry. The EC's 'price assistance' (for example to its farmers), is a euphemism *Butter mountains and wine lakes*

Leading exporters and importers in world merchandise trade, 1988

(Billion dollars and percentage)

			EXPORTS	
Rank			1988	
1978	1988		Value	Share
2	1	Germany, Fed. Rep.	323	11.2
1	2	United States	322	11.1
3	3	Japan	265	9.2
4	4	France	168	5.8
5	5	United Kingdom	145	5.1
6	6	Italy	129	4.5
9	9	Canada	117	4.0
7	8	USSR	111	3.9
8	9	Netherlands	103	3.6
10	10	Belgium-Luxembourg	92	3.2
27	11	Hong Kong[a]	63	2.2
20	12	Korea. Rep.	61	2.1
21	13	Taiwan	61	2.1
12	14	Switzerland	51	1.8
14	15	Sweden	50	1.7
33	16	China	48	1.6
18	17	Spain	40	1.4
31	18	Singapore[a]	39	1.4
22	19	Brazil	34	1.2
15	20	Australia	33	1.1
23	21	Austria	31	1.1
40	22	Mexico[d]	31	1.1
24	23	Denmark	28	1.0
16	24	German Dem. Rep.	28	1.0
25	25	Czechoslovakia	25	0.9
		Total	**2398**	**83.3**
		World	**2880**	**100.0**

[a] Includes substantial re-exports.
[b] Imports f.o.b.
[c] Includes substantial imports for re-export.
[d] Includes estimates of trade flows through processing zones.
Source: US Information Agency.

		IMPORTS		
Rank			*1988*	
1978	*1988*		*Value*	*Share*
1	1	United States	460	15.4
2	2	Germany, Fed. Rep.	251	8.4
5	3	United Kingdom	189	6.4
4	4	Japan	187	6.3
3	5	France	179	6.0
6	6	Italy	139	4.6
10	7	Canada	115	3.8
8	8	USSR[b]	107	3.6
7	9	Netherlands	99	3.3
9	10	Belgium-Luxembourg	92	3.1
23	11	Hong Kong[c]	64	2.2
12	12	Spain	61	2.0
11	13	Switzerland	56	1.9
29	14	China	55	1.8
19	15	Korea, Rep.	52	1.7
30	16	Taiwan	50	1.7
12	17	Sweden	46	1.5
24	18	Singapore[c]	44	1.5
16	19	Australia	36	1.2
15	20	Austria	36	1.2
34	21	Mexico[d]	27	1.0
17	22	German Dem. Rep.[b]	27	0.9
20	23	Denmark	27	0.9
26	24	Czechoslovakia[b]	23	0.8
28	25	Norway	23	0.8
		Total	**2446**	**81.8**
		World	**2990**	**100.0**

for subsidies to undercut foreign imports. Not surprisingly, butter mountains and wine lakes develop as a result of protecting local farmers. The 1984–5 suffering in the American farm-belt, and the ensuing risks to the banking system from thousands of bankruptcies, is evidence of the social and economic costs of failure to protect home producers. In terms of global international trade the complaints of the poorest nations about agricultural tariffs carry little weight.

Trade blocs   The real clout remains with the richer countries of Europe, East Asia and North America whose trade has grown so interdependent that trade wars would be fatal. There are a series of MAD (Mutual Assured Destruction) relations that link Japan, the EC and the North Americans in a *de facto* suicide pact in trade. Any attempt to wage a trade war will do serious damage to everyone's economy. Thus slanging matches across the Atlantic about the EC's protectionist practices in agricultural imports, are matched by the United States and Japan trading insults over the so-called structural impediments to trade. Just to complete the triangle, the EC squeezes Japan into accepting 'voluntary export restraints' as a way of keeping the temperature of trade disputes under control.

Keeping trade   With the Communist states either collapsing or the survivors
open   wanting to join the international market economy, it seems as if the arguments in favour of free trade are winning. In 1987 Canada and the United States negotiated a free trade agreement and the EC has been opening its doors to new members and international agreements. The risks of trade wars between the three main trading blocs of the capitalist economy seem less than earlier in the 1980s, although an unhealthy suspicion persists, especially on the part of those whose economy is not doing quite so well. In late 1990, as the developed world drifted into a recession and worry about the impact of the Gulf War increased, the Uruguay round of the GATT talks seemed thwarted by United States-EC disputes over agriculture and the fading faith in the United States for a genuinely open market in services. But for all the fury about the failure to conclude the GATT round, the reality of complex international trade meant that it was unlikely the world market economy would collapse just because trade negotiators could not agree on further liberalization.

The real market   The statesmen of the major market economies like to pretend
forces   that they control trade policy and they can keep the system open and thriving. But the real decision-makers are the myriad company executives who make daily decisions about what currency to use, where to open new operations to avoid tariffs, and which company to buy in order to expand or share risk. In the modern world where American firms in Japan sell more to the United States than the total of the Japanese trade surplus with the US, it is impossible

Car company tie-ups: The engine of growth

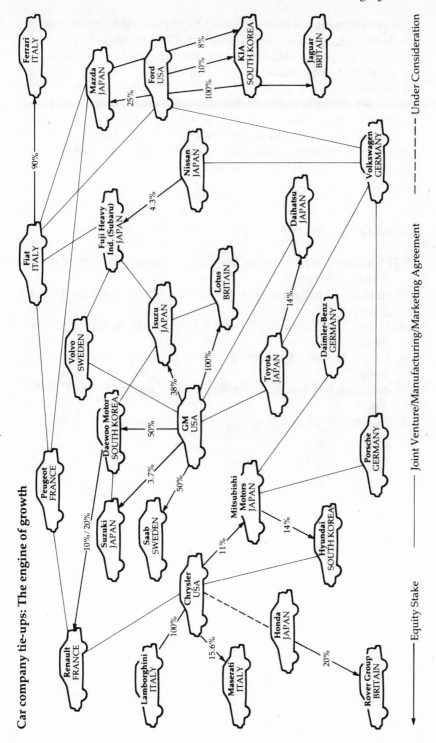

——— Equity Stake   ——— Joint Venture/Manufacturing/Marketing Agreement   - - - - Under Consideration

for governments to know whether to impose trade restrictions in order to enhance the national interest. Can anyone control a complex trading process where Korean cars, designed by Germans, are marketed by Americans? The ex-British Prime Minister, Margaret Thatcher, argues the case in Europe for Japanese companies who have set up operations in Britain. Individual companies avoid higher taxes or rises in currency value by locating production overseas. This is clearly a complex economy, far beyond the control of governments unless they operate together. Even then, supporters of the market, live and die by its arcane and often perverse ways.

Reading

J.H. Jackson, *Restructuring the GATT System* (London: Frances Pinter, 1990).

D. Julius, *Global Companies and Public Policy* (London: Frances Pinter, 1990).

A. Oxley, *The Challenge of Free Trade* (New York: St. Martin's Press, 1990).

E. Luard, *Economic Relationships Among States* (London: Macmillan, 1984).

P. Nicolaides, *Liberalizing Service Trade* (London: Frances Pinter, 1989).

S. Strange, *States and Markets* (London: Frances Pinter, 1988).

The Politics of Oil

One of the most enduring currencies of power in the post-war world has been oil. The transition from control by Western multi-nationals (Exxon, BP, Shell, Texaco, Socal, Mobil, CFP) to the Organization of the Petroleum Exporting Countries (OPEC) has been one of the major events since 1945. By the 1980s, when OPEC was fracturing, the age of oil seemed to be fading. But the Iraqi invasion of Kuwait, and the threat to do the same to Saudi Arabia in August 1990, raised the spectre of one state controlling nearly half the world's oil supply. Now the concern was no longer OPEC, but the risk of war when access to oil was threatened.

OPEC was established at the initiative of Venezuela in September 1960 and initially included Iran, Iraq, Kuwait and Saudi Arabia; later members are Algeria, Ecuador, Gabon, Indonesia, Libya, Nigeria, Qatar and the United Arab Emirates. OPEC members today produce about 30% of total world petroleum (compared with 55% in 1973) and possess about 67% of known reserves. The Soviet Union produces 23% and the United States some 18% of world oil. The immediate reason for the establishment of OPEC was a conjunction of political and economic trends. Politically, as part of the decolonization process, developing countries became more assertive in controlling their own resources. Economically, as a

Discovering the power of oil

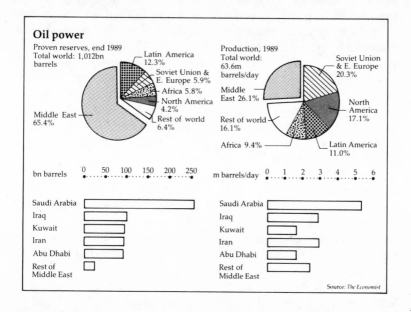

Oil power

Proven reserves, end 1989
Total world: 1,012bn barrels

Middle East 65.4%
Latin America 12.3%
Soviet Union & E. Europe 5.9%
Africa 5.8%
North America 4.2%
Rest of world 6.4%

Production, 1989
Total world: 63.6m barrels/day

Middle East 26.1%
Soviet Union & E. Europe 20.3%
North America 17.1%
Latin America 11.0%
Africa 9.4%
Rest of world 16.1%

bn barrels 0   50   100   150   200   250

Saudi Arabia
Iraq
Kuwait
Iran
Abu Dhabi
Rest of Middle East

m barrels/day 0   1   2   3   4   5   6

Saudi Arabia
Iraq
Kuwait
Iran
Abu Dhabi
Rest of Middle East

Source: *The Economist*

43

result of the competition between new independent oil companies, new oil producers and some new state oil companies, the international price began to fall.

Pumping and prices

Although the immediate objective of halting the falling price of oil was successful, OPEC members realized that only when they controlled levels of production could they effectively control the price. It was not until the coup by Colonel Qadafy in Libya in 1969 that such control could be asserted. Because of the closure of the Suez Canal in 1967, Libyan oil was in high demand in Europe. Qadafy was able to put pressure on the independent oil firms to raise prices and cut back production. Algeria, and then OPEC states individually, followed suit. Coupled with a boom in Western economies in 1972, demand for oil was high. The 1973 Arab–Israeli War led OPEC to impose an embargo on the United States and the Netherlands and, because of the paucity of spare oil production capacity, the price rose from $2 per barrel in June 1973 to over $11 in December. The market price of world oil output rose from 0.5% to 2.5% of gross world product. Further price rises followed in the 1970s, and OPEC members moved swiftly to nationalize large sections of foreign oil company operations and to establish their own 'downstream' refining facilities.

The oil shock

Real oil prices declined to a certain extent in the late 1970s as recession hit Western economies (the so-called oil shock), inflation rose and demand fell. But economic recovery in 1979 increased demand, and the Iran–Iraq War in 1980 reduced supply so a further burst of price rises ensued (from $13 a barrel in early 1979 to $39 at the end of 1980, back to under $20 in early 1991, and then fluctuating wildly as the risks of war in Gulf were perceived to rise and fall). Yet because of the fall in the value of the United States dollar, 'real' oil prices (oil is priced in dollars) fell to mid-1970s levels. In 1985 world oil sales accounted for 5% of gross world product and in 1990 for 40% of world energy use. The primary variable determining the price of oil was the need of capitalist economies, and OPEC members could affect these demands by alterations in their prices. However, the needs of OPEC members were never uniform, with the major cleavage between the 'spenders' and the 'savers'.

Spenders versus savers

Although all OPEC members had taken advantage of the huge shift of resources resulting from the rise in oil prices to spend lavishly on their own development, some members, such as Nigeria or Iran, had particularly pressing needs for a steady flow of oil to finance grandiose plans. They were aware that their resources were limited and therefore had to hope that the rise in prices would not undermine demand in the short term. Others, such as Saudi Arabia, had massive supplies and could afford to leave oil in the ground and so develop more slowly (except for what was needed to cover overseas deficits on purchases). They feared that inflated prices would undermine the 'age of petroleum' by making alternative sources of energy more feasible. The spenders sought increased production, but depended on the savers, especially Saudi Arabia, to cut production and so keep prices high. The savers recognized that increased production would undermine prices. Of course, both wanted to increase oil prices; the difference was how and by how much.

The issue was decided by factors only partially in the control of OPEC. The organization had never been a collection of ideologically like-minded states. It was always an organization of economic convenience. Meanwhile, Western economies built up vast oil reserves, enabling them to ride out short-term fluctuations in price which in the past had helped drive up overall prices. Western states also became more conscious of the need for conservation and therefore controlled demand, even while their economies were growing. Finally, such non-OPEC producers as Mexico, Britain and Norway felt little compunction in cutting prices to keep up their own full production. OPEC, which had fought so hard to make itself the marginal producer in the tight market of the 1970s, now found itself stuck at that marginal position in a softening market. Prices were still set at the margins, but the buyers now were reasserting more control, forcing OPEC into cutting either prices or production.

The OPEC collapse begins

By the 1980s there was a growing recognition among many OPEC Gulf states, especially those of a more conservative political persuasion, that they had an even greater vested interest in the stability of the international market economy. Many had dreamt of the oil bonanza providing the ability to buy modernity, but only a few states, such as Kuwait, were successful in buying economic modernity, while refusing to modernize its political system. Others, such as Iraq, squandered their funds on grandiose projects or costly wars. Compared to the success of the NICs, OPEC states wasted an unrepeatable opportunity for growth. For some, such as the smaller Gulf states, their most profitable investments were abroad in developing economies, and these investments prospered with a low international oil price.

Investment choices

The conflicting objectives between those such as Kuwait who could live with a low and stable oil price, and those such as Iraq which wanted more revenue and cared less about the stability of the international market economy, erupted in August 1990 when Iraq invaded Kuwait. The conflict had more complex causes, but certainly a feature was the emerging rift in OPEC about the best way to husband their resources. It is thought that at present rates of use, the known oil reserves will last for thirty years, and another thirty years if new extraction techniques are used. In the short

War within OPEC

term, as we have already seen, a conflict in the Gulf brings greater uncertainty about the price of oil. On the other hand, a sudden discovery of vast new oil fields might bring about a price reduction. But in the end the oil will run out, its price will be bound to rise, and other ways of generating energy will become more profitable.

The greening of oil

In addition, the new concern with limiting greenhouse gases has increased the chances that oil consumption will be limited by more energy-efficient technology. Backlash against the oil business after damage caused by such oil spills as the 11 million gallons that gushed from the Exxon Valdez in Alaska in March 1989 will also hit the oil business hard. Although 3 million barrels of oil were spilled into the delicate environment of the Gulf, and Iraq torched hundreds of oil wells, at least this case of massive pollution could be blamed on the war in 1991 rather than on the oil industry. But with alternative sources of energy more viable, those oil-rich states that by then have squandered their chances to buy their way into a modern economy by spending fleeting oil revenues, are unlikely to get a second chance. If it has not already been destroyed by war, OPEC, like its cherished oil, will run out.

Ten worst oil-spills

Date	Location	Tanker(s)	Estimated spillage (US gallons m)
July 1979	Trinidad	Atlantic Empress, Aegean Captain	92
August 1983	South Africa	Castillo de Bellver	77
March 1978	France	Amoco Cadiz	68
March 1967	Britain	Torrey Canyon	36
December 1972	Gulf of Oman	Sea Star	35
May 1976	Spain	Urquiola	31
February 1977	Northern Pacific	Hawaiian Patriot	30
March 1970	Sweden	Othello	18–31
June 1968	South Africa	World Glory	14
March 1989	Alaska	Exxon Valdez	11

Source: 1989 World Almanac

Reading

'Cheaper oil', *The Economist*, 6 July 1985.

Y. Sayigh, *Arab Oil Politics in the 1970s* (London: Croom Helm, 1983).

I. Skeet, *OPEC* (Cambridge: Cambridge University Press, 1989).

F. Venn, *Oil Diplomacy in the Twentieth Century* (London: Macmillan, 1986).

D. Yergin, *The Prize* (New York: Simon & Schuster, 1991).

2

SHAPING THE NEW AGENDA

Islam and Other Ideologies

It is often possible for states to keep their people cooped up and restrict the range of their trade. But ideas may prove more powerful than narrow-minded leaders, for they can percolate through to people and lead to a popular uprising. However, the power of ideas is variable, and waxes and wanes in seemingly sudden waves. Consider the 1980s, when the ideal of Communism was recognized as bankrupt, while the attraction of Islam seemed to revive in many parts of the developing world.

Islam and other religions Some 32% of the world's population are said to be Christian, but only 60% of these are practising church members. But except for a few sects or cases where they are in conflict with other active religions, Christians are not a powerful political force. By contrast there is the case of Islam, comprising some 20% of the world's population. There are thirty-three countries when the majority of the population is Islamic, yet some of the largest numbers of believers are in countries such as India where Muslims comprise less than half the population. Indonesia and Bangladesh have a huge Islamic majority, but it is still estimated that India has a larger Muslim population than the neighbouring Islamic state of Pakistan. The supposedly atheist Soviet Union has more than 30 million Muslims and China has over 20 million.

Islamic foundations The founder of Islam was the prophet Muhammad, born around 570 AD in Mecca in present-day Saudi Arabia. He proclaimed the worship of one God, Allah, and fought with opponents to assert his position as the prophet of Allah. The sacred book, the Koran, was revealed to Muhammad and it lays down certain social and moral rules. In subsequent centuries additional laws were welded into the Islamic system. Despite some factional disputes, Islam spread by conquest throughout the Middle East into North Africa, Southern Europe, and eventually through Central Asia to India and Southeast Asia. At various times, different rulers in the Islamic world sponsored magnificent art and architecture not to mention science and technology. But the rise of European power on its Christian base eventually subjugated most of the Islamic world and helped carve it up into various states.

Sunnis and Shi'as Over 80% of Muslims are Sunni – followers of the Sunna, or the Way of the Prophet. The Shi'as are associated with the party of Ali and although they are meant to have few fundamental differences from the Sunni, they give their spiritual leaders greater autonomy to interpret the proper application of the rules. Although Islam makes no essential distinction between religion and politics, the differences within the religion have assumed major political importance.

The heartland of traditional Islam in Saudi Arabia received a major boost in the 1970s with the formation of an effective strategy to raise oil prices and take control of the resource from Western companies. Funds were used to support Islam around the world, undermining both socialist governments in the Arab world, and 'permissive Western practices' in other states. Perhaps the most high profile success for Islam was the victory of the Ayatollah (high religious leader) Khomeini in Shi'ite Iran who deposed the corrupt, but Western-oriented Shah. Alcohol was banned, Western culture attacked, and women veiled in accordance with traditional beliefs. Persecution of religious and secular opponents was a major part of the revolution in the early 1980s.

Islamic revival

The resurgence of Islam has helped intensify a number of conflicts both inside the Arab world and without. The war of Afghan guerillas against the heathen Soviet Union in the 1980s was simple in comparison to either the warring factions of Islam in the Lebanon, the Iran–Iraq confrontation or the Iraq–Kuwait conflict. But Islam, like any ideology, soon discovered the rude pragmatism of international affairs. While Iran denounced the United States as 'the great satan', it supported the same anti-Soviet forces in Afghanistan as the Americans.

Islam in confrontation

With the death of Ayatollah Khomeini in 1989, Iran looked like passing into a less revolutionary phase. Indeed the wave of Islamic optimism seemed to have crested. The oil weapon was shown to be of limited use, and the Gulf was divided by wars between Iran and Iraq and then Iraq and the Allied Forces, resulting from the invasion of Kuwait and the threat to Saudi Arabia. Islamic fighting forces, whether in Afghanistan or Lebanon, tended to fight each other as much as they fought non-believers. With the decay of the Russian empire, even the greater independence for Moscow's Islamic colonies in Soviet Central Asia merely looked like producing a clutch of Afghan-like rivalries.

New issues for Islam

Indeed, ideology everywhere seemed in retreat before the power of pragmatic politics. The post-1945 world's main ideological struggle had pitted those espousing Marxist-Leninist dogma against supporters of the free-market and the rights of individuals. The Communist world had been led by the Soviet Union since the Russian Revolution of 1917, but seventy years on from the revolution, the ideology was in retreat.

Collapsing Communism

By the end of 1989 the ideology that claimed to be leading socialist states towards Communism was nearly routed. The causes of the collapse are complex. By the late 1980s it had become

Why Communism failed

clear to the rulers of the Soviet Union that its notion of class struggle had led to the impoverishment of their own country as well as those of their allies. As Moscow agreed to the restructuring (*perestroika*) of their system, they also decided to allow their closest allies in Eastern Europe to choose their own path to modernity. The unleashing of pent-up discontent in Eastern Europe led to the removal from power of the Communist Party in Poland, East Germany, Czechoslovakia, and Hungary. Changes in leadership in Bulgaria and Romania led Communists to rename their party but cling to power reaffirmed by the verdict of the ballot box. By early 1991 even the Soviet Union was inching towards multi-party government, albeit in a system that looked like collapsing into a welter of rivalries.

Where are the Communists now?

By mid-1990 it was hard to find anyone in Europe who would own up to being a Communist. Even reclusive Albania saw challenges to its Communist Party by late 1990, although elections in the spring of 1991 produced the first case of a more or less fairly elected Communist Party government. Communist parties that remained in power were those who came to power as a result of an indigenous revolution. China, Vietnam and Cuba were the prime examples where Communism had been nurtured by nationalism into a more natural government. The other Communists still in power – North Korea, Mongolia, Laos and Cambodia – were all, interestingly, in East Asia. Was there something in common that kept them Communist?

From Communism to Confucianism

With the exception of Cuba and Albania, all remaining states ruled by Communist parties were part of the Chinese cultural zone of Confucianism. Although Confucianism has nothing that can be called a coherent set of beliefs necessary to qualify as a formal ideology or religion, it does lay the basis for an acceptance of authoritarianism and group rights, rather than the rights of the individual. Indeed it was hard to find anything that might be described as a genuinely multi-party, free-market society anywhere in the Confucian zone of East Asia, including those states not ruled by Communist parties.

National Communism

Of course, there were important variations in these East Asian states' ideologies. Thus Communism was not likely to last in some states, and probably those without an indigenous revolution were the most likely to find their own type of authoritarian government. This is not to say that Communism would become an irrelevance, for even if China and Vietnam remain as the last two Communist-ruled states on earth, more than one-fifth of humanity will still be ruled by those who claim some inspiration from 19th-century European revolutionaries.

Reading

P. Bannerman, *Islam in Perspective* (London: Routledge, 1988).

A. Dawisha (ed), *Islam in Foreign Policy* (Cambridge: Cambridge University Press, 1983).

D. Hiro, *Islamic Fundamentalism* (London: Collins, 1988).

B. Lawrence, *Defenders of God* (New York: Harper and Row, 1989).

J. Piscatori, *Islam in a World of Nation States* (Cambridge: Cambridge University Press, 1986).

K. Dawisha, *Eastern Europe, Gorbachev and Reform* (Cambridge: Cambridge University Press, 1990).

D. Armstrong and E. Goldstein, *The End of the Cold War* (London: Frank Cass, 1990).

G. Stern, *International Communism* (Brighton: Wheatsheaf, 1990).

People Power and Human Rights

In the new pragmatism of the 1990s, there is a sense that all that needs to be done is to get the people out on the streets, and any tyrant can be deposed. Was not President Marcos of the Philippines toppled like that in 1986? Did not the dictators of Eastern Europe, including the barbaric Ceausescu clan in Romania, succumb to the power of unarmed, peaceful demonstrators in 1989? Yes, but the counter-examples are also powerful. In 1989 Communist China used its troops to massacre demonstrators right before the eyes of Western television cameras. And even some of those countries who used people power to clear out old dictators, soon chose replacements that looked nearly as incompetent as their predecessors (the Philippines, Bulgaria and Romania).

Revolutionary conditions

Of course the mass of people united behind a single cause can be unstoppable. Russian and Chinese Communists came to power on the wave of such sentiment, and the inhabitants of the present-day United States also won their independence with similar popular power. But the masses can go in a number of directions, and indeed they can often do serious damage in the process. Iran is certainly a poorer place after its revolution, even if more spiritually pure. There is no pattern to what the masses might do, largely because there is no common pattern to politics in this multicultural world.

Multi-culturalism and human rights

Indeed, multiculturalism is also the main reason why it is so hard to identify something that might be called an international standard of human rights. The atrocities that human beings commit against each other range from large-scale genocide to individual acts of terror and cruelty. Most of these inhuman acts are carried out in the name of some political principle and frequently the individuals under threat have little recourse against the vicious state power. Unfortunately, since different states operate on different principles, the definition of the rights enjoyed by human beings around the world is so different. Such early documents as the United States Bill of Rights or anti-slavery treaties attempted to codify human, political and minority rights, but they were by no means universally accepted.

The Declaration of Human Rights

In response to the unprecedented barbarities of Nazi Germany, new impetus was given to the idea of codifying universal human rights. On 10 December 1948, the United Nations General Assembly passed, unopposed, the Declaration of Human Rights. The Soviet bloc, Saudi Arabia and South Africa abstained. The

Human Rights Commission of the United Nations had been established in 1946 and it drafted the declaration and the covenants required to implement it. The first covenant on economic, social and cultural rights and the second on civil and political rights were passed by the General Assembly in 1966, but did not enter into force until 1976. The second covenant also established a Human Rights Committee to implement these rights, but it has been consistently hindered by governments' refusal to cooperate. For example, Israel has refused to cooperate with investigations of its activities in territories it occupied after the 1967 war.

Although a legal basis was established for individuals to hold their governments to international standards on human rights, the United Nations efforts lacked the teeth to implement them. The basic problem is that sovereign states can, and often do, ignore treaties using various excuses. Some states claim that 'human rights begin at breakfast' and they cannot afford to implement the luxuries of international law when they are engaged in the tough process of state-building. Others claim that rights of individuals are secondary to rights of classes or groups. Some claim that the freedom from want for society as a whole also overrides certain freedoms for individuals, such as the right to own property. States even find it difficult to agree that the right to life is so basic that it cannot be taken away, as by capital punishment. *The UN's soft teeth*

Certain regional groupings have, however, been more successful in implementing human rights policy. The Council of Europe's Convention on Human Rights was signed in Rome on 4 November 1950, and came into force on 3 September 1953. A European Commission on Human Rights determines whether petitions are admissible and the Court of Human Rights then rules on the cases that are presented. It has heard cases regarding Greece, Northern Ireland, and also issues involving individuals. The worse sanction it has against states is to expel them from the Council, but the real power is in the attention that a free press and public opinion can bring to bear as a result of a case being brought to the Court. So long as the states of Western Europe have such a free press and open politics, the Convention can help protect individuals from their governments and help harmonise laws in Europe. Because of the screening procedures of the Commission, the prestige of the Court is, in fact, increasing. It has of course so far only operated at the margins of unclear law, but the Convention has been able to build on the common consensus in democratic politics and the rule of law. *Regional human rights*

Other regional human rights efforts have been far less successful. The 1975 Helsinki Conference on Security and Cooperation in Europe (CSCE) included concern for human rights. But East European opposition groups, such as Charter 77 in Czechoslovakia, had little success in improving their situation, because their political system provided for fewer individual rights. In any case, the Helsinki document is a declaration, not a binding treaty. Also, the Arab League set up a Permanent Arab Commission on Human Rights in 1969 but it has had even less impact. The 1969 American Convention on Human Rights entered into force in 1978 but has run up against the problem of differing political systems in Latin America.

Amnesty
International

Some smaller non-state human rights groups have had a greater impact than many regional, inter-state conventions. Amnesty International, a private monitoring group launched in Britain in 1961, seeks to obtain freedom for prisoners of conscience. It has been instrumental in bringing attention to cases of human rights abuses in Europe (for example in Northern Ireland and Greece) and beyond. It concentrates on gathering information and on education and pressuring Western governments to act against both their friends and enemies.

The triumph of people power in much of Eastern Europe clearly had a great deal to do with the fact that those like the signatories of Charter 77 were organized campaigners for human rights with international support. One of their leaders, Vaclav Havel, even became President of post-Communist Czechoslovakia. But with thousands of prisoners of conscience around the world, only a few can hope for such complete satisfaction. In the end the most important support the non-Communist world gave to the dissidents on the other side of the continent was the power of positive example – non-Communist Europe worked and prospered.

Reading

J.I. Dominguez *et al*, Enhancing Global Human Rights (New York: McGraw Hill, 1979).

J. Donnelly, *Universal Human Rights in Theory and Practice* (Ithaca: Cornell University Press, 1989).

C. Humana, *World Human Rights Guide* (London: Hutchinson, 1983).

B. Roberts, 'Human Rights and International Security', *Washington Quarterly*, Spring 1990.

A.H. Robertson, *Human Rights in the World* (Manchester: Manchester University Press, 1982).

Migration and Refugees

One thousand years ago there were no Germans in Berlin, no Russians in Moscow, no Thais in Bangkok and only native Americans in the United States of America. For thousands of years open borders were essential to the development of world politics and indeed such migration was a basic human right. It may have been physically more difficult to cross mountain ranges and long distances in those days, but people moved more freely than in our modern age of a supposed 'global village' and ever-closer interdependence. The migrants were then more able to seek a better life than in the modern world where larger gaps between rich and poor, free and oppressed, create far more reason for the rich and free to defend their space.

The past and passports
Over thousands of years, people migrated across the planet to populate nearly every region. It was not until the 16th century in Europe that political units such as nations and states began burdening the traveller with passports in order to control the flow of humanity. But these same Europeans were also responsible in one way or another for some of the most massive shifts of population. Under British colonialism, some 28 million Indians left for other British dominions. In the century from 1815 some 55 million Europeans went abroad, mostly to the Americas. In the aftermath of the Second World War, 15 million Germans were on the move and in the decade from 1945 some 45 million people moved around the world, most notably 15 million in the India-Pakistan resettlement in 1946–7.

Migration as a market mechanism
To some extent these shifts in population were merely the mechanism by which the political market made sure people lived with their own kind when politics changed borders and economic prospects. Wars and decolonization altered the shape and content of countries, leaving a window of opportunity for those who felt they needed to move. It was usually the most persecuted and most ambitious who did so, although once a new status quo began to take shape, it was harder for anyone to change places. Yet even in the post-war world, major migrations did take place. Some 3.5 million people fled East Germany before the Berlin Wall went up in August 1961 and still nearly 300,000 more managed to get out in the following twenty-five years.

Modern patterns
By the 1980s the flows of refugees and migrants as a whole were largely confined to specific regions with very little transcontinental flow. The war in Afghanistan created 4 million refugees,

56

with the largest portion heading for the Pakistan border. In the thirty years of Communism in Cuba, some 10% of the population moved to the United States. With the collapse of Communism in Eastern Europe, hundreds of thousands fled West, especially from East Germany, before the revolutions provided new governments.

One of the few exceptions to the restricted number of transcontinental migrants was the special case of the 2 million refugees from Vietnam in the decade after the end of the war in 1975. Because the United States had been so closely involved in the war, it ended up taking half of the total, but only after a major international relief effort was organized. The United Nations helped obtain international agreement for an Orderly Departure Program in 1979 under which Vietnam promised to stop all illegal departures and Western states agreed to take the refugees then forsaken in camps around Southeast Asia. But as the refugees continued to trickle out in the late 1980s, 'compassion fatigue' clearly set in, especially as the wounds of guilt about the war began to heal in the United States. The refugees from Vietnam, who increasingly came out in search of economic prosperity rather than political freedom, remained stuck in squalid camps.

The Vietnamese challenge

On a broad measure, the world now contains some 15 million refugees and most are in the developing world. While many would

Refugees in the 1990s

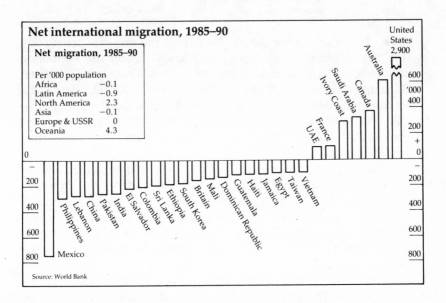

Net international migration, 1985–90

Where they come from

Countries of origin of asylum-seekers in Western
Europe, the United States and Canada

1983–88*

Iran	140,000
Turkey	110,000
Poland	108,000
Sri Lanka	80,000
Ghana	45,000
Lebanon	40,000
Romania	31,000
Yugoslavia	31,000
Czechoslovakia	29,000
Chile	27,000
India	26,000
Pakistan	26,000
Hungary	25,000
Zaire	24,000
Ethiopia	23,000
Iraq	15,000

*Excluding applications from Central
Americans   *Source*: UNHCR

like a better life in the developed world, the majority are merely
the victims of upheavals caused by wars. Consider the 3.6 million
Afghans in Pakistan and 2.3 million in Iran. There are 1.2 million
Mozambicans in central and southern Africa, 900,000 Palestinians
in Jordan, 660,000 Eritreans in Sudan, 350,000 Somalis in Ethiopia,
320,000 Cambodians in Thailand and 250,000 Central Americans
in each other's countries. Europe (minus Turkey) has less than
150,000 refugees.

Finding   The easiest solution for all concerned is that once the cause of
solutions the upheaval is resolved, usually a war, the refugees should return
home (as 41,000 Namibians did in 1989). Indeed that is what is
likely to happen to all the major groups of modern refugees. But
the problem of migrating people is far from over, because even
without war, people will continue to seek a better life in the richer
and freer world.

Economic   These so-called economic migrants continue to come to the
migrants   United States from the south. Some 95% of 125,000 official refugees
admitted to the United States in 1989 were from Communist states,
but a far larger (and hard to count) flow surged across the Mexican
border in search of a higher standard of living. Western Europe
also confronts a similar problem with people from North Africa.

France has 3.6 million immigrants in total and Italy has 1.3 million (of which two-thirds are illegal immigrants). Once into the EC, these migrants find that the lifting of internal border controls allows them to roam around in search of a better life. And looking east from the EC there is the spectre that now the Iron Curtain has been removed, millions of frustrated or even starving East Europeans might seek a better life in richer Western Europe. It is a paradox that as the borders within the EC come down, they seem to have to go even higher on the outer fringe.

At the rich world's door

Asylum-seekers in Western Europe, the United States and Canada

	Applicants	Backlog	Costs* $ Billion	Acceptance rate %	Proportion that stays %
1983	90,000	60,000	0.5	40	90
1985	200,000	100,000	2	35	90
1987	240,000	360,000	3	25	90
1989†	450,000††	400,000	5	20	90
1991**	550,000	500,000	6	15	90

* Includes social assistance for those awaiting verdict   ** Forecast   † Estimates
†† Excludes East Germans, Bulgarian Turks, Soviet Jews and other Soviet emigrés

Source: UNHCR

Bearing the burden

The ability of the rich to absorb these migrants depends on a complex mix of factors. Larger countries may have more space but if they have a sparse population they may not want the ethnic balance to change quickly, if at all. If they have a large population they may claim they are already too crowded to absorb more. Germany may take millions of ethnic Germans from the East, but absorbing Turks is far more difficult. Politically liberal states like Sweden have now discovered the limits of their liberality, whereas the United States continues to absorb hundreds of thousands into its melting pot of migrants.

New flows

The flow of migrants looks set to continue. Some even suggest that with global change in the climate and increasing famine, the pressure on the rich will become intolerable. Supporters of the 'market mechanism' seem to think that under such conditions the rich will simply build higher fences while more people die in the developing world. Global warming might make Canada and the Soviet Union more able to absorb larger populations in a more hospitable climate.

Yet some economic migrants will find a better life. The boat people of Southeast Asia will continue to trickle around the developing world, albeit in smaller numbers than before. The yacht people of Hong Kong will find places in Canada, Australia and the United States because they have skills and even money that makes their resettlement far easier. But if local wars and famines in the developing world do get so bad that the immediate pressure on people to leave is so great, the developed world will have to do more than simply build higher walls. They might even have to help solve the problems of the poor.

Reading

A. Dowty, *Closed Borders* (New Haven: Yale University Press, 1987).

'The Year of the Refugee', *The Economist*, 23 December 1989.

K. A. Hamilton and K. Holder, 'International Migration and Foreign Policy', *The Washington Quarterly*, Spring 1991.

G. Loescher and L. Monahan (eds), *Refugees and International Relations* (Oxford: Oxford University Press, 1989).

W. McNeill and R. Adams, *Human Migration* (London: Indiana University Press, 1977).

Food and Famine

Food is a basic human need, but not until recently has its supply become an international issue. The pathetic pictures of starving children on the television screens of the developed world contrast with EC butter mountains and overflowing grain silos in the United States. Few issues illustrate the huge divide between rich and poor on this planet more than the question of who eats and who starves. International efforts to relieve the most acute famines have been mounted but, despite the fact that famines can be predicted well in advance, relatively little has so far been done to prevent the deaths of millions in the poorest parts of the world.

In the past, any absence of food led to famine or migration. *Learning to* Hardly any food was traded across long distances and millions of *trade food* people died without most of the world knowing about it. But in the 19th century, North American grain, Argentinian beef and Southeast Asian rice were traded in increasing quantities. The coming of steamships and refrigeration made food transport more economic. Some states, such as Britain, abandoned the policy of self-sufficiency in food and relied on cheap food imports. But by the end of the First World War, only Europe was in any significant way dependent on food imports.

By the 1980s the picture was radically altered with only North *Increasing* America and Australia effectively independent of food imports. In *world food* 1980, 70% of the grain on the international market came from *production* North America. Poor countries found it harder to increase their yield as fast as such grain-growing, developed states as Canada and the United States. Yet total world food production had consistently increased in the 1970s – about 3% higher on an annual average, with many states such as Brazil, Korea, Morocco or Cuba showing even greater increases.

There were few shortages of food in the developed and fast-developing world. Better health care kept more people alive and there were demands for better levels of nutrition; but there was also a clear trend towards controlling population growth. In developed states the increase in population slowed as living standards and education levels rose. Better, and more widespread, use of contraception and later marriages in developed states helped ensure that there were few food problems. Similar trends were evident in newly-industrialized countries and were often enhanced by tough measures to control population growth, as in China and Indonesia.

Threats of
famine

Yet the world's population is expected to increase by the year 2000 to 6 billion souls. The main problem, and pressure on food supplies, comes from unchecked population growth in some parts of the Third World. Not only are there more mouths to feed, but unrestrained urban sprawl reduces cropland and new fields are often less productive. Few people actually die of malnutrition; most become weak and die of related diseases such as diarrhoea or dysentry. Obviously it is urgent for some parts of the less-developed world that food supplies double in the next twenty years. Given the low crop yields in many Third World states, especially Africa and Andean Latin America, this is certainly feasible.

The location of
the starving

The worst problems seem to be in sub-Saharan Africa, in which there are twenty-three of the world's thirty-six poorest states. But it is only since the early 1970s that the area has run seriously short of food. Production of food had dropped since 1968, while it was increasing in most of Asia and Latin America. In 1984 total African food production rose 3.6%, but in the Sahel states (Sudan, Chad, Niger, Mauritania, Mali, Burkina Faso) where population growth was one of the highest on the continent, it fell by 5%. The difficulties can in part be attributed to climate, and especially years of drought, but some states, such as Chad, still have rich soils.

Problems with
food aid

From 1984, Africa received more free food aid (7 million tons in 1984–5) than ever. Yet food aid is not a solution to the long-term threat of famine for a number of reasons. First, food aid tends to go to cities rather than the worst-affected rural areas. Sixty per cent of EC and 30% of American food aid is 'programme aid', which is given to governments to sell, usually in cities, providing funds which often go to buy tanks rather than seeds for the next season's crops. Second, food aid also cuts food prices, reducing incentives to farmers to grow their own crops and creating long-term dependence. Thirdly, the aid is often provided without the necessary transport and therefore rots on quaysides and airport tarmacs. Fourthly, problems are exacerbated by the types of régimes governing starving people. They often insist on controlling food supplies and will feed their armies before they are prepared to help the starving.

Western relief organizers are well meaning but often squabble among themselves and sometimes are incompetent amateurs. Their aid is usually very expensive to transport and poorly used. Of the 1975–81 aid to the Sahel, 35% was spent on shipping, 30% on infrastructure, and only 4% on growing crops and 15% on tree planting and conservation. Africa received ten times the aid of South Asia on a per capita basis in the 1970s and still many more Africans died. Finally, the building of camps for dispensing aid creates 'food drones'. Patterns of migration are upset and peasants

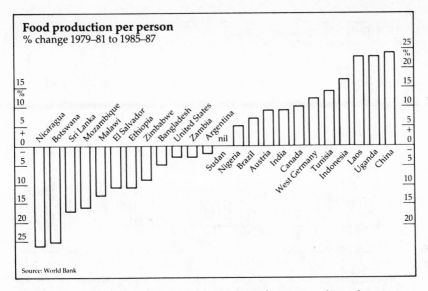

Food production per person
% change 1979–81 to 1985–87

Source: World Bank

are enticed away from returning to their farms to plant the new crop. The resulting 'aid culture', seen vividly in the 1985 and 1987 Ethiopian famine, creates long-term dependence.

International agencies

The international agencies dealing with food supply are well-meaning, but most have a poor record. In October 1945 the United Nations set up a specialized agency, the Food and Agriculture Organization (FAO). In 1963 it began administering the World Food Programme to encourage more food production but ended up as a bloated bureaucracy, spending far too much time gathering figures. The 1973–4 African food crisis led to the creation of the World Food Council to monitor world food production. Because famines are rarely sudden they can be predicted well in advance. The United Nations also set up the International Fund for Agricultural Development to undertake practical aid work. But by far the most effective aid organizations are those with local expertise and 'barefoot doctors' able to make on-the-spot decisions on priorities.

Roots of famine

However, with all the goodwill in the world, the root of the food problem lies beyond the reach of international agencies. Several key reforms in famine areas are urgently needed. First, food production can be increased by creating good markets with adequate prices. If prices are held too low, so as to satisfy town dwellers, farmers will not farm or will not sell what they grow. Monopoly purchasers in centrally planned economies often do not respond to the market and, consequently, unreal prices are set. Second, more effective communication, vehicles and storage are required to get more food to the people who need it and to keep it for longer. Third, more consumer goods need to be produced to be sold to farmers in exchange for their food. Farmers will not be productive if they have nothing to buy. Fourth, effective

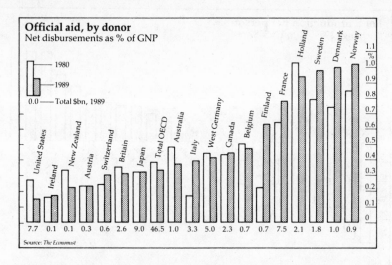

Official aid, by donor
Net disbursements as % of GNP

1980
1989
0.0 — Total $bn, 1989

United States
Ireland
New Zealand
Austria
Switzerland
Britain
Japan
Total OECD
Australia
Italy
West Germany
Canada
Belgium
Finland
France
Holland
Sweden
Denmark
Norway

7.7 0.1 0.1 0.3 0.6 2.6 9.0 46.5 1.0 3.3 5.0 2.3 0.7 0.7 7.5 2.1 1.8 1.0 0.9

Source: *The Economist*

production of food requires a broad and stable demand, which means creating a market for food among the population at large, not merely heavy consumption by a governing élite. It is ironic that large proportions of many developing states' food import bills include tinned fish, Uncle Ben's packaged rice or powdered milk. These non-essential items satisfy the urban élites' desires for what they perceive to be a Western pattern of consumption.

The need for land reform

Fifth, farmers need land reform. A rough equality of resources such as land, water and farming techniques will encourage competition and realistic prices. Sixth, investment in Third World states needs to be geared first to agriculture rather than the high prestige heavy industrial projects. Foreign investment needs to be similarly directed. Unfortunately, heavy foreign debt makes such future investment hard to obtain, leading to further economic problems. It is not surprising that, in 1984, twenty-three of thirty-one states rescheduling their debt were in sub-Saharan Africa.

The politics of famine

Third World régimes are often to blame for failing to undertake necessary reforms. One-party states tend to ignore famine warnings (as happened in Ethiopia) for fear of undermining confidence in the régime. India, a poor peasant democracy with 740 million people, has a land size only one-third larger than Sudan, but now more than feeds itself (albeit at three-quarters of the Sudan's average daily calorie intake). China suffered 20 million famine-related deaths after the 1958 Great Leap Forward, but, with recent agricultural reforms, has effectively removed the threat of massive famine. Finally, the existence of often unnatural state frontiers, for example in Africa, prevents migration of people from poor agricultural land, as in Ethiopia, Niger or Mauritania, to nearby richer land in Chad, Sudan, or Mali.

The problems are immense, but most are political and demographic. Famine is, therefore, largely a man-made disaster and one that requires fundamental reforms in local governments. International aid can fill glaring gaps for short periods but can make matters worse in the long term. Perhaps the most effective aid that developed states might offer (apart from limiting the debt burden of the poorest states and reducing farm surpluses in rich countries) is to keep out. Developing states that have reformed themselves have booming economies, falling population growth rates and, mostly, full stomachs.

Reading

'Aid to Africa', *The Economist*, 20 July 1985.

G. Hancock, *Lords of Poverty* (London: Macmillan, 1989).

Independent Commission on International Humanitarian Issues, *Famine: A Man-made Disaster?* (London: Pan, 1985).

R. Riddell, *Foreign Aid Reconsidered* (Baltimore: Johns Hopkins, 1987).

W. Shawcross, *The Quality of Mercy* (London: André Deutsch, 1984).

H. Singer, J. Wood, T. Jennings, *Food Aid* (Oxford: Oxford University Press, 1987).

Disasters and their Relief

It is a safe, if macabre, bet that every year there will be a number of major disasters, such as earthquakes, hurricanes, floods or volcanic eruptions. In the 1970s, an average of 40,000 people a year died in earthquakes. In 1990 over 50,000 people died in an earthquake in Iran and in 1991 a cyclone killed over 200,000 in Bangladesh. Most disasters will take place between the Tropics of Cancer and Capricorn and hit the under-developed states hardest. Most earthquakes strike along the 'ring of fire' that girdles the Pacific. By and large they will occur no matter what people or states do. Of course, after the fact, much aid can be provided (30–40% of the aid on average comes from outsiders) but little can be done to prevent the disaster happening again. Sometimes, future casualties can be reduced by better planning and improved rescue techniques.

The Red Cross The leading international disaster relief organization is the International Red Cross and Red Crescent. It comprises three bodies. The International Committee of the Red Cross was founded in 1863 and operates in wartime. There are also one hundred and forty-three national societies. The peacetime League of Red Cross and Red Crescent Societies (LRCS) was founded in 1919, is based in Geneva and specializes in relief operations, especially supply and logistics aid to local national relief groups.

Griefbusters In developed states, disasters often cause greater damage to property but fewer deaths. Certainly, developed states are better able to recoup their losses. For example, the United States has the 1972 Example State Disaster Act in order to help set out professional standards for coping with disasters. In 1976 the Red Cross published a detailed handbook on disaster relief. Some bright spark has even suggested the need for an international team of professional 'griefbusters', ready to sell their services to governments in need. Their expertise, equipment, and co-ordination would overcome the most serious problems that afflict well-intentioned but incompetent rescuers.

Warning of disaster But in the end relief comes best from a tough central command structure able to rely on local knowledge. Regional warning stations, for example the North Pacific system for the warning of tidal waves that links the USA, Japan and the Soviet Union, can give relief organizations a head start. Public education on a broader scale, for example China's success in preparing its people to cope with earthquakes, can train the population for crisis.

The effect of disasters can be remarkably different depending *Rich and poor deaths* on whether they strike the rich or poor. In 1989 an earthquake measuring 7.0 on the Richter scale killed a handful of people in San Francisco, while a quake of the same size in Armenia in 1988 killed over 25,000 and one at 7.3 in Iran in 1990 killed over 50,000. The Tangshan earthquake (7.8 on the Richter scale) in China in 1976 killed a quarter of a million people, while only one hundred died in the 9.2 monster in Alaska in 1964. A quake measuring 6.5 struck in 1987 in the water off Tokyo, but only 2 people died in this well-built, 'earthquake proof' metropolis. The main difference seems to be the level of development in the different regions. Rapid, uncontrolled urbanization in Nicaragua, Mexico and China resulted in cramped, poorly-built homes, and the state was unprepared to cope. A chemical leak at Bhopal in India in 1984 killed thousands in a shanty town built too close to the plant.

North American earthquakes

Year	Location	Intensity	Deaths	Cost($)*
1989	Loma, Prieta, Ca	7.0	+8	–
1988	Quebec	6.0	2	18m
1987	Whittier, Ca	5.9	8	236m
1985	Mexico City	8.1	8,000	3.4bn
1983	Coalinga, Ca	6.5	0	23m
1971	San Fernando, Ca	6.6	58	900m
1964	Prince William Sound	8.4	131	1bn
1952	Kern County, Ca	7.7	12	150m
1949	Olympia, Wa	7.0	8	80m
1946	Unimak Island	7.4	173	90m
1940	Imperial Valley, Ca	6.7	9	33m
1933	Long Beach, Ca	6.2	115	266m
1918	Mona Passage, P.Rico	7.5	116	29m
1906	San Francisco	8.3	700	2bn

*In 1979 dollars
Source: Federal Emergency Management Agency
The Economist, 21 October 1989

The level of development of states is of course a problem *Disasters and development* beyond the scope of disaster relief. But disasters, however unwelcome, can provide an opportunity to rebuild with priorities of development in mind. Unfortunately, many relief organizations established their procedures in Europe in 1945 when the priority was rehousing refugees. When applied to the Third World, these principles are often a hindrance. The 1970 earthquake in Peru killed 70,000 people, over half of whom perished in the village of Yungay. Ninety per cent of the earthquake deaths resulted from building collapse, yet the new housing is hardly better built. Similarly, cyclones and landslides are often far more serious because of human misuse of the soil. The deaths in 1974 from a hurricane which struck Honduran squatter settlements is a case in point. At times, drastic reform is undertaken. After the Tangshan earthquake in China in 1976, the authorities rebuilt industry before housing so as to create a more rational living pattern. The 1970 Bangladesh earthquake helped trigger a revolution, and the great Lisbon earthquake on All Saints Day in 1775 shocked the Age of Enlightenment. But most disasters have a less dramatic political impact.

Relief priorities   The problems in disaster relief are myriad and priorities are not always obvious. Saving life is usually paramount but, depending on the nature of the disaster, there is also a need to restore public services, repair communications, prevent epidemics and provide compensation. Earthquakes and hurricanes kill more people than other disasters (yet, car crashes alone kill 55,000 Americans each year), but depending on where they strike their effects can be very different.

Clearly, disaster relief needs to be more geared to local conditions. For example, earthquake victims do not necessarily need food, clothes or medicines for the prevention of epidemics as much as they need cash to rebuild. Outsiders on the spot are often a hindrance. Cyclone victims on the other hand, often do require food relief, and there is usually a risk of epidemics. In fact, in most disasters, the first aid to arrive is rarely very helpful. Effective aid is longer term and should aim at the sort of reconstruction that helps limit the damage if there is a next time. Local aid agencies are often better equipped and more knowledgable about requirements.

The bias of the aid donor   Of course, sometimes the aid does not do the job it was intended for, in part because it is provided for a variety of motives. Some humanitarian aid comes from foreign individuals, but it is often given via huge bureaucracies that squander a great deal on infrastructure. Other assistance, such as the pop music world's 'Live Aid' fund-raising for Ethiopian famine, tries to bypass large organizations but in turn lacks its own local staff with expert knowledge. Some states give aid for political reasons and some religious institutions because they hope their image and 'cause' will be enhanced. These competing motives often mean competing aid organizations, where a more coordinated programme could be more effective. Reliance on volunteers may be cheaper, but also less efficient. Of course, local authorities also have their particular motives in dispensing aid and in making use of the international media to serve their own domestic political ends.

The view given of disasters is often that of victims who cannot cope 'without your help'. The image is mostly misleading. Aid that distorts local self-help mechanisms may do long-term damage. But aid that is not concerned with furthering the development of the area may only ensure that the same thing happens again. Aid donors and recipients are inevitably caught between wanting help and not wanting advice which they sometimes need.

Reading

F. Curry, *Disasters and Development* (London: Oxford University Press, 1983).

S. Green, *International Disaster Relief* (New York: McGraw Hill, 1977).

R.C. Kent, *Anatomy of Disaster Relief* (London: Frances Pinter, 1988).

E. Linden, *The Alms Race* (New York: Random House, 1976).

United Nations, *Disaster Prevention and Mitigation* (New York: United Nations, 1984).

Earth Matters

Human beings not only do nasty things to each other, they also kill other living creatures and the environment around them. This is not only a tragedy for animals and plants but it provides humans with an unhealthy atmosphere and can lead to catastrophic changes in peoples' lives and politics. Of course the global biosphere (the domain of life on earth) has always been messed about, but only in recent times has our wreckage been so devastating.

Safeguarding the earth's environment would seem an obvious area for international cooperation. But only in the last century have even sporadic efforts been made in a few wealthy countries to protect some species and preserve some wilderness. The real efforts at global cooperation are much more recent and are proceeding far too slowly. Apart from a number of national and regional conservation organizations, the only major international institution is the United Nations Environmental Programme (UNEP) established in 1972 in Stockholm. Like many other international bodies, UNEP has been marred by conflicting national interests and inflammatory rhetoric but it has helped identify the main areas of environmental crisis.

First, human beings kill thousands of living creatures, thereby depleting the genetic stock of life. When the slaughter is for food, most people (except vegetarians) understand the motivation. When the killing is for frippery, like perfume (in part obtained from whales) or fashionable fur coats (skinned from baby seals) there tends to be a greater outcry. While it may be easier for concerned citizens in wealthy Western countries to get worked up about whales and cute seals, it is the elimination of the more obscure life forms that is often more important in the long term. The vast majority of species are endangered in other ways, as for example when new dams flood natural habitats. The 1973 Convention on International Trade in Endangered Species has been signed by eighty countries and prohibits international commercial trade in the rarest six hundred or so species of animals and plants. But in a commercial world where a rare orchid or an Amazon parrot can fetch up to $5,000 the attempt to preserve genetic diversity is never going to be easy.

By reducing our pool of genetic resources, we undermine our ability to recover when disaster strikes. For example, the United States' sugar industry in the 1920s was saved by the transplantation of the rare Java (Indonesia) sugar cane. Or take the case of the unloved armadillo, an animal, like man, which contracts leprosy. Experimentation on the poor creature suggests a cure for human beings is possible. Most recently, the dramatic progress in biotechnology depends on a wide stock of peculiar genetic types around the world. Of course, species have been destroyed in the past (remember the ancient dinosaur or the more recent dodo bird) but by destroying so much more, so quickly, we deplete our chances of survival and development.

Next, the poorest parts of the world suffer from desertification – the encroachment of desert on to farmland. The Sahel region of Africa is a prime example where poor people eke out an existence on marginal farmland. But when, for the sake of short-term gain, the peasants allow animals to destroy vegetation by over-grazing, marginal land becomes desert and millions starve to death. *Desertification*

The 6% of the earth's surface that is tropical forest is being destroyed by population growth in developing states. Often because of unequal distribution of land in poor states (as in Latin America's Amazon), poor people seek space in forests. Trees are destroyed for cheap energy and to provide farmland. But the earth is invariably poor, crops fail and the poverty increases. What is worse (unlike the forests which existed in Europe and North America before deforestation) tropical forests seem to provide vital rainfall and oxygen for the planet as a whole. Without these tropical forests, the build-up of carbon dioxide traps heat in the earth's atmosphere (the so-called greenhouse effect) and is likely to change temperatures worldwide. The polar ice packs may melt, coastal areas will flood, the American grain areas will turn to dust and the Soviet Union will become the breadbasket of the world. To make matters even more complicated, in addition to the 48% that is carbon dioxide, the greenhouse effect is also composed of other gases including 18% methane and 14% chloroflurocarbons (CFCs). *Shrinking forests*

Assuming that global warming is taking place (and there is some dispute on this matter), the impact will obviously be worse for some. Most developed countries, which have so far emitted most of the greenhouse gases, are rich enough to clean up their industry and even pay for the necessary adjustments if patterns of global weather change. Most poor countries look set to be the main contributors in future to greenhouse gases, but they can neither afford to clean up or avoid the impact of climate change. The poor will be the main losers and thus the solution of making the polluter pay will not work so easily. One of the more innovative ideas is to agree tradable permits for pollution which would allow those who are willing and able to clean up cheaply to do so and then make money by selling spare permissions to those for whom cleaning up would be more expensive. International coop- *The growing greenhouse effect* eration is needed, but it can be made to work with the grain of the international economy that plays such a key role in creating the pollution in the first place. Of course, as concern with protecting the environment grows, so it may well conflict with those opposed to trade protection and the consequent damage to free trade.

Counting gases and blame

But who is to pay how much for what? CFCs are not a problem in India's total greenhouse gas emission, but they are significant for Germany. Methane is a major portion of India's contribution and Brazil throws out mostly carbon dioxide. What is more, if emissions are measured on the basis of gases per-person or per-unit of GNP, the table of culprits can be made to look very different. Yet if those responsible for the problem are those who will face the most problems in coping with change in the climate, they must eventually face the problem. Sadly, so far the negotiators have had a tendency to add merely more hot air to the debate.

Coping with CFCs

CFCs trap heat ten thousand times as well as carbon dioxide and they are mostly used in replaceable luxuries such as air-conditioners and fast-food containers. They also help destroy the protective ozone layer in the stratosphere, thereby letting in more dangerous ultra-violet rays from the sun, which causes cancer. Stopping CFC production by the end of the century would probably cut greenhouse warming, after a lag, by up to 15%. A UNEP meeting in Montreal in 1987 resulted in a protocol to reduce CFC production by half. With only a few large corporations making the offending gases, it looked likely that targets could be met, although India and China refused to sign unless they were offered money to help cut CFC production. In subsequent meetings in 1990, both India and China accepted the protocol on the condition that the promised aid and transfer of technology would take place.

A climate convention

But if treatment of CFCs provide some grounds for optimism, a more general convention on protecting the climate is further off because there will be winners – usually the cooler countries. Rich countries are also loath to pay for poor countries who seem determined to repeat mistakes made by the rich and refuse to have schemes that interfere in development programs by subsidizing green policies. The United States, with its particularly profligate use of energy, also feels that the costs of its own adoption of strict targets on carbon dioxide emissions will be more than the effect of global warming. Washington is also loath to transfer the high technology necessary for solving these problems to countries with whom it disagrees on other issues.

Acid rain

Indeed the United States often seems to act like a developing country on environmental matters. With its coal-intensive power generating (like China) and its gas-guzzling cars, it puts out twice as many tonnes per person of carbon dioxide as Britain. It also

We polluters

Net per head emissions*of greenhouse gases, 1987 tonnes of carbon

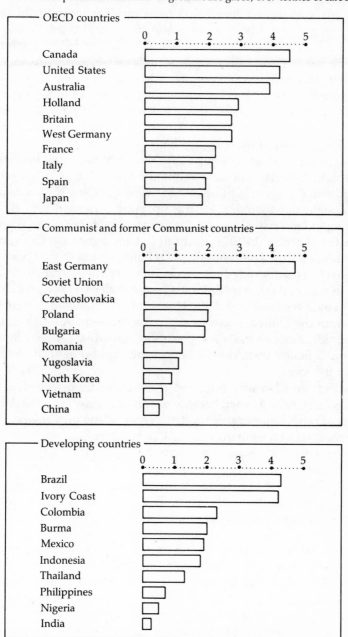

* Main three such gases (a) converted into their equivalent – in heating terms-
  in carbon dioxide and then (b) measured as tonnes of carbon

Source: Heroic estimates from World Resources Institute, Washington DC

releases sulphur dioxide and nitrogen dioxide – or acid rain which turns rivers and lakes acidic, killing fish and other life. Changes in the soil structure of forests kill trees and dependent wildlife. Acidic smog shortens people's lives and attacks buildings. Globally there is a rough balance between natural and man-made sulphur in the air but in Europe and North America 90–95% is man-made. Acid rain is composed of roughly 70% sulphuric acid and 30% nitric acid; the annual production of both doubled in Europe from 1950–70. The substances drift down to earth in rain, snow or smog and form sulphates or nitrates. Electricity manufacturing is the key culprit, followed by vehicle exhausts.

Downwind of the acid   States have been slow to cope with the problem in part because of the cost, especially in hard economic times, but also because the acid rain can drift for hundreds of miles, dumping the problem on the state downwind. Clearing up your own acid rain may only benefit your neighbour. A classic case therefore for concerted international action. In 1979, thirty-five states signed the Convention of Long-Range Transboundary Air Pollution but little of practical value was achieved. It took decisive action by 'downwind' states to start real reforms. In 1980, Canada (half of whose problem drifts in over the border with the United States) obtained an agreement from the United States to study the problem. Although the Reagan administration stalled the effort, growing concern from the United States' own victims of acid rain has brought the issue back to the fore.

The greening of Europe   Sweden and Norway have led the way in Europe as victim states. West Germany then became deeply concerned in 1983 after reports of rapid deterioration in its forests and the growing political importance of the environmental Green Party. Bonn formulated a ten-year plan to reduce emissions by 50%, at a cost of $2–3 billion. West Germany also bullied its EC partners to consider the problem, as 75% of Europe's sulphur dioxide comes from Britain, France, Germany, Italy and Spain. The EC Parliament's environmental committee reported in January 1984 that $380 billion worth of damage was done each year by acid rain in Europe. In March the environment ministers agreed on regulations for new power plants and in May steps were taken to introduce lead-free petrol. The Soviet Union also became concerned, although most of its problem is self-generated and eventually dumped in a haze over the Arctic.

Chernobyl   In 1986 the release of nuclear material from a Soviet power plant at Chernobyl showed just how far, and lethal, air pollution can get. Nuclear power plants are much cleaner than coal-fired ones in terms of producing acid rain, but when they go wrong they can clearly go much more devastatingly wrong. The impact of choices of energy are hard to compare, but are clearly some of the most vital issues of modern public policy.

In June 1984, the United States and the Soviet Union agreed to exchange information on the acid rain problem. In July 1985, under the auspices of the United Nations Economic Commission for Europe, Canada and nineteen European states agreed to a protocol pledging 30% cuts (from 1980 levels) in sulphur dioxide by 1993. Britain refused to join the '30% club', claiming that it had already made substantial cuts (about 40%) in levels from the 1970s and was being penalized for its earlier diligence. The United States also balked, claiming it had already made 26% cuts. In 1980 the United States was the world's second greatest producer of sulphur dioxide, after the Soviet Union. Britain ignominiously led the European table. Poland also refused to sign, claiming economic hardship. The cost of the necessary 'gas scrubbers' for power stations was estimated at $180 million per station and recently new power stations have cost 30% more because of environmental protection measures.

The 30% club

Some progress has already been made, as the British and American claims make clear. There is already improved technology for purification of power plants, major energy savings have reduced the need for power and there are limits on motor vehicles' exhaust and lead in petrol. Environmental groups are, however, caught in a bind when it is pointed out that the much-despised nuclear power is not an acid rain producer. Already, sulphur dioxide levels seem to be stabilizing although nitrogen oxide levels are not.

The technology of purification

Although few scientists dispute that control of sulphur dioxide levels from power plants is useful, it appears that many of the early scientific studies were too hasty. As the sulphur dioxide levels are being controlled, it is clear that insufficient attention has been paid to the nitrogen oxide problem. Thus the focus of environmentalists is likely to shift to nitrogen oxides and, thankfully, the technology for limiting emissions (as on car exhausts) is already available and relatively inexpensive.

It was the most free-market of Prime Ministers, Margaret Thatcher, who said 'No generation has a freehold on this earth. All we have is a life tenancy – with a full repairing lease'. Indeed the very economic priorities that were so crucial in causing the disrepair of the environment can be harnessed to the cause of environmental protection. At the moment, humanity is not only failing to carry out necessary repairs, it is actually subsidizing the destruction of the building. But if water cost $1 a gallon and petrol $20 a gallon perhaps the full repairing lease could be maintained.

Life tenancy

Reading

D. Adamson, *Defending the World* (New York: St. Martin's Press, 1990).

L. Brown *et al*, *State of the World* (New York: Norton, 1990).

F. Cairncross, *Costing the Earth* (London: Economist Books, 1991).

'Costing the Earth', *The Economist*, 2 September 1989.

M. Grubb, *Energy and the Greenhouse Effect* (Brookfield Vt: Dartmouth, 1990).

V. Helman, 'The Environment', *Washington Quarterly*, Autumn 1990.

S. Schneider, *Global Warming* (San Francisco, Sierra Club Books, 1989).

S. Simpson, *The Times Guide to the Environment* (London: Times Books, 1990).

World Commission on Environment and Development, *Our Common Future* (Oxford: Oxford University Press, 1987).

The Sea and Politics

Seventy per cent of the earth's surface is covered by sea and thus few states are landlocked. Understandably, most governments are concerned with how the sea around them is used and misused, and any attempt to draw up international rules of the sea naturally grabs the attention of most governments. But like many other international issues, this one has been obscured by the sterile vocabulary of both East–West and North–South conflict. Some attempts have been made to resolve these messy disputes, but so far there remains merely a whirlpool of conflicting interests.

Until the 1950s, few states claimed much of the sea, preferring instead to follow the long-established principles of freedom of navigation. States usually claimed sovereignty over coastal waters to a distance of three nautical miles (nautical miles are about 15% longer than land miles). But as the prospect of large profits from fishing and offshore mineral rights loomed larger, claims were extended to twelve miles and then in some cases (mainly in Latin America) to two hundred miles. *Territorializing the sea*

In 1958, eighty-six states met in landlocked Geneva (albeit by a lake) for the United Nations Conference on the Law of the Sea (UNCLOS). By 1960 they had failed to agree on a major treaty, with the group split mainly between countries such as the Superpowers and Britain, who did much of their fishing on the high seas and wanted to restrict coastal waters, and local states, such as those in Latin America with long coastlines to exploit. The issues were primarily political and economic rather than military. UNCLOS did agree on four minor conventions concerning territorial waters, fishing, and oil and gas on continental shelves. *UNCLOS*

The United Nations General Assembly decided in 1967 to set up an ad hoc committee to establish a new conference. The stamina of all concerned was severely tested when between 1974–82, over one hundred and sixty states met for UNCLOS III. In April 1982, after ninety-three weeks of talks and eleven sessions, a Convention was approved by 130 to 4 (United States, Israel, Venezuela, Turkey voted against) with seventeen abstentions (including West Germany, Britain and the Soviet Union). So far, one hundred and thirty four states have signed the Convention but only fourteen have ratified it. It was agreed that each state would have a twelve mile coastal limit and a two hundred mile 'exclusive economic zone' (EEZ) in which it could control mineral and fishing rights as well as mineral rights on the continental shelf up to three hundred *Inventing EEZs*

77

and fifty miles out, and in certain cases beyond. The EEZS were one of the most notable achievements of the conference and were acceptable to the United States. Thus one-third of the ocean was brought under control of the EEZS, giving some islands control over 130,000 square miles of sea. Of the total 25 million nautical square miles covered by the EEZS, ten states have 53%, including the United States (8.7%), Australia (8%), Indonesia (6.2%), New Zealand (5.5%), Canada (5.3%), Soviet Union (5.1%), Japan (4.4%), Brazil (3.6%), Mexico (3.2%), Chile (2.6%). The top twenty-five states control over 76% of the EEZS.

Muddy EEZs   As yet it is difficult to tell what impact this new sea régime will have. Although freedom of navigation through the zones was declared, limits could be imposed to control pollution risks. The EC's decision to restrict access to its waters to Community members only suggested that in the end freedom of navigation would be more restricted. It is also no accident that during the Falklands War, Britain declared an 'exclusion zone' of precisely two hundred miles (like the EEZS). The convention also guaranteed free movement through such international waterways as the straits of Dover or Gibraltar, but not those under national control like Suez, Panama or the Turkish straits.

Free-market sharks   The real reason why the United States and other Western states did not sign the treaty was the provision that minerals (e.g. manganese, cobalt, copper, nickel) beyond the EEZ are 'the common heritage of mankind'. An international régime, the International Seabed Authority, is to be established one year after UNCLOS III is ratified by sixty states to ensure that the minerals do not simply go to those who can dig them out (most likely the developed world's multinational mining companies). The United States and other so-called free-market sharks objected to this enactment of the New International Economic Order. Wealthy states would be forced to transfer technology to states which may follow hostile ideologies and without any means of protecting the investment of the high-risk companies involved. This clash of 'maritime theologies' (freedom of the sea versus the common heritage of humanity) appeared to defy compromise.

UNCLOS stalled   When the 9 December 1984 'deadline' for signing the treaty passed, fifteen states had missed it, including West Germany, Britain, the United States, Albania, Turkey, Ecuador, Syria and Israel – an odd bunch of bed-fellows. No NATO or Warsaw Pact state ratified the treaty. Only one Arab, one Asian, two Latin American, and six of the fifty-one African states did ratify UNCLOS III. The abstainers can choose to join if they wish at a later date. But there does not seem to be any hurry.

There appears to be little pressure on the wealthy non-signers to capitulate. Certainly they control most of the technology necessary to make exploitation of the sea possible and in any case it seems it will not be economic to do so until well into the 21st century. The most attractive minerals appear to be in the North Pacific, almost as far as is possible from the developing world. It is difficult to believe that the states of the South will be able to force those who have the technology to cooperate. Nevertheless, those aspects of the treaty that follow common sense and recent practice, such as the EEZs, will be implemented with or without UNCLOS III. The more controversial demands for international régimes and new economic orders seem likely to be ignored by those whom the treaty is intended to hold in check.

Reading

K. Booth, *Navies and Foreign Policy* (London: Croom Helm, 1977).

K. Booth, *Law, Force and Diplomacy at Sea* (London: Allen & Unwin, 1985).

B. Buzan, 'A Sea of Troubles?', *Adelphi Paper* No. 143 (London, 1978).

R. Ogley, *Internationalizing the Seabed* (London: Gower, 1984).

C. Sanger, *Ordering the Oceans* (London: Zed Press, 1987).

The Drug Trade

The use of deadly drugs is not an obvious international issue; the suffering caused by drug abuse primarily affects individuals and the society they live in. But controlling the supply of drugs is, in large part, an international worry. The United States has long been concerned about the ruin of people's lives and the related crimes caused by drug abuse. But West European states have only recently become similarly motivated to control the pernicious problem. By 1985 there were 14,000 officially reported drug addicts in West Germany, 25,000 in Italy and even 5,000 in Poland. Although United States narcotic addiction in 1900 was one-third higher than at present, it is now four times higher than the 1950s. The 1984 United States drug market was said to have done $100 billion worth of business. Western Europe has some 300,000 heroin addicts; the United States has about half-a-million. Addiction rates in Hong Kong, Thailand, Malaysia are reportedly even higher.

From poor to rich   Unlike the trade in weapons, the drug trade is from poor to rich countries and is opposed by most governments. Drugs, unlike arms, are not a useful instrument of state policy. The benefits (i.e. the huge profits) accrue to a few big criminal dealers. The problem of controlling the drug trade is therefore neither an East–West nor a North–South issue.

Differing views of drugs   Some drugs are needed for medicinal purposes, especially in the developed world. Others are difficult to define as dangerous. Compare the attitudes towards alcohol in France where wine is the national beverage, to Libya or Saudi Arabia where use of alcohol invites flogging or worse. Compare the use of coca leaves in Peru and the United States or cannabis in parts of India and in Europe. But drugs of abuse, such as heroin, are generally accepted as dangerous and their control has evolved into an international problem akin to attempts to control the slave trade.

Reaping what you sowed   Developed Western states are to a certain extent reaping what they – often literally – sowed. For example, imperial Britain shaped the opium trade in the 19th century, by selling Indian-produced opium to China (causing millions to become addicted to the drug) in exchange for silk and tea. In the 20th century Britain and other Western states have changed their minds and begun to counteract the international drug trade. The United States led the way in the 1920s and the United Nations later took over with the creation of the Commission on Narcotic Drugs.

Cannabis Production
1984–7

Gross Cultivation in Hectares

	1984	1985	1986	1987
Belize	1,270	1,220	3,030	1,090
Colombia	10,000	8,000	12,500	13,085
Costa Rica	133	135	145	300
Guatemala	200	225	275	325
Jamaica	2,575	2,365	4,800	1,330
Lebanon	16,000	20,000	16,000	16,000
Mexico	8,700	5,865	8,430	9,000
Morocco	–	13,000	14,000	15,000
Panama	400	400–500	250–275	30–40
Paraguay	–	–	3,000	3,000
United States*	1,700*	2,100*	4,300*	5,300*

Source: International Narcotics Control Strategy Report, 1987, 1988
US Department of State; Drug Enforcement Administration

* United States-Metric Tons. U.S. numbers reflect only those figures supplied by state and local agencies participating in the U.S. Domestic Eradication Program.

Coca Production
1984–7

Gross Cultivation in Hectares

	1984	1985	1986	1987
Bolivia	37,500	34,000	37,000	40,300
Colombia	17,000	15,500	25,000	25,000
Ecuador	895	1,025	695	510
Peru	100,000	95,200	107,500	109,500

Source: International Narcotics Control Strategy Report, 1987, 1988
US Department of State

Opium Production
1984–7

Gross Cultivation in Hectares

	1984	1985	1986	1987
Afghanistan	–	–	9,950	18,500
Burma	65,000	70,000	144,600	108,080
Egypt*	1.4*	2.5*	2.5*	2.7*
Guatemala	200	225	275	325
Laos**		[16,000 to 47,000]**		
Lebanon	125	250	400	1,800
Mexico	5,200	7,500	6,000	7,360
Pakistan	1,750	2,770	7,805	11,270
Thailand	6,933	8,780	4,750	6,900

Source: International Narcotis Control Strategy Report, 1987, 1988
US Department of State

* Egypt – Metric Tons.
** Laos – Estimated Annual Cultivation.

UNFDAC   The United States is keen to make use of international and United Nations machinery to combat the drug problem. In 1961 the Single Convention on Narcotic Drugs banned a wide range of drugs, including cannabis, but left amphetamines (synthetic stimulants) untouched. By 1984, one hundred and fifteen states adhered to the Convention but, as the emphasis was placed on national control of the problem, it had little except moral success. In 1971 the United Nations Fund for Drug Abuse Control (UNFDAC) was established and the United States, Germany, Sweden and Norway have led the way in funding the body. Also in 1971, the Vienna Convention on Psychotropic Substances was agreed, to control the trade in amphetamines and hallucinogens.

Controlling the killing   But the most effective measures of control have come in bilateral initiatives. The United States, as the leading 'victim nation', has signed bilateral accords with a number of states, some of which include the stationing of American drug control officers abroad, as in Thailand and France. Thailand and the 'golden triangle' used to be the principal heroin producers, but tougher United States policies, in coordination with the Thai government, controlled the trade for a while. Unfortunately, if somewhat predictably, Pakistan then took over as the leading heroin producer. It is a deadly embarrassment to the United States that the war in Afghanistan was in part funded by rebels in the heroin trade. Similarly, pro-US Contra rebels in Central America supported their operations by running cocaine and other drugs. The Panamanian strong-man, General Noriega, apparently had been a key part of the South American drug traffic that connected Colombia, the Contras and Panama with markets for cocaine in the United States.

Multinational cartels   Latin America's thriving drug business was described by a former Peruvian president as the region's 'only successful multinational'. Retail sales in 1987 of South American cocaine in North America and Europe topped $20 billion, equivalent to the world retail sales of diamonds, or total liquor sales in the United States. Some estimates for 1990 suggest the North American market in cocaine alone was worth over $100 billion, although Colombian exporters 'merely' earn some $10 billion each year. If Colombia's Medellin drug cartel were a corporation it would rank with the oil giants on the *Fortune* 500. Although only a fraction of the profits actually return to South America, the trade has supported Colombia's relatively good economic performance and has enabled a whole new class of entrepreneurs to buy land, build properties and subvert authority.

Narcodollars and narco-terrorism   Indeed, these developing states have grown increasingly concerned about the domestic and international problems caused by the drug trade. The flow of narcodollars helped fuel inflation in Bolivia, Peru and Colombia, as well as financing the narcoterror-

Value added

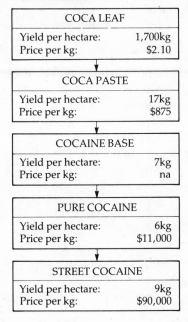

COCA LEAF	
Yield per hectare:	1,700kg
Price per kg:	$2.10

COCA PASTE	
Yield per hectare:	17kg
Price per kg:	$875

COCAINE BASE	
Yield per hectare:	7kg
Price per kg:	na

PURE COCAINE	
Yield per hectare:	6kg
Price per kg:	$11,000

STREET COCAINE	
Yield per hectare:	9kg
Price per kg:	$90,000

ism of Left and Right. Corruption linked to the drug trade has hit nearly every producer country, not to mention neighbours and trans-shipment points. Vast tracts of land are governed by drug barons and politicians who oppose the trade are gunned down in public.

However, this is a problem in North–South relations where developing states are able to get the developed world to help. The substitution of crops, funded by developed states, is intended to solve the problem at source. But it is difficult to see how the drug trade can ever be eliminated. Apart from the already obvious political dilemmas, there is the problem that growing areas are often remote and beyond government control. Also, the new crops are rarely as financially attractive as the drugs. Western states are sometimes loath to use sanctions against producer states which are often their allies in Third World conflicts. There is evidence, too, that cocaine is seen as a greater problem than heroin in the United States, in part because it affects the richer segments of the population.

New, souped-up versions of cocaine, such as crack, have zipped around the US from California. Some one million users were ensnared in the first six months of 1986. Heroin too has seen a new lethal offshoot, black tar – also known as bugger, candy, dogfood, gumball or tootsie roll. With a purity ten times that of

Crack and black tar

*The fear of
synthetic drugs*

normal street heroin, it is selling faster and spreading quickly from its first importation from Mexico.

Perhaps more worrying for the future is the move to more synthetic drugs. Old measures are obviously ineffective against drugs produced in home laboratories. Yet, more positively, a shift to synthetic (psychotropic) drugs may well mean more production in the developed world, which at least holds out hope that the common interest of the states affected will make for a tougher policy. In the final analysis, the use of most damaging drugs seems greatest among the poor and deprived. Therefore only social and economic change in developed states will finally end the problem.

Reading

B.M. Bagley 'Colombia: The Wrong Strategy', *Foreign Policy*, Winter 1989–90.

K. Brunn *et al*, *The Gentleman's Club* (London: University of Chicago Press, 1975).

A.S. Trebach, *The Heroin Solution* (New Haven: Yale University Press, 1982).

Plagues

Diseases show no respect for international borders. They may be infectious, genetic or environmental and can be carried in the water or in the bloodstream of animals or people. But wealthier states with higher standards of medical care and education are usually able to protect their citizens from the worst diseases, or at least give their people the knowledge and support to limit the damage the disease may do. Modern diseases such as AIDS, like the far more pervasive killers of old, have encouraged international cooperation to control their spread.

Rats, lice and virus have played a critical part in shaping history. The plagues of biblical times were perhaps exaggerated by Israelite chroniclers, but there is no doubting that roughly one-third of all Europeans died in the 14th century's Black Death. The European influenza of 1556–60 killed 20% of the British population. More devastating still was the death that Cortez and his Spanish supporters brought to the Americas in the 16th century. Smallpox and other diseases killed 80% of the local population and the population of central Mexico fell by 30 million by 1568. The isolated world of the Americas was simply unprepared for the virulent viruses bred in the cities of Europe. *Rats, lice and virus*

War, religion and commerce were the main transporters of past diseases, and they fed on sheltered people lacking modern medicine and public health care. Syphilis and typhus were stoked up and spread in the Italian wars of 1494–1559 and then spread east by Portuguese soldiers and traders. But by 1700 most diseases had shifted from the epidemic to the endemic type. Yet the First World War and the presence in Europe of African, American and European troops provided the feeding grounds for the great influenza of 1918–9 that killed 20 million people. *War, religion and commerce*

Improved sanitation, better food and the advances of medical science blunted the impact of disease. Religion, with its pilgrimages that spread such diseases as cholera from India in the 19th century, also fell victim to modern medicine. When science could explain death and even prevent it while bypassing the local religious teaching about 'the will of God', the power of organized religious authorities was diminished. More democratic governments were first given the task of promoting public health and basic medical services. *Victims of modern medicine*

Those societies that successfully modernized have had the greatest success against disease. Average life expectancy in the *World Health Organization* developed world is seventy-two years, while it is fifty-five in less developed states and merely fifty in Africa. International cooperation to rectify these figures can be dated from the establishment of the International Office of Public Health in Paris in 1903 which was reconstituted as the World Health Organization by the United Nations in 1946.

Malaria remains endemic

Malaria remains the biggest international killer. Major successes in control have been achieved in the 1970s by health programs in China and India; 48% of the world's population, or 2,266 million people, live in regions where risks persist while efforts at control are pursued. Some 8% of the world's population, or 400 million people, mainly in tropical Africa, live in regions where malaria remains endemic. More general success has been achieved in eradicating smallpox as part of a 1974 WHO program. Apart from the usual stress on primary health care and better education, vaccination campaigns have been organized. Africa still does least well.

Smoking and cancer

Some diseases such as cancer, diabetes or heart disease, are considered non-communicable, although environment and viral infection may well play a part in their spread. In developed countries, these diseases kill millions of people every year. For many people, especially non-smokers, smoking and the cancer it causes can be considered a communicable epidemic. But at least in more developed societies, improved public health education may someday relegate smoking to the category of spitting in the streets – a recognized danger to public health.

Viral hepatitis

In recent years, at least as much attention has been focused on more obviously communicable diseases such as viral hepatitis. According to the WHO in 1987, 200 million people were carrying hepatitis-B, and bubonic plague was still not eliminated. International efforts coordinated through international organizations are regularly made to tackle infectious diseases. They even operate in wartime, as seen in the four-day ceasefire in the Lebanon civil war in 1987 in order to allow mass immunization of children against smallpox.

AIDS and HIV

One of the new diseases in the 1980s has been Acquired Immune Deficiency Syndrome (AIDS), which is thought to be caused by the human immunodeficiency virus (HIV). Yet it is now known that there are many AIDS cases who have no trace of the virus and there are many perfectly healthy HIV carriers without AIDS.

It is also known that the expected exponential growth of AIDS has not yet taken place, all of which suggests the problem is more complex than first thought. While some 10 million Africans may be infected with the AIDS virus, nothing like the expected 1.5 million Americans by 1989 were similarly affected. AIDS recorded deaths in 1989 in the USA were 8.6 per 100,000, about the same rate as for homicide, and ranking 15th as a cause of death. Without certain 'co-factors', more of which are present in poor Africa, the threat is far smaller than thought in the late 1980s.

AIDS is a communicable disease but only through very identifiable and controllable ways. It enters the bloodstream almost entirely through anal sex or the use of an infected needle. In an effort to raise public awareness in developed countries there has been an effort to 'democratize' AIDS – public health campaigns that seek to demonstrate that no social group is immune to the AIDS threat. But, for example, in the United States, white heterosexuals made up only .5% of all AIDS cases, or 254 of all 41,250 reported by late 1987. Among heterosexuals, AIDS still seems to be caught mainly from prostitutes. As unfair as it may sound, discussing AIDS without mentioning homosexual behaviour or drug abuse is like discussing syphilis without mentioning sexual intercourse.

A discriminating threat

Because the disease has so far been largely confined to the homosexual and drug-taking communities, various efforts have been made to keep its impact limited. Although AIDS is far more difficult to spread via heterosexual sex, (women are thought to act as a sort of firebreak) it can happen and does spread quickly in such communities as Brazil's large bisexual population. Some would-be-controllers put their faith in blood tests, other, more extreme arguments are for the quarantine of AIDS victims and even of homosexuals. Generally, European governments have been most forthright in using public health campaigns to reach their endangered populations.

But like most diseases in the world today, poor countries and poor people in wealthy countries are still those most at risk. Whereas careful sexual behaviour will be enough to save most people in wealthy countries, homosexuals and drug users will remain at risk. African countries are too poor to afford such necessary public health measures as sterile needles and safe supplies of blood. Most AIDS victims will continue to die in poorer countries.

Poor at risk

Reading

J. Adams, *The HIV Myth* (London: Macmillan, 1989).

A. Crosby, *Ecological Imperialism* (Cambridge: Cambridge University Press, 1986).

W. McNeill, *Plagues and Peoples* (London: Penguin, 1979).

R. Shilts, *And the Band Played On* (London: Penguin, 1988).

S. Sontag, *AIDS and its Metaphors* (London: Allen Lane, 1989).

3
MODERN WARFARE

The Nuclear Weapons Revolution

With the invention of nuclear weapons, and their first use on Hiroshima in August 1945, war would never be the same again. Humankind had acquired the deadly ability to destroy civilization as we know it. The fundamental change was that whereas previous wars could be conceived of as useful instruments of policy, a nuclear war would only result in the death of the planet. We would be left with a 'republic of insects and grass'.

Awesome destruction
By the standards of modern nuclear weapons, the first nuclear weapon was puny. The Hiroshima bomb had the explosive power equivalent to 20,000 tons of TNT (i.e. 20 kilotons) but the typical Superpower weapons of 1991 were much more devastating and were measured in megatons (millions of tons of TNT). For example, a one megaton bomb exploded over Detroit, would destroy all brick houses in a three-and-a-half mile radius, kill half-a-million people outright and many more from wounds and radiation. Incredibly enough, the Superpowers had some 13,000 megatons in their combined arsenals in 1991. Strategists euphemistically call this excess 'overkill'.

Defining deterrence
The United States was the first to develop nuclear weapons but was slow to formulate a new strategy in appreciation of the new nature of war. In August 1949 the Soviet Union broke the American monopoly and shook the West's complacency. In Washington, policy-makers, and mostly civilian ones at that, began to conceive of nuclear weapons as instruments of deterrence. The age-old Roman concept, 'if you want peace, prepare for war', was adapted to argue that if you wanted to prevent nuclear war it was best to be in a position to threaten the enemy with unacceptable damage if he chose to start one. This doctrine was remarkably crude, but it managed to prevent war between East and West.

Making deterrence credible
In 1954, American Secretary of State Dulles took deterrence to mean that the threat of massive retaliation would prevent any unwanted Soviet activity around the globe. This was nonsensical, as it was soon realized that for the threat at the heart of deterrence to work, it had to be credible to the opponent. It was incredible, for example, that the United States would threaten nuclear war if Soviet troops invaded Hungary (as they did in 1956). Thus it was recognized in the United States that credible deterrence required (1) survivable forces that could ride-out a pre-emptive Soviet strike, and (2) flexible or graduated types of weapon to respond to different levels of threat.

The American build-up of forces in the 1950s and 1960s achieved these two requirements. The Soviet Union was not far behind. Although in 1957 the Soviets were the first to test an intercontinental ballistic missile (ICBM), through the 1960s the United States had more weapons and warheads. The Americans developed a triad of forces (sea, land and aircraft-based) so that if war should come, at a minimum, one-fifth to one-third of the Soviet population could be killed in a retaliatory strike and a half to two-thirds of Soviet industry destroyed. Once again in the clinical language of nuclear strategy, this was called 'assured destruction'. When the Soviet Union began to evolve towards a similar capability, there was said to be a balance of deterrence based on Mutual Assured Destruction (MAD). The acronym was certainly apt. *Assured destruction*

Yet the evolution of more accurate and flexible weapons undermined the notion of MAD. Because there were now more flexible weapons that could strike small and specific targets, in theory at least, not all nuclear wars need become total all-out wars. With the ensuing discussion, especially in the 1970s, of 'limited strategic options' some strategists speculated that nuclear weapons might, after all, be a useful instrument of policy. Military planners could move away from targeting people, as in MAD, and get back to the good old type of war that targeted the enemy's military sites instead. For example, if a Soviet invasion of Europe could not be halted with conventional weapons, then a limited, accurate nuclear strike at a Soviet military target might demonstrate strength of purpose and bring the war to a halt. Unfortunately, as sensible as that strategy may appear in theory, it also undermined the deterrence element of MAD by suggesting general nuclear war might not necessarily ensue from gradual escalation of limited nuclear strikes. It had become increasingly acceptable to think about the unthinkable – nuclear war. *A MAD strategy*

The talk of limited war also raised other problems. It required yet more sophisticated capabilities for command, control, communication and intelligence (C³I). It also suggested that some form of nuclear war might be 'safe' (i.e. safely fought in Europe and not on the territories of the Superpowers). Yet, confusingly, advocates of limited nuclear options suggested this kind of war-fighting posture was, in practice, the only way to deter war from breaking out. In fact, they urged more spending on defensive technologies such as civil and air defence in order to make survival in a limited war more possible. MAD, which held each side's population hostage for the good behaviour of both, was crumbling. Western advocates of limited nuclear options also insisted that the Soviet Union had anyway never accepted MAD. They pointed to Soviet *Limited nuclear options*

deployments of a range of nuclear forces and to Soviet civil and air defence programmes to back up their argument.

*Attacking
arcane
strategies*

MAD also came under increased attack in the 1980s from a very different quarter. The anti-nuclear movements claimed that all the strategies of reinforcing deterrence through limited nuclear options merely made war more likely. They became exasperated with the arcane discussions among strategists and urged instead a complete abolition of the nuclear threat. But as attractive as these simplistic notions might appear, they were difficult to translate into policy. Since nuclear knowledge could not be unlearned, there was no going back to a pre-nuclear age.

*The arms
control solution*

The problem for those in the middle of this nuclear debate was how to evolve a strategy that, given the number of weapons that existed, was practical and not just simply imaginable. Those in the middle argued that stable deterrence in the nuclear age could best be shaped through great power arms control. They felt it relatively safe to settle for a small number of credible, survivable, nuclear weapons of varying types. For example, a fleet of missile-carrying submarines was safer than land-based weapons which were easy to find, and therefore more likely to be fired in haste for fear they would be lost in a pre-emptive strike by the opposite side.

*Threats to the
negotiations*

The protracted arms control negotiations of the 1970s were intended to place walls and a ceiling around the arms race and then reduce the ceiling on the number of weapons to acceptable levels. Yet there were basic problems that made negotiation difficult and protracted. Foremost among these were differing Soviet and American strategic doctrines, new technologies under development, mistrust, and of course stupidity and narrow self-interest.

*Caution in
crisis*

Yet it is difficult to argue that the Superpowers are any closer to a nuclear war. Crises in which one side or the other resorted to nuclear threats have been few. Since the 1962 Cuban missile crisis, there has only been one minor alert during the 1973 Arab–Israeli War. It is, however, true that in 1969 the Soviet Union threatened a pre-emptive strike against Chinese nuclear installations.

But as time passes, the pressure against the first use of any nuclear weapon seems to increase. As long as both Superpowers (and any other set of states in a nuclear stand-off) retain an invulnerable second strike (and they all, so far, do), no attacker can have a reasonable hope of escaping unscathed from nuclear retaliation. The proliferation of warheads makes the potential for nuclear war even more destructive but even if there were a gross imbalance in numbers of warheads, neither side would have a usable superiority. In an age of survivable retaliatory forces, superiority in numbers only means you can make the rubble bounce higher.

For some, this essentially robust deterrence in a nuclear age seems safe enough. For others, the risks still seem too high and they argue that nuclear weapons must be abolished entirely. Those on the extreme of the debate are countered by yet other extremists who suggest there is a technological fix to the nuclear age, by reasserting the dominance of defensive weapons over offensive ones.

Robust deterrence

Finally, there are those who would prefer to tinker with MAD to enhance its robustness by means of arms control. They believe that weapons themselves are not the roots of the conflict and that the real risk of war can only be eliminated when international conflict is moderated. Yet even in the 1990s when Superpower détente had broken out, there seemed little chance that nuclear weapons would be abolished. It appeared more likely that arms control agreements could be reached that would limit the most dangerous features of the nuclear age, but that the weapons, once invented, would remain in the arsenal to cope with an uncertain world.

Reading

D. Holloway, *The Soviet Union and the Arms Race* (London: Yale University Press, 1983).

L. Freedman, *The Evolution of Nuclear Strategy* (London: Macmillan, 1989).

M. Mandelbaum, *The Nuclear Revolution* (Cambridge: Cambridge University Press, 1981).

G. Segal *et al*, *Nuclear War and Nuclear Peace* (London: Macmillan, 1988).

ICBMs and their Control

Before the nuclear weapons revolution, war was largely confined to the battlefield or restricted to the range of aircraft. Bombs could only be 'delivered' as quickly (or as slowly) as aircraft could fly. Although the first atomic bombs were also delivered by aircraft, it was only with the invention of intercontinental ballistic missiles (ICBMs) that large numbers of devastating warheads could be delivered on a distant target in a matter of minutes. Because these first missiles were relatively inaccurate, they were aimed at large targets, such as cities. Thus, ICBMs made it possible for the full horror of the nuclear age to loom over millions of people and threaten the end of civilization.

Types of weapon   Intercontinental nuclear weapons (known in the jargon as 'strategic delivery vehicles') now take three forms. They can be land-based intercontinental ballistic missiles (either fixed in silos or mobile), long-range bombers, or submarine-launched ballistic missiles (SLBMs). Both SLBMs and ICBMs now carry several multiple independently-targeted re-entry vehicles (MIRVs). ICBMs are the most accurate type of intercontinental weapon, but also the most vulnerable to pre-emptive attack because their location on land is usually well known. SLBMs are safest from pre-emptive attack, as the submarines that carry them can disappear into the huge oceans. Bombers are much easier to detect and therefore are less useful in a pre-emptive strike, and because they are slow, they are also less likely to reach their target. However, on balance, bombers are safer. Because they are manned, they can be recalled before their bombs are released if an error has been made.

SALT I   The United States had more strategic delivery vehicles than the Soviet Union until the early 1970s and it still leads in the number of warheads. But in the late 1960s, when it was clear that the United States was prepared to allow the Soviet Union to catch up and reach strategic parity, Moscow accepted Washington's offer to discuss limits on strategic weapons. The first Strategic Arms Limitation Talks (SALT I) opened on 17 November 1969, and concluded in Moscow on 26 May 1972. The SALT I talks were largely carried on in a serious, secret atmosphere, where each side was surprised to learn a great deal about the other's perspectives. The SALT I accords comprised two unequal parts.

The ABM treaty   The first and more comprehensive, the Anti-Ballistic Missile (ABM) treaty, included an agreement that neither country should build for 'defence of the territory of its country' more than two

ABM sites. The location of early warning radar was limited and observance of the treaty was to be verified by 'national technical means' (e.g. satellites). The treaty, of unlimited duration, would be reviewed every five years. Six months notice had to be given before either side could withdraw and to avoid that happening, a standing consultative commission would resolve disputes. In a 1974 protocol, both sides agreed to deploy only one ABM system.

This treaty, the jewel of the arms control crown, was remarkable in that it enhanced deterrence by ensuring both sides would be vulnerable to threats of assured destruction. It also limited spending (estimated at a minimum of $106 billion in the United States for a skeleton ABM) on defensive systems which were generally assumed at the time to be unworkable. Offence still dominated defence in the nuclear age.

This judgement was encouraged by the rapid development of offensive nuclear weaponry and established the link to the second, less effective, treaty signed in SALT I. The interim offensive agreement limited the United States to no more than 1,054 ICBMs, and 656 SLBMs, while the Soviet Union was limited to 1,618 ICBMs and 740 SLBMs. The United States could have no more than 710 missiles on 44 submarines, while the Soviets were restricted to 950 missiles on 62 submarines. Moscow agreed that the United States and its allies could together have 50 submarines with 800 missiles. ICBMs could be modernized, but not increased in size by more than 10–15%.

Roomy walls and high ceilings

No limit was placed on the number or accuracy of MIRV warheads, where the United States held a wide lead. Sadly, this lost opportunity to cap the growth of MIRVs meant that in the era of arms control the number of warheads actually grew rapidly. SALT I therefore at best set roomy walls to the arms race but no real ceiling. Nevertheless, an atmosphere of success and Superpower stability was achieved and, even when those intangible elements faded in the late 1970s, both sides agreed to abide by the treaty after it ran out in 1977.

The SALT II process was delayed by ill-will over conflict in the Third World, President Nixon's resignation in 1974 and the settling in of the new President Carter in 1977. The SALT II treaty was signed on 18 June 1979 in Vienna but has never been ratified by the US Senate. It placed a ceiling on SALT I's roomy walls by limiting the number of missile launchers to 2,400. The ceiling was to be lowered to 2,250 by January 1981, a level which would require the Soviet Union to dismantle some launchers. Of these, only 1,320 could be MIRVed and no more than 820 could be on ICBMs. The ceiling was fixed in place by limiting the launch-weight and throw-weight of heavy missiles and the number of warheads on each missile. No new fixed-site heavy ICBM could be built and

SALT II

no light ICBM could be converted to a heavy one. The limits on modernization were strict, although each side could build one new light ICBM. The parties also agreed that verification by national technical means should not be hindered.

Attacks on SALT II

The treaty was attacked by the Right as not being sufficiently airtight (for example, there were some loopholes on verification) and for not having achieved sufficiently deep cuts in the Soviet missile force. The Left attacked SALT II as not doing enough to make the walls around the nuclear arsenals smaller and the ceiling lower. Supporters claimed refinements would come later. But the critics on the Right triumphed in the United States on a wave of more general concern about America's loss of international stature. The Reagan administration came to power with a vow to deal with the 'decade of neglect' of United States defence and to drive a harder bargain than what it claimed to be the 'fatally flawed' SALT II agreement.

START

To placate supporters of arms control at home and among the European allies, President Reagan agreed to begin the Strategic Arms Reduction Talks (START) on 29 June 1982. The official United States position was that it desired deep cuts in total numbers of nuclear weapons and especially in the main area of Soviet advantage, land-based ICBMs (70% of the Soviet arsenal was of this type and only 25% of the American force). The proposals were manifestly unnegotiable from the Soviet point of view and the talks stalled. In the meantime, both sides agreed to abide by the terms of SALT II.

Umbrella talks

The Soviet Union stormed out of the START talks in November 1982 after the NATO decision to deploy new intermediate-range-nuclear forces (INF). But new 'umbrella' talks opened on 12 March 1985. The umbrella covered the old START, INF and new space weapons talks, but they were soon deadlocked on the Soviet demand that all future progress be linked to a limit on American plans for the Strategic Defence Initiative (SDI). The Soviets argued it is impossible to discuss limiting offensive weapons if it is not known whether the weapons to be deployed in the future will have to penetrate a heavy defence. The Americans argued that SDI was merely a research program to match similar Soviet research. Because the United States refused to abandon SDI and the Soviet Union insisted they do precisely that, the START deadlock remained unbroken at the Reykjavik summit in October 1986.

Politics in command

In the last years of the Reagan presidency it became increasingly clear that the Soviet Union under Gorbachev was serious about improving East-West relations. It was also clear that the SDI could not work and would not be funded by Congress in the new mood of détente and a rising budget deficit. Politics and technology drove the two sides to a deal, but politics also slowed down the talks. In the year of revolutions in Eastern Europe in 1989, and continuing uncertainty in Kremlin politics, strategic weapons talks were simply not important.

On 1 June 1990 at the Washington summit, the Superpowers *The* agreed to something less than the 50% cuts in their arsenals they *Washington* had promised the world. Indeed the cuts of about 30% merely *summit* took the world back to the balance of just before the START talks. Despite notional limits of 6,000 on the number of each country's 'warheads', it was clear that the difficulty of counting cruise missiles on bombers and submarines meant the real numbers would be higher. Although both sides would be destroying obsolete weapons, they would still be free to modernize within the treaty's limits. An arms race will continue, albeit in a more limited form, and the state of the Soviet economy will have far more to do with the pace of the race. Indeed, as the Soviet Union's economic and political crisis deepened in 1991, more conservative forces in Moscow ensured that the final details of the START accord could not be agreed.

Still more than enough

		Intercontinental ballistic missiles	Submarine-launched ballistic missiles	Bombers	START accountable warheads*	Actual warheads*
Before	**USA**	1,000	560	263	8,457	11,974
START	**USSR**	1,356	930	162	10,407	11,320
After	**USA**	850	378†	224**	5,903†**	9,498
START	**USSR**	689	300	167	5,983	6,888

* Warhead figures depend partly on estimates of number of weapons on each bomber. ** Assumes 32 operational B-2 bombers. † Assumes 72 submarine missiles are exempted by 'discounting'. Sources: IISS; Natural Resources Defence Council; *The Economist* database

And yet the START deal is important in less legalistic ways. As *Maintaining* the first major Superpower accord in over a decade, it demon- *stability* strates that the Superpowers are determined to get on with each other and maintain basic stability. They both intend to retain an assured second strike capability, but seem inclined to enhance stability by limiting more dangerous weapons and creating a more cooperative atmosphere. Although arms control is not entirely a matter of trust, it is easier to trust an adversary when the conflict seems to be easing and there is a record of progress and amicable appreciation of each other's genuine security concerns. The new agenda for START will be to enhance stability in these ways. Yet there remains a distinct limit to this process, especially as neither Superpower, or indeed any great powers, seems willing to abandon these weapons of last resort.

Reading

C. Blacker and G. Duffy, *International Arms Control* (Stanford: Stanford University Press, 1984).

R. Cowen Karp (ed), *Security with Nuclear Weapons?* (Oxford: Oxford University Press, 1991).

H. Feveson and F.N. von Hippel, 'Beyond START', *International Security*, Summer 1990.

L. Freedman, *The Evolution of Nuclear Strategy* (London: Macmillan, 1989).

J.P. Rubin, 'START Finish', *Foreign Policy*, Fall 1989.

G. Segal *et al*, *Nuclear War and Nuclear Peace* (London: Macmillan, 1988).

S. Talbot, *Endgame* (New York: Harper and Row, 1979).

War in Space

Voyages to the planets and outer space have long captivated earth-bound imaginations. But the fantasies of the inter-galactic politics beyond our earthly politics were most often conceived of as a variation on the familiar theme of competition for influence and power through military means. War in space was expected to be technologically more glamorous, but no less deadly. In reality, the space age has been slow to develop and far less uplifting than many had hoped.

The space age began with the launch of a Soviet satellite, *The space age* Sputnik, on 4 October 1957. The militarization of space was not far behind. Since 1958, 75% of all satellites have been for actual or potential military purposes. In 1984 alone, one hundred and five such satellites were launched into this new military 'high ground'. So far, unlike the Buck Rogers scenarios of war in space, the space age has developed much more slowly and proved more peaceful than the age of airpower did before it. Most of the satellites are for communication or surveillance and they are essential tools of arms control since they provide checks that agreements are being observed. The 1967 Outer Space Treaty prohibited the deployment of weapons of mass destruction in space, but it has not prevented the deployment of anti-satellite weapons (ASAT).

There is a military purpose in destroying satellites since both *ASAT and the* Superpowers depend heavily on space-based communications and *Soviet Union* intelligence. In 1981 the Soviet Union was said to have tested a killer satellite, but only at altitudes up to five hundred miles out in space. Most satellites, especially the important ones, operate much higher. The United States has also been active in ASAT research and in 1982 established a Space Command to coordinate war in space. In 1983 the Soviet Union announced a moratorium on anti-satellite tests and in June 1984 Moscow's proposed ASAT talks did not materialize after the United States set unacceptable terms.

The American administration was not interested in nego- *ASAT and the* tiations because it had a major testing programme underway. In *United States* September 1985 the United States tested its first anti-satellite weapon which struck a satellite three hundred and forty-five miles high. Unfortunately for Moscow, more Soviet than American satellites are in these lower orbits. In December 1985, the US Congress imposed a ban on ASAT tests against objects in space so long as Moscow keeps to its moratorium. Both sides agree that there is an opportunity to halt this type of technology before it goes too far but the issues are really more linked to other space-related weaponry.

Negotiating ASAT

An ASAT agreement would cause serious problems for the American Strategic Defense Initiative (SDI). Thus it seems most logical that ASAT and SDI need to be discussed in the same forum. It is not yet clear whether the Soviet Union now wishes to retain the option of an ASAT capability to destroy weapons deployed in space under an American SDI.

Star Wars is born

The complications that SDI causes for ASAT can be traced to President Reagan's speech, on 23 March 1983, launching SDI. The idea was to render nuclear weapons obsolete by creating a series of defensive measures to block and destroy incoming Soviet missiles before they reached American territory. This 'Star Wars' plan would possibly make use of lasers, particle beams and electromagnetic cannon, either based in space or on land, to shoot down Soviet missiles. The massive SDI program is still in its infancy and its future success is uncertain. In its most ambitious, and apparently now abandoned, form it would end the nuclear threat by stopping all weapons from hitting people or military sites. The staggering costs and technical problems led to a scaling down of objectives to the more prosaic protection of land-based ICBMs, as the original ABM systems were expected to do.

Making SDI work

For such a system to work, it would need to be more effective and cheaper than any addition of offensive weapons or other counter-measures. Initial, hopeful ideas envisaged a multi-layered defence to find and destroy most weapons in their boost phase before they spill out their MIRved warheads. Sophisticated command and control with unheard of sophistication in computer software would have to be built to handle such complex and swift 'battle management'. In 1985, the American space shuttle tested a laser fired from the ground which might play a part in SDI, but in January 1986 a shuttle exploded on takeoff, thereby demonstrating just how complicated even the most basic steps in space could be. Needless to say the Soviet Union has its own souped-up ABM type research program, but even according to American supporters of SDI, Moscow has fallen behind American research.

SDI or ABM?

Of course, there remains a simple appeal in SDI. The notion of assured survival instead of assured destruction is enticing because it offers the prospect of somehow untying the nuclear weapons knot. But the scaled down version of SDI, a glorified ABM defence of missiles, offers only survival for ICBMs, not people. As an anti-nuclear proposal it is therefore both over-sold and over-priced. Land-based missiles might be better protected, but well before the system is deployed, less vulnerable SLBMs will be able to carry out all the military tasks for which ICBMs are said to be so important (accurate strikes on Soviet military targets). It would make far more sense to scrap the land-based weapons and if that does not seem like enough reassurance, put more weapons out to sea.

SDI is peculiar in that it is a doctrine in search of a capability, *The SDI mule* rather than the more usual opposite way round. Taking the most benign view, SDI is a bit like the French folk story of the Pope's mule. The Pope offered vast sums of money to anyone who could teach his mule to speak. One day a simple peasant went to see the Pope and returned with the prize. The peasant had promised to teach the mule to speak within ten years. When asked how he could make such a pledge since mules cannot speak, the peasant replied: 'In ten years either the Pope will be dead, or I will be dead, or the mule will be dead'. Indeed, the Bush administration has quietly smothered SDI, at least until some other perceived threat and new technology revives the debate about defence in the nuclear age.

Reading

A. Carter and D. Schwartz, *Ballistic Missile Defense* (Washington: Brookings, 1984).

D. Graham, *High Frontier* (New York: Tor Books, 1983).

T. Karas, *The New High Ground* (New York: Simon and Schuster, 1983).

'New Technology and Western Security Policy', *Adelphi Papers* No. 199 (London, Summer 1985).

P. Stares, *The Militarization of Space* (London: Croom Helm, 1985).

Union of Concerned Scientists, *The Fallacy of Star Wars* (New York: Random House, 1984).

Nuclear Test Ban

Because nuclear weapons have revolutionized world politics, it is only natural that politicians have struggled with various schemes to control the risks of nuclear war. One of the most persistent, and possibly productive, means of nuclear arms control is the effort to halt the testing of nuclear arms. These efforts are based on the principle that no one is going to risk using nuclear weapons unless they are pretty confident they will work. A test ban would undermine such confidence. Nuclear weapons would then become museum pieces.

Dangers of a test ban   Although this simple idea may be attractive, it also has its dangers. For example, nuclear deterrence is based on the knowledge that the opponent can devastate any attacker with a second strike. If a test ban makes the devastation in the deterrent less credible, the deterrent itself may not be believed. The nuclear age with added test bans might become more unstable. What is more, not all weapons are equally dangerous and a sensible test ban might eliminate all defensive or less dangerous technology.

The dangers from fall-out   Not surprisingly, it has been difficult to agree on test bans. Concern about nuclear weapons testing has essentially taken two forms. Initially it focused on the fall-out from above-ground tests and the pollution of air and water which later came into contact with people. In the late 1950s, various Soviet and American propaganda proposals were made for a test moratorium. In November 1958 the Superpowers and Britain (then the only three nuclear powers) began serious talks on a test ban. An ad hoc moratorium was observed until September 1961 when, after the United States announced it would return to testing and France carried out its own program of tests, the Soviet Union broke the moratorium.

The partial test ban treaty   Following the Cuban missile crisis in 1962, the negotiations were given a new impetus. On 5 August 1963, a limited test ban was signed in Moscow. Tests in the atmosphere, outer space, underwater (and underground, if they caused fall-out outside national territory) were banned. The treaty entered into force on 10 October 1963 and has been ratified by over one hundred states (though not France or China – both nuclear weapons states). Although it limited the fall-out, the partial test ban did nothing to limit the nuclear arms race. New technology allowed states to test effectively underground and still stay within the terms of the treaty.

Verification   Thus concern now shifted to limiting testing so as to prevent an arms race. The logic was that if new weapons could not be tested there would be no certainty that they would work and therefore there would be no point in deploying them. Yet negotiations foundered on the same problem that bedevilled the partial test ban talks – verification. How much on-site inspection was needed to verify that an earthquake was not a nuclear test, and how much inspection of sensitive military sites should be allowed to a potential enemy? About one hundred and fifty events larger than four on the Richter scale (which measures earthquakes and other seismic phenomena) take place in the Soviet Union every year. The Soviet Union was opposed to widespread on-site inspection and so the United States claimed no progress could be made. But in the meantime, the technology for independent verification of tests has improved.

It became clear in the late 1960s that few tests could be carried out without visible surface effects, verifiable with satellites. Since a series of tests would be needed for full confidence in a weapon, supporters of arms control claimed a tough treaty was possible which would ban all tests above 10–20 kilotons without on-site inspection. Unfortunately, by that time most of the Soviet tests of MIRVs were below 20 kilotons, and in any case the Soviets were also using more peaceful nuclear explosions for civilian purposes, for example in major construction projects. *A threshold test ban*

In the spirit of East–West détente, in 1974 the Superpowers signed a Threshold Nuclear Test Ban, prohibiting tests above 150 kilotons without any on-site inspection. They also agreed to exchange geological data on test sites. In 1976 a treaty restricting peaceful nuclear explosions to the same limit was agreed and for the first time the Soviet Union accepted on-site inspection. However, neither treaty came into force officially as the United States Senate refused to ratify them. Both Superpowers, nevertheless, agreed to abide by the treaties.

In 1977 the Superpowers and Britain opened a new round of talks on a comprehensive test ban. Although initial agreement was reached on a limited term treaty (it would be unlimited if France and China joined), with national technical means of verification and some on-site black boxes (called passive means), the United States suspended the talks in 1980. The Soviets had also agreed in 1978 to 'challenge inspections', where the United States could quit a treaty if Moscow refused to allow an inspection. The Reagan administration ended the talks because of a desire to test new weapons and because of domestic pressure from military laboratories and sections of the armed forces. *Comprehensive test ban talks*

As with much of the rest of the Superpower nuclear weapons negotiations agenda, the ending of the Cold War led to renewed optimism that some progress might be made on a test ban. *New caution*

Estimated number of nuclear explosions 6 August 1963–31 December 1989

a = atmospheric
u = underground

Year	USA[a]		USSR		UK[a]		France		China		India		Total
	a	u	a	u	a	u	a	u	a	u	a	u	
6 Aug.–31 Dec.													
1963	0	15	0	0	0	0	0	1					16
1964	0	38	0	6	0	1	0	3	1	0			49
1965	0	36	0	9	0	1	0	4	1	0			51
1966	0	43	0	15	0	0	5[b]	1	3	0			67
1967	0	34	0	17	0	0	3	0	2	0			56
1968	0	45[c]	0	13	0	0	5	0	1	0			64
1969	0	38	0	16	0	0	0	0	1	1			56
1970	0	35	0	17	0	0	8	0	1	0			61
1971	0	17	0	19	0	0	5[b]	0	1	0			42
1972	0	18	0	22	0	0	3	0	2	0			45
1973	0	16[d]	0	14	0	0	5	0	1	0			36
1974	0	14	0	18	0	1	7[b]	0	1	0	0	1	42
1975	0	20	0	15	0	0	0	2	0	1	0	0	38
1976	0	18	0	17	0	1	0	4	3	1	0	0	44
1977	0	19	0	18	0	0	0	8[e]	1	0	0	0	46
1978	0	17	0	27	0	2	0	8	2	1	0	0	57
1979	0	15	0	29	0	1	0	9	1[f]	0	0	0	55
1980	0	14	0	21	0	3	0	13	1	0	0	0	52
1981	0	16	0	22	0	1	0	12	0	0	0	0	51
1982	0	18	0	31	0	1	0	6	0	1	0	0	57
1983	0	17	0	27	0	1	0	9	0	2	0	0	56
1984	0	17	0	29	0	2	0	8	0	2	0	0	58
1985	0	17	0	9	0	1	0	8	0	0	0	0	35
1986	0	14	0	0	0	1	0	8	0	0	0	0	23
1987	0	14	0	23	0	1	0	8	0	1	0	0	47
1988	0	14	0	17	0	0	0	8	0	1	0	0	40
1989	0	11	0	7	0	1	0	8	0	0	0	0	27
Total	0	590	0	458	0	19	41	128	23	11	0	1	1271

[a] See note *a* below.

[b] One more test was conducted this year, but it did not cause any detonation.

[c] Five devices used simultaneously in the same test are counted here as one explosion.

[d] Three devices used simultaneously in the same test are counted here as one explosion.

[e] Two of these tests may have been conducted in 1975 or 1976.

[f] This explosion may have been conducted underground.

Estimated number of nuclear explosions 16 July 1945–31 Dec. 1989

USA[a]	USSR	UK[a]	France	China	India	Total
921	643	42	177	34	1	1818

[a] All British tests from 1962 have been conducted jointly with the United States at the Nevada Test Site. Therefore, the number of US tests is actually higher than indicated here.

Source: Stockholm International Peace Research Institute Yearbook, 1990.

Although some people felt it might be possible to obtain a comprehensive test ban, the Superpowers seemed unpersuaded that they should go that far. As they edged towards acceptance that their nuclear weapons should be retained for minimum deterrence, they also saw the need to keep a minimum level of testing. Furthermore, the Superpowers were not persuaded that a complete ban would stop threshold nuclear powers such as Iraq obtaining their own weapons. If a complete test ban could not be fully verified, it could not halt nuclear proliferation.

Yet the Superpowers were coming to accept that there were less radical limits on testing which might be useful. Limiting the number of tests would limit the risk of environmental pollution from the venting of tests and would slow the pace of development of new weapons. Reducing the size of underground tests to the 10–20 kiloton range would also reduce the risk of venting while still allowing the triggers for thermo-nuclear weapons to be tested and deterrence to be kept robust. By not reducing the limit any lower, the Superpowers might also encourage other nuclear powers to join in an international accord. With intrusive on-site inspections in such an arms control agreement an increasing confidence about the intentions of other, sometimes rival, powers, would occur.

New hopes

The debate over a comprehensive test ban indicates the extent to which improvements in technology can be made to serve the cause of peace, as well as war, through weapons development. Of course, the difficult details and effective verification will require complex negotiations between all existing nuclear weapons powers. Not a simple task.

Reading

C. Blacker and G. Duffy, *International Arms Control* (Stanford: Stanford University Press, 1984).

J. Evenden, 'Politics, Technology and the Test Ban', *Bulletin of the Atomic Scientist*, March 1985.

A. Greb and W. Heckrotte, 'The Long History of the Test Ban Debate', *Bulletin of the Atomic Scientist*, August 1983.

Nuclear Proliferation

If you think it is dangerous enough living in a nuclear age, with the five great powers all brimming over with nuclear weapons, imagine a world with dozens of nuclear powers. Picture a nuclear confrontation in the Arab–Israeli or India–Pakistan conflict and you can understand the dangers of nuclear proliferation. It is true that nuclear weapons have proliferated faster vertically (within one state's arsenal) than horizontally (by spreading to more countries). But while there is reasonable confidence that the proliferation by the great powers is roughly balanced and under control, there is deeper concern about the spread of nuclear weapons to less 'reliable' states. Such concern is long-standing but may be fading as few states show signs of joining the nuclear club and the most worrying case, Iraq, was hit hard by a UN sanctioned coalition in 1991.

The IAEA The dangers of nuclear proliferation have been faced in a variety of ways. In 1956 the International Atomic Energy Agency (IAEA) was established to control the supply of uranium (the fuel needed to make a nuclear weapon) and especially to monitor the expansion of peaceful uses of nuclear energy. Although well-meaning, the IAEA is toothless since it cannot force extensive inspections of nuclear facilities in states thought likely to be about to 'go nuclear'. Apart from the Soviet Union and the United States, nuclear weapons have spread only to Britain (in 1957), France (in 1960), China (in 1964) and India (in 1974). These states all shared the view that genuine political independence or regional supremacy required an independent nuclear force. Since their allies were unlikely to provide them with such weapons, they had to develop nuclear forces on their own. But because of the concern that this 'logic' would later extend to a wide variety of states, and because the IAEA was obviously ineffective, two types of effort were undertaken to limit the spread of nuclear weapons.

Nuclear free zones The first effort focused on the concept of establishing nuclear-free zones. The oldest treaty to that effect is the 1959 treaty banning all nuclear weapons in the Antarctic. It was hoped that such a 'non-armament' measure would be easier to enforce than the withdrawal of weapons already deployed. The second such pact, signed at Tlatelolco (Mexico) in February 1967, bound Latin American states not to maintain nuclear forces and to use nuclear material and facilities only for peaceful purposes. All nuclear plants in the region were to be placed under IAEA safeguards. But the implementation of the treaty has been patchy at best. Brazil, Chile, and Trinidad and Tobago said they would only be bound when all the other Latin American states had ratified it. Argentina signed but did not ratify; Cuba and Guyana have not signed. A protocol commits states to respect the denuclearization of Latin America and not to use or threaten the use of nuclear weapons against any party. All five major nuclear powers have ratified the protocol.

In 1967 an Outer Space Treaty was signed, banning the place- *Newer zones* ment of nuclear weapons in space, on the model of the Antarctic pact. In 1971 similar arrangements were agreed in the Seabed Treaty (which covers the sea beyond twelve miles from the coast). Various other proposals have been made for nuclear free zones, including the Pacific, the Nordic countries, Africa and the Mediterranean area. Some European anti-nuclear groups have gone so far as to propose the establishment of nuclear-free zones for individual towns and cities. But the idea of a Pacific zone is the only one to have made any serious progress. In 1975 the United Nations General Assembly approved the plan, but only China among the nuclear powers accepted it. On 5 August 1985, 8 South Pacific states agreed to a treaty along the lines of Tlatelolco. In 1987 the Soviet Union and China agreed to abide by the treaty, while the United States and France refused.

Despite all the goodwill that lies behind such treaties, the *The* problem with nuclear free zones is that they usually cover areas *proliferation* where there is little reason to believe states would wish to deploy *problem* nuclear weapons anyway. To date, there is no case of a nuclear or potential nuclear power being deterred from acquiring such weapons by the existence of a nuclear-free zone. Therefore most attention in controlling proliferation has focused on limiting the spread of the weapons themselves. The main impetus for a non-proliferation treaty came from small states in the late 1950s. Progress became easier in 1965, when the United States abandoned its idea of transferring nuclear weapons to allies in the so-called Multilateral Force in Europe.

The Non-proliferation Treaty (NPT) was signed in July 1968. *The NPT* Signatories promised not to transfer nuclear weapons or the means to build them to non-nuclear states and IAEA safeguards were to be used to inspect nuclear plants designed for peaceful purposes. The Superpowers agreed to reduce the incentive for acquiring nuclear weapons by themselves seriously pursuing arms control. They also agreed to support non-nuclear signatories of the NPT if they were threatened by a nuclear state. But the Soviet Union refused to undertake not to threaten non-nuclear states because the United States stationed nuclear weapons in allied states (e.g. in West Germany). The treaty entered into force in March 1970, with ninety-seven signatures and forty-seven ratifications. By 1990 it had one hundred and forty-one adherents. France and China are the most notable non-adherents, though both have been careful not to violate the treaty's provisions. In 1985 China agreed to IAEA inspections of some civilian nuclear plants. Other important countries which have not signed are Brazil, India, Israel, Pakistan, Saudi Arabia and South Africa. Argentina has said it will sign, if the Superpowers agree to a comprehensive test ban.

Reviewing the NPT

The five-yearly NPT review conferences were intended to reassure the faithful that non-proliferation was working but the treaty had serious limitations from the start. The 1980 review conference ended without a joint declaration, largely because no agreement was possible on criticism of both East and West for failing to halt vertical proliferation. At the 1985 review conference, a compromise resolution criticized the nuclear powers for failing to agree a comprehensive nuclear test ban treaty. With Britain and the United States reserving their positions, the Soviet Union accepted the declaration. The 1990 review conference ended without any formal declaration.

The risks of proliferation

Although the NPT has serious gaps, the failure of the Superpowers to halt their own vertical proliferation has encouraged cynicism that the pact is merely a ruse for Superpower control of nuclear weapons. The weakness of IAEA safeguards, especially as different types of nuclear fuel cycle have been developed, inspires little confidence in 'safeguards'. The oil crisis in the 1970s also encouraged the spread of nuclear power plants for peaceful purposes and the consequent risk that fuel could be diverted for military ends. By 1980, 22 states operated 235 nuclear reactors and in 1985, 26 countries were running 344 plants. It is true that the issue of nuclear power had become the focus of environmentalists and that this political opposition limited the spread of these plants. But the use by India of reactor material supplied from a Canadian-produced plant suggested safeguards were woefully out-of-date. And of course, the Indian test merely encouraged Pakistan to obtain its own nuclear weapon.

The most acute fears about proliferation have focused on the Middle East. Israel is generally agreed to have a 'bomb in the basement' in case it should ever face military defeat at the hands of its Arab neighbours. But Israel does not wish to encourage its neighbours to obtain their own weapons, so it has made clear that it will not be the first to introduce nuclear weapons to the area. However, neither would Israel wait to be the second. A novel, strategic doctrine.

The risks of non-proliferation

Israel has also taken a more active and dangerous part in keeping the risks of nuclear war in the Middle East under control. In 1981 it destroyed Iraq's nuclear reactor in an attempt to fore-

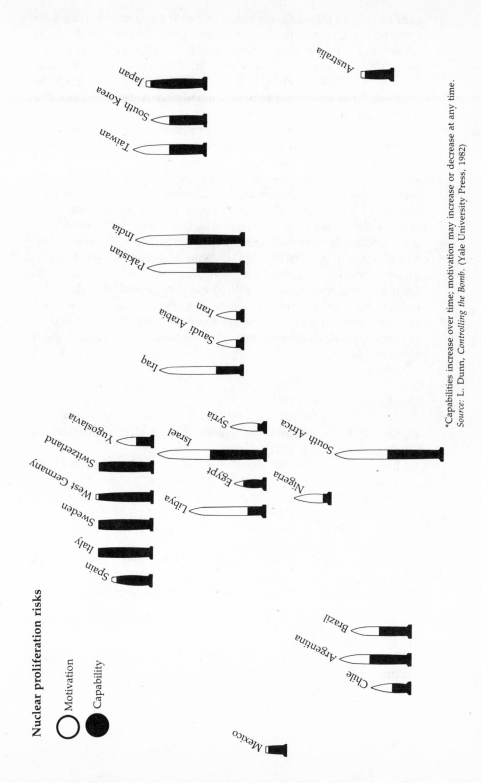

Nuclear proliferation risks

○ Motivation

● Capability

Japan
South Korea
Taiwan
Australia

India
Pakistan
Iran
Saudi Arabia
Iraq

Yugoslavia
Switzerland
West Germany
Sweden
Italy
Spain

Israel
Syria
Egypt
Libya
Nigeria
South Africa

Brazil
Argentina
Chile

Mexico

*Capabilities increase over time; motivation may increase or decrease at any time.
Source: L. Dunn, *Controlling the Bomb.* (Yale University Press, 1982)

stall having to take its own bomb out of the basement. It was an extreme but apparently effective short-term tactic of non-proliferation. In 1991, the allied forces which forced Iraq to withdraw from Kuwait, also made sure that Iraq's nuclear potential was destroyed. Less hair-raising support for non-proliferation has been obtained in negotiations between Brazil and Argentina since the latters' return to democratic rule.

Enhancing
security
The essential tool in preventing proliferation is to enhance the security of states who feel threatened without nuclear weapons. Some states are attracted to the security of insecurity, otherwise known as nuclear deterrence. Others, such as Libya or Iraq, simply want the weapon to threaten others. Some, such as South Africa, Taiwan or Israel, feel beleaguered and can trust no one but themselves for their security. But despite all this international insecurity it is remarkable how little overt proliferation has taken place. The NPT's major success is in helping create a climate hostile to open proliferation. No doubt, bombs are kept in various basements from Pretoria to Jerusalem. But by refusing openly to admit the existence of these weapons, some stability is maintained. Of course, Superpower control of vertical proliferation and a reduction in international insecurity would make matters even more stable.

Reading

R. Cowen Karp, *Security with Nuclear Weapons?* (Oxford: Oxford University Press, 1991).

L. Dunn, *Controlling the Bomb* (London: Yale University Press, 1982).

L. Dunn, 'The Nuclear Non-proliferation Record', *Washington Quarterly*, Summer 1990.

T. Greenwood *et al*, *Nuclear Proliferation* (New York: McGraw Hill, 1977).

J. Simpson and A. McGrew (eds), *The International Nuclear Non-proliferation System* (London: Macmillan, 1984).

G.C. Smith and H. Cobban, 'A Blind Eye to Nuclear Proliferation', *Foreign Affairs*, Summer 1989.

K. Waltz, 'The Spread of Nuclear Weapons', *Adelphi Papers* No. 171 (London, 1981).

J. Yager, *Nonproliferation and US Foreign Policy* (Washington: Brookings, 1984).

Chemical and Biological Weapons

Nuclear warfare is not the only horrific military threat to civilization in the modern era. Although the effect of environmental warfare may take longer to show, and although chemical and biological weapons may 'only' kill living things, rather than destroy buildings, this kind of weapon could be even more destructive of life than nuclear war.

Biological weapons (BW) are designed to distribute living organisms, usually bacteria or viruses, that can kill by causing disease. Crops may also be targeted. Research in the United States on biological weapons began when it was feared that Nazi Germany was exploring their use. However, it soon became clear that biological agents are of limited military use because there is an incubation period before they take effect and they are difficult to contain within a designated target area. On the other hand, chemical weapons (CW), which use toxic compounds, such as nerve gas, are lethal enough to kill in minutes.

Killing chemicals and biology

The Hague Conventions of 1899 and 1907 considered bans on chemical weapons, but some (mustard gas, chlorine, phosgene) were used in 1915 during the First World War. They accounted for 20% of all artillery shells fired and caused 15% of all casualties but only 1.4% of total deaths. The Geneva Protocol of 1925 which prohibited the use of both CW and BW, entered into force in 1928 (but was only ratified by the United States in 1974). Most parties reserved the right to use CW agents against an enemy who used them first. The Protocol did not ban the development and stockpiling of CW, as was done by both sides in the Second World War.

The Geneva Protocol

Chemical weapons have rarely been used since the Protocol. Defoliant chemicals were used by Britain in Malaya (1948–60). Italy used other types of CW in Ethiopia in 1936, and Egypt used yet others against the Yemen in 1963–7. But it was the larger scale use of CW in the Vietnam war that stimulated international efforts to limit their use.

Using CW

President Nixon agreed in 1969 to put forward the Geneva Protocol for American ratification and to suspend development of BW (and destroy stockpiles). America also ceased unilaterally to produce and test CW at this time. In 1970 the ban was extended to cover toxins (poisonous chemicals produced by micro-organisms). Britain and the United States announced they were ready to accept an unverified ban on BW in order to prevent a possible arms race. They were unwilling to do so for CW where large stockpiles already

A new treaty

111

existed. On 10 April 1972 the Convention on Prohibition of the Development, Production and Stockpiling of Biological Warfare and Toxin Warfare and on their Destruction was signed. It provided for no on-site inspection, but the United Nations Security Council could insist on an investigation where evidence suggested that agreements were being violated. Unlike the case of the Non-proliferation Treaty, France and China acceded to this treaty.

Deadlock on CW control

However, the cw treaty negotiations (which have continued since 1972) are still blocked by disagreements over verification. Problems are exacerbated by the fact that some research in the field is of commercial value. Pressure for a treaty comes from repeated claims that cw have been used in recent conflicts. Since 1979, Vietnam has been accused of using 'yellow rain' in Cambodia but a 1981 United Nations report could not reach a conclusive judgement. In May 1984 the United Nations did confirm that cw were being used by Iraq against Iran and Iraq later used them against its own Kurdish population. In December 1984 a leak at an American civilian chemical factory in Bhopal (India) killed 3,500, suggesting just how lethal warfare with similar substances might be.

CW stockpiles and Europe

Until the ending of the Cold War, the main danger of cw was in Europe, where both East and West stockpiled weapons and trained to cope with chemical warfare. The United States and France each reportedly held up to 433 tons of cw agents in Europe. Although some American studies confirm that cw might well be an ineffective military tool, in the 1980s efforts were stepped up to deploy a new generation of cw. The United States binary weapons program for nerve gas was designed to deploy weapons that are divided into two sections and which are safe when separate.

Binary weapons

Talks about controlling these weapons continue in the United Nations. The United States insisted more modern cw were required to deter the Soviet Union and after the end of the Cold War cited the stockpiles in Iraq as a threat. It is thought that some twenty other states have a cw capability and some non-governmental organizations (such as terrorists) could all too easily obtain access to cw. The United States is quick to point out that binary technology is less subject to hijack by terrorists. Washington also points out that, in 1979, in the Soviet city of Sverdlovsk, there was apparently an accident with anthrax (a bw agent) suggesting Soviet experiments continue.

Superpower agreement

As the Superpowers recognized their state of diminished influence in the 1990s, they began to focus on those areas where agreement between themselves might help preserve their pre-eminence. Thus in 1990 the Superpowers agreed to cut their cw arsenals by 80%. The hope was that by creating a climate conducive to arms control, there was a chance that lesser powers might not acquire the same kind of lethal arsenals as the Super-powers hold. The failure of Iraq to use its chemical weapons in the 1991 war suggested that the Americans might have less to fear and less reason to block a cw accord. Yet the once Superpowers also know that in such a climate of uncertainty, it would also be folly to disarm completely.

Reading

V. Adams, *Chemical Warfare, Chemical Disarmament* (London: Mac-millan, 1989).

C. Blacker and G. Duffy, *International Arms Control* (Stanford: Stanford University Press, 1984).

E. Spiers, *Chemical Warfare* (Chicago: University of Illinois Press, 1986).

Stockholm International Peace Research Institute, *Yearbook* (Oxford: Oxford University Press, 1990).

V. Utgoff, *The Challenge of Chemical Weapons* (London: Macmillan, 1990).

The Arms Trade

As devastating as nuclear arms might be, they have rarely been used in anger. Most wars are still fought with conventional weapons, and better control of the means of war might help cut the scale of deaths or risks of conflict. Until the late 1980s, the vast majority of weapons was bought by the poorer parts of the world, but with mounting debt problems, the falling price of oil, and even the ending of many wars, total arms sales to the developing world began to shrink.

The exporters   The Superpowers continue to dominate the trade in major conventional weapons, with the Russians accounting for 37% of the world total and the United States 34% in 1989. The overall situation, with France, Britain, China and Germany taking up the remaining leading places, has not changed much in the past several years.

The leading exporters of major weapons, 1985–9

The countries are ranked according to 1985–9 aggregate exports. Figures are in US $m., at constant (1985) prices.

Exporters	1985	1986	1987	1988	1989	1985–9
To all countries						
1. USSR	12 796	14 579	14 718	12 464	11 652	66 209
2. USA	8 800	10 272	12 529	10 505	10 755	52 862
3. France	3 970	4 005	2 896	2 199	2 732	15 802
4. UK	1 699	1 429	1 665	1 297	1 620	7 711
5. China	1 088	1 193	1 960	1 842	779	6 862
6. FR Germany	1 025	1 108	674	1 432	780	5 019
7. Czechoslovakia	497	497	570	548	546	2 658
8. Italy	646	456	388	438	149	2 077
9. Sweden	163	324	489	577	323	1 877
10. Netherlands	88	240	265	532	631	1 756
11. Brazil	188	150	507	356	183	1 385
12. Israel	227	250	346	133	228	1 183
13. Spain	139	193	160	212	404	1 109
14. Canada	132	472	387	75	37	1 103
15. Egypt	124	159	194	232	62	771
Others	922	710	1 089	777	938	4 432
Total	**32 504**	**36 037**	**38 837**	**33 619**	**31 819**	**172 816**

Source: SIPRI data base.

The importers   In 1989, for the first time in twenty years, the Middle East was not the leading importing region. South Asia, largely because of deliveries to India and Afghanistan, took top spot as Middle East importers were hit by falling oil prices and the needs were reduced because of the ending of the Iran-Iraq War. India topped the world table of imports with 10% of the total in 1989. Iraq and Japan were the second and third largest importers, each accounting for some 6% of the world total. Saudi Arabia, once a high-flyer on these tables, was down to fourth place with just under 5% of the world total of arms imports. But with the sparkling performance of high technology weapons in the allied attacks on Iraq in 1991, the Gulf region looked set to import a whole new generation of technology. Other regions of the world might also reconsider their need for better and 'smarter' equipment.

The leading importers of major weapons, 1985–9

The countries are ranked according to 1985–9 aggregate imports. Figures are in US $m., at constant (1985) prices.

Importers	1985	1986	1987	1988	1989	1985–9
All countries						
1. India	1 876	3 683	4 585	3 383	3 819	17 345
2. Iraq	2 871	2 447	4 247	2 005	418	11 989
3. Japan	1 634	1 745	1 771	2 343	3 062	10 554
4. Saudi Arabia	1 447	2 395	1 956	1 770	1 196	8 764
5. Syria	1 690	1 508	1 169	1 172	336	5 876
6. Egypt	1 282	1 665	2 347	348	152	5 795
7. Czechoslovakia	1 332	1 086	967	1 067	828	5 280
8. North Korea	977	876	487	1 383	1 553	5 275
9. Spain	270	1 039	1 513	1 580	749	5 152
10. Turkey	604	621	1 153	1 238	1 134	4 751
11. Poland	427	1 057	983	1 063	1 118	4 649
12. Afghanistan	82	611	687	939	2 289	4 610
13. Angola	694	975	1 135	890	24	3 719
14. Canada	877	828	732	526	444	3 408
15. Libya	969	1 359	294	65	499	3 186
Others	15 472	14 142	14 811	13 847	14 198	72 463
Total	**32 504**	**36 037**	**38 837**	**33 619**	**31 819**	**172 816**

Source: SIPRI data base.

Of course, all these figures appear more precise than they really are. Figures for arms imports and exports are notoriously difficult to obtain in the often secretive military world. Some arms transfers are sales, some are grants and some are aid packages that include training and often greater dependency on the supplier than simple sales of equipment to developed states. Thus, it would be wrong to overemphasize the facts and figures of the arms trade, for it is politics that lies at the heart of the process.

The secretive game

Weapons are transferred for a number of often overlapping reasons. First, they are sold or provided to close allies, for example the Superpower transfers to European states. The idea is to shore up the defences of states which are seen as vital to the defence of the supplier. Some other states, such as Israel, can be counted in

Weapons for allies

this category of American transfers. In accordance with the Nixon Doctrine of the 1970s, the United States tried to encourage as many of its allies to stand on their own without the need for American troops.

Weapons for influence

Second, weapons are transferred to enhance political influence. Both Soviet and American weapons transfers to the Middle East demonstrate this objective as well as the difficulty of ensuring that states thus armed then pursue policies favourable to the donor. In fact, there are a wide variety of political motives, many of which amount to little more than causing a nuisance, where few direct gains are expected.

Weapons for profit

The final motive for arms transfers is economic gain. In order to cut the costs of research and development by having longer weapons production runs, middle-ranking powers, such as the Europeans or China, and smaller states such as the two Koreas or Brazil, have discovered the value of arms exports. These states therefore manage indirectly to maintain a more independent foreign policy by virtue of being less reliant on foreign arms manufacturers. This was certainly the initial Israeli motive for arms production.

Why buy weapons?

However, it would be unfair to blame the arms trade only on the sellers and not on the consumers. Weapons can be transferred only if there are states and movements who want to acquire them. Indeed, the motives of purchasers are most important. Weapons are obtained for a variety of reasons: (1) to attack an enemy (for example, Egypt and Syria attacked Israel in 1973); (2) to defend against a potential attack (for example, West European purchase of American weapons); (3) to satisfy the armed forces who like new toys (as happens in many Latin American states which face no real enemy, except possibly those at home).

The new games of the 1990s

The winding up of the East-West conflict and the slowdown of some conflicts in the developing world are likely to have major impacts on the arms trade business. Arms sales among developed states will undoubtedly decelerate although not end completely. There is likely to be much closer integration of companies in the defence sector as new market shares are divided. Exports to the developing world had already slowed before the Iraqi invasion of Kuwait but the new conflict looked like proving correct those who noted that the fading of the East-West conflict did not mean that smaller wars in the developing world would end. Arms sales will be possible where local conflicts flare and great powers become drawn into the fray.

The MTCR

Much concern has already been focused on the Middle East and the apparent start of an arms race in middle-range ballistic missiles. This more sophisticated technology can be provided by the major arms exporters, or may result from co-production arrangements among developing states. Seven Western industrialized powers agreed in the April 1987 Missile Technology Control Régime not to spread ballistic missile technology with a range above 300 kilometres and a payload of over 500 kilograms to the developing world. The régime, which in 1991 had 15 formal adherents, now also monitors the proliferation of cruise missiles and is now supported by a wider range of developed states. But the local rivalries are likely to continue and Israel has already shown it can develop such weapons itself. The use of missiles as part of the Gulf conflict of 1990–1 made it plain that new warriors would find new ways of waging war.

Obviously, the move to halt the arms trade needs to concentrate on the different motives of sellers and consumers. In this field, no one strategy for arms control will be effective, or indeed sensible. On balance, the main problem seems to lie with the wide range of motives on the part of those who acquire weapons. Suppliers provide the weapons, but they often soon lose control over the policy whose ends the weapons are meant to serve. They may threaten not to resupply an awkward client, but recipients can often go elsewhere, or threaten collapse and so cast doubt on the prestige of the supplier. Apart from arms supplies to close allies, there can be little confidence that lasting political influence will be 'earned' from the trade in arms. Thus, if the objective of arms controllers is to control conflict, they might do better to concentrate on controlling the politics of the conflicts that drive states to buy arms. The reasons for buying arms are almost as numerous as the causes of war.

The problem of arms control

Reading

N. Ball and M. Leitenberg, *The Structure of Defence Industries* (London: Croom Helm, 1983).

A. Gilks and G. Segal, *China and the Arms Trade* (London: Croom Helm, 1985).

M. Kaldor, *The Baroque Arsenal* (London: André Deutsch, 1982).

T.G. Mahnken 'Security Implications of Missile Proliferation' *Washington Quarterly*, Winter 1991.

J. Nolan, *Trappings of Power* (Washington: Brookings, 1991).

A. Pierre, *The Global Politics of Arms Sales* (Princeton: Princeton University Press, 1983).

Terrorism

It is the terror in terrorism that almost makes it modern day political theatre on our television screens. But despite the 'good copy' that hijackings, shootings and bombings provide, there is little evidence that all the sound and fury actually has forced great political change, although it has affected our travelling lives, particularly in the Western world.

Who is a terrorist?

The trendy slogan is that 'one man's terrorist is another person's guerrilla freedom fighter'. It is true that many people in the radical and Arab world applauded when Palestinians killed Israeli athletes at the 1972 Munich Olympics, seeing it as part of the struggle against the Zionist oppressors. But most people saw it as a callous attack on innocent sportsmen competing in the spirit of goodwill. Trying to define terrorism in such an emotional atmosphere is next to impossible.

Yet, somewhere between a common criminal and a guerrilla who fights by the rules of war, is a terrorist. This terrorist kills civilians in order to sow terror in support of their political struggle. By contrast, common criminals have no political motives while guerrillas do not intentionally kill civilians.

Types of terrorist

The means of sowing terror are all too numerous. Aircraft can be hijacked, bombs thrown at train stations, busloads of schoolchildren gunned-down and pubs bombed. Outside the political extremes of Left and Right, probably most people would readily agree that no cause justifies such violence. But what of the terrorism of bombing cities as happened in the Second World War to destroy enemy morale? Indeed, what of the threat to destroy millions in a nuclear war – the essence of our nuclear strategy called Mutual Assured Destruction? All these are also terrorism, albeit not what we normally mean by the term.

Why terror?

Small-scale terrorists are most often Left-wing radicals violently opposed to the existing order. However, it is true that several European countries have also experienced terrorism by extreme Right-wing groups. They usually resort to terror because they are too weak and the opposing state too strong to be challenged in more conventional guerrilla warfare or via the ballot box. Thus an upswing of terrorism is often a sign of stability, rather than imminent collapse.

The media

The would-be terrorist, plotting against an unsuspecting government, has a number of advantages. First, modern society is highly dependent on fancy gadgetry such as airplanes, television and computers. By striking soft targets, such as innocent civilians, the terrorist needs few weapons and little training. All he needs is zeal.

Above all, the terrorist can count on modern media to report terrorist attacks. Even though the terrorist will be criticised, he will receive far more publicity than he could hope to win by publishing a few illegible political pamphlets that no one will read. The temptation to strike, and then teach other dissatisfied movements by example, is obvious. For example, Palestinians taught supporters of Castro the art of aircraft hijacking in the early 1970s.

Despite all the coverage, relatively few people die as a result of terrorism. Adopting the broadest definition of terrorism, some 1,500 people were killed in the decade from 1968. Between 1980–5, 1,000 Americans died at the hands of terrorists. Israel, seemingly the number one target, has suffered around 500 deaths since the modern wave of terror began in 1968. More than ten times that number of Israelis died in accidents on their country's lethal highways in that time. *The death toll*

Virtually no country is immune from the attention of terrorists. Aircraft have been hijacked in the Soviet Union and China, as well as the Middle East and the United States. Africa and East Asia seem least affected, while Western Europe, the United States and the Middle East are the most frequent targets. *The range of targets*

There are literally thousands of organizations which have committed terrorist acts. By far the most numerous are the various Arab factions fighting Israel, America and fellow Arabs. In December 1988, 259 people were killed when a Pan Am plane was destroyed over Scotland. Yet the single most murderous terrorist act was the destruction of an Air India 747 over the Atlantic in June 1985, apparently the handiwork of Sikh extremists in which 329 people died. In 1987, North Korean agents destroyed a South Korean aircraft on a flight over Southeast Asia. *The range of terrorists*

Despite the loss of life and the personal suffering it causes to victims' families, terrorism has had remarkably little impact on modern day politics. To be sure, politicians and diplomats now need extra protection and that costs time and money. It is a nuisance to have your baggage checked in public places or to have to turn up an hour earlier before a flight for a security check. Many Americans, worried by threats of reprisals in Europe for the American raid on Libya in 1986 or the attack on Iraq in 1991, rearranged their travel plans, even though statistically speaking European cities remained far safer than the streets of the United States. *The impact*

Yet there are few signs that governments have changed their policies as a result of terrorism. Some European governments close their eyes to Arab terrorists because they fear that if they act *Civil liberties*

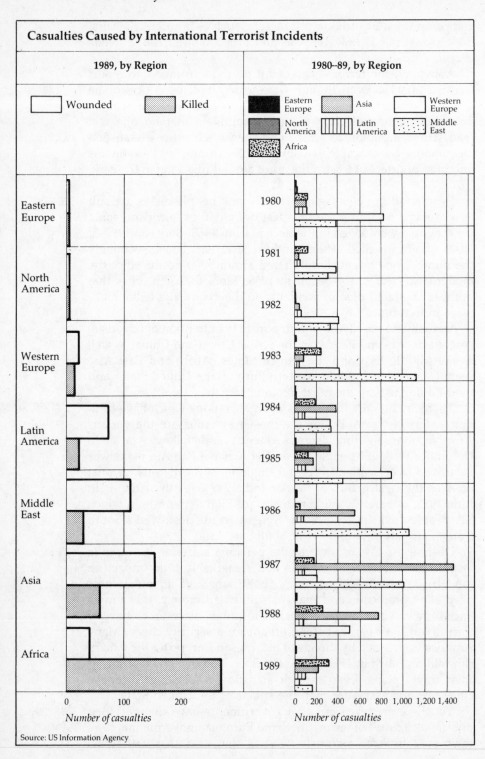

Casualties Caused by International Terrorist Incidents

Source: US Information Agency

against them they will be future targets. But fear of the oil weapon is a far more potent explanation for Western governments' reluctance to deal harshly with governments who harbour or support terrorist groups. The First World War supposedly began because of the assassination of the Archduke Ferdinand, but the guns of opposing armies were clearly primed well before. The most important potential impact of terror is that liberal democratic governments will descend to the level of terrorists, impose draconian laws and restrict civil liberties. So far, despite the adoption of anti-terrorist legislation in most European countries, and especially in Britain and Italy, there is little evidence that the terrorists have achieved this much.

Britain has tough anti-terrorist laws on its books to combat the IRA that allow civil liberties to be suspended for a time, but there is little evidence of anything more than occasional misuse of those laws. Canada imposed a state of emergency during its terrorist crises in the 1970s, but no lasting damage was done. Israel operates under a system of press censorship, but that was imposed because it had been under threat from its neighbours for decades before the terrorist threat. Most Western governments faced with the threat of terrorism have managed to direct the law against the terrorists themselves without abolishing the civil rights of the rest of their population.

Various strategies have been adopted against the terrorist threat. The most obvious is simple defence, such as putting armed guards at embassies or soldiers at airports. Protecting all possible targets is impossible, but these guards have been known to save the day, for example when an Israeli security guard shot a hijacker while the plane was coming in to land in London. The risk from such action is high, but a success or two which attracts media coverage also sends a message to the would-be terrorist. *Defending against terror*

Terrorists can also be deterred by less violent means such as using sniffer dogs to detect explosives or X-ray machines to detect weapons. Israeli airlines deter most hijackers by making it clear that they search bags more often and more thoroughly than other airlines. Some countries, like Greece, are said to be havens for terrorism because the Greek authorities are notoriously lax about security. Of course some countries, notably Libya and Syria, actually encourage terrorist groups by providing training facilities and money. *Deterrence*

The most energetic response to terror is to strike back hard. Most industrialized states now have anti-terror squads designed to liberate hijacked people. An Israeli commando squad freed captives in Entebbe in Uganda in 1976 and a year later the West Germans did the same at Mogadishu. Britain's SAS has broken up an embassy siege in London. The more ambitious have not just *Terrorizing the terrorist* waited to be attacked, and have gone in search of the potential terrorist. Once again the Israelis have led the way, killing Arabs in Europe and launching bombing raids as far away as Tunisia. Other liberal–democratic régimes have also struck covertly, sometimes killing the wrong people in the cause of anti-terrorism. In April 1986 the United States launched raids on Libya in retaliation for terrorism. In October Britain led its European partners in taking limited diplomatic measures against Syria because of its complicity in an attempt to destroy an El Al plane in flight.

The legal option   The more genteel anti-terrorist would make use of the law. There are a number of conventions to prevent aircraft hijacking, but all have failed because no sanction is provided against those who support the terrorist. The United Nations General Assembly has regularly condemned terrorism, but then it has also supported struggles for national liberation. In 1977, two protocols to the 1949 Geneva conventions were formulated to help identify terrorists as killers of civilians, but even Western nations have been reluctant to support this.

The legal solution is never likely to stop terrorism which by its very nature disdains the rules of the international game. But the laws also run the risk of legitimizing certain types of attack, for example on soldiers or diplomats. The United States in particular suffers far more from attacks on its soldiers and diplomats, for example in Beirut and Tehran. Among those who support Catholic or Protestant extremists in Northern Ireland, there are many who prefer to see British Army soldiers as targets than women and children in a church.

Living with terror   Since the upsurge of terrorism in the late 1960s, there has been no trend of increasing terror. The targets and methods change, but the problem remains one of the lesser challenges to international order. Greater vigilance and more direct counter-action will help control the problem, but offers no solution. Neither will resolving the roots of political conflict and terrorism, for even in the unlikely event that there should be a peace settlement, say in the Middle East, there will always be a dissident fringe ready to throw bombs from the sidelines. Perhaps with the passage of time, there will be greater recognition that terrorism feeds off our more morbid motivations, and is better minimized as the flea-bite of international affairs that it is.

Reading

L. Freedman *et al*, *Terrorism and International Order* (London: Routledge & Kegan Paul, 1986).

P. Janke, *Guerrilla and Terrorist Organizations* (Brighton: Harvester, 1983).

W. Laquer, *The Age of Terrorism* (London: Weidenfeld, 1987).

G. Rosie, *The Directory of International Terrorism* (London: Mainstream, 1986).

P. Wilkinson, *Political Terrorism* (London: Macmillan, 1974).

P. Wilkinson, *Terrorism and the Liberal State* (London: Macmillan, 1986).

Spies

Spying, glibly known as the second oldest profession, is as old as politics. From Joshua's biblical spies to KGB defectors, the rationale for spying remains the same. It is in the interest of adversaries to know as much about their opponent and his thinking as possible. In the edgy atmosphere of the Cold War, spy scandals were the equivalent of gunfire. In the confused mood of the new détente, spies are hastily running for new cover and revealing long-cherished secrets.

The spy trade

The methods of spying have, of course, changed. Modern intelligence is gathered in two main ways, one far more glamorous than the other. The less flashy, but more often useful, work is called 'sigint' (signal intelligence) and 'elint' (electronic intelligence). Whether it comes from the 'national technical means' of spy satellites or the mass of antennae on 'fishing trawlers' off enemy coasts, or shadowing naval fleets, the information provides most of the reliable knowledge about enemy deployments. With satellites that can read newspaper headlines from space, or early warning airborne aircraft (such as AWAC) that can 'see' over the horizon and hundreds of miles to the enemy's rear, the problem for intelligence agencies rapidly becomes how to digest all the information available rather than the failure to gather data.

Telling the hardware where to look

By far the largest proportion of Western budgets for spying goes on the American National Security Agency and the British GCHQ, rather than the better known Central Intelligence Agency (CIA) or the Secret Intelligence Service (SIS). The CIA, and its 'humint' (human intelligence) is primarily concerned with assessment of intelligence by analysts behind desks. But most public attention has focused on that part of humint which harks back to Biblical times – spies out in the cold of enemy territory. The reason for continuing to rely on this type of espionage is the belief that, while sigint or elint may be able to gather information on enemy capabilities, only humint can assess enemy intentions. Somebody has to tell all the hardware where to look.

Turning spies

Yet the difficulties in assessing humint are legendary. Is a spy still working for the side he started with, or has he been 'turned' by the enemy? Or, more confusingly still, has the double-agent been turned yet again, and back again . . .? Of course he may be working for a third party. And even if treachery can be discounted, spies are fallible human beings and could be fed 'disinformation' by the enemy. These natural human uncertainties and paranoias make the spy game wonderful material for the master spy-story teller or newspaper editors anxious to sell a scoop. But they also make humint of dubious practical value.

The value of information from spies varies with the conditions and the characters concerned. During wartime, information is of much greater value. The breaking of the German Enigma code in the Second World War gave the Allies important strategic and even tactical advantages over the enemy. Although the war was not won by breaking Enigma, it was certainly an important factor. In post-war conflicts, similar information obtained by humint continues to be important. In the Arab–Israeli conflict of 1967, the spy Eli Cohen provided key information on enemy dispositions and was instrumental in making the Israeli pre-emptive strike so devastating. Israeli intelligence about PLO operations allows it to strike with such pinpoint accuracy at targets as far away as Tunis, as it did in raids on PLO headquarters in October 1985 and January 1991. Of course failure of such intelligence, as in the 1973 surprise Arab attack on Israel, also suggests that humint in wartime continues to be of the utmost importance.

The value of spies

In the less pressing tensions of post-war international politics, agents continue to be widely used. American CIA agents tried to kill Castro with exploding cigars and the Bulgarians, using Turkish Right-wing terrorists, are said to have tried to kill the Pope, perhaps on behalf of the Soviet Union. Israel regularly kills PLO men around the world and in the past has made use of its own agents to free hostages from captive aircraft as far away as Entebbe in Uganda. American agents were used in the botched attempt to free American hostages in Iran in 1980 and more successfully in the war against Iraq in 1991.

Exploding cigars

It was far more difficult to judge the effectiveness of spies and agents when the conflict was less immediate, as in the East–West Cold War. Although most post-war spy stories used this East–West backdrop, it is not clear how important such spying is until war breaks out. For example, as a legacy of the last war, the four powers agreed to a form of licensed spying in East and West Germany. In 1985 an American officer was killed while carrying out his duties observing military activities in East Germany. But some cold war spying can be said to be of importance to national security, even if only temporarily.

Spies in from the cold war

In the 1940s, the atom bomb spy, Klaus Fuchs, stole enough American information to allow the Soviet Union to detonate its first atom bomb eighteen months earlier than expected. In 1985, the Walker family was arrested in the United States for passing sigint information to Moscow that seriously undermined America's confidence in its ability to track Soviet ships. But, as in the Fuchs case, the damage is often reasonably short term. Adjust-

Philby and Penkovsky

ment in deployments and codes by the side being spied upon is possible because war has not broken out. In other cases, the management of crises can be improved when inside information on the other side's intentions is provided. Kim Philby was said to have provided such information to Moscow in the early days of the Cold War, as did Oleg Penkovsky for Washington before the Cuban missile crisis in 1962. Arkady Shevchenko's defection in 1978 apparently provided the United States with more recent insights into Soviet diplomatic strategy. Obviously, none of these spies was crucial for national defence but they did help inform policy. As long as states hope to keep information confidential from an adversary – and the Superpowers still see each other as adversaries – such spying will be of value.

Why change sides?   It is also difficult to judge precisely why spies change sides, although you have to feel sorry for East German spies who find their enemy in West Germany is now the boss. The vast majority of spies who went east did so for money, as a result of blackmail (usually sexual), or because they bore grudges. Most spies who defected westward did so for ideological reasons. Now that the Cold War is over, the political upheaval will mean that while there will be unemployment for some, this is also a time which will produce new recruits to new causes. Counter-intelligence directors have a thankless job, just as spy novel writers have a whole new set of characters to invent.

Planting professional spies   Planting professional spies is more reliable than counting on spontaneous defections from the other side. For one thing, professionals know what to look for and how to look after themselves. But it is more difficult to plant such spies in the higher echelons of government where they might be most useful. Periodic embassy expulsions, are in part attempts to sweep out agents who run 'sleepers' or cultivate new agents. Some expulsions are merely undertaken to make a political point. But, apart from Kim Philby who was a planted agent, the most important Cold War defectors have been officials who turned. The Shevchenko case in the 1970s is a case in point. But the defection of Vitaly Yurchenko, reported to be number five in the KGB, in 1985 and his return to Moscow several months later suggests the risks of dealing with these turn-coats.

Shady business   It is not surprising that such treachery is often seen as a dirty business, even though when 'our side' gains, the motives are invariably described as highly principled. Certainly the dirty tricks departments of the American CIA and the French DGSE (in sinking the Greenpeace ship, *Rainbow Warrior*, in 1985) feed the worst assumptions about this 'dishonourable' profession. Top spies or their masters can rarely escape such opprobrium. It is true that Yury Andropov moved from controlling the KGB to controlling the

Soviet Union as a whole, but he had to wipe his shoes for a few months in a civilian post before he could take the top job. As John Le Carré expresses so vividly, the shady business of spying also shades very smoothly into highest foreign policy.

States will always be hyper-sensitive about security and some – like the British government of Mrs Thatcher – will not know when to give up trying to protect the unprotectable. The memoirs of Peter Wright were published in 1987 almost everywhere but in Britain, and the vain attempts to stem the tide brought ridicule on the British government. All in the name of security.

The need for, and fascination with, spies will continue as long as there is political conflict. But the methods of intelligence gathering have clearly moved away from humint and towards sigint and elint. As new technologies revolutionise information-gathering, this trend is likely to continue; a pity, because somehow it is difficult to see a publisher taking an interest in the treacherous tendencies of a computer or satellite.

Reading

J. Barron, *KGB Today* (London: Hodder & Stoughton, 1984).
C. Dobson and R. Payne, *The Dictionary of Espionage* (London: Harrap, 1984).
C. Pincher, *Their Trade is Treachery* (London: Sidgwick & Jackson, 1981.
T. Powers, *The Man Who Kept Secrets* (London: Weidenfeld & Nicolson, 1980).
P. Wright, *Spycatcher* (New York: Viking, 1987).

4

THE NEW EUROPE

Securing Democracy

In the last six months of 1989, the six allies of the Soviet Union in Eastern Europe found their independence. But in the subsequent six months the euphoria turned to anxiety as democratic elections were held – but with democratic values and capitalist prosperity hard to find. Western Europe may have won the Cold War, but is Eastern Europe losing the peace?

Paths to revolution   The paths to freedom for all the East Europeans began in Moscow. Just as these six states – Poland, East Germany, Czechoslovakia, Hungary, Romania and Bulgaria – all found their 'Communist revolutions' in the baggage train of Russian military power at the end of the Second World War, so they could not mount their real revolutions without a change of direction in Moscow. It was the decision by Mikhail Gorbachev, some time after he came to power in 1985, that he could not modernize his own country while grappling with unruly 'allies' to his west that opened the way to the revolutionary events of 1989.

But of course it only dawned on Gorbachev that you cannot herd people into paradise and post sentries at the gate (in the phraseology of the former Soviet leader, Nikita Khrushchev), because the East Europeans themselves had indicated that they were not happy with Russian rule. But they all had coped with the Soviet empire in different ways, in keeping with their differing pre-Communist political traditions. All were members of the military Warsaw Treaty Organization and the economic Council for Mutual Economic Assistance, but after forty years of socialist paradise, all had found their own mix of reform, local culture and national interest. Not surprisingly, when Russian power retreated in 1989, the old patterns distorted by recent revolutions emerged.

Poland   Poland is easily the largest of the six with a population larger than that of the GDR, Hungary and Czechoslovakia combined. This 'country on wheels', as Churchill described it, has been invaded so often by its German and Russian neighbours that its sense of nationhood is as fierce as its politics is unstable. Poland was the first to have freeish elections in Eastern Europe (June 1989), the first to show that Communists were unpopular and that Gorbachev was happy for this reality to be demonstrated at the polls.

As a vital member of the Warsaw Pact, Poland's defection had been delayed in the Brezhnev years. Martial Law was imposed in 1981 after an independent trade union, Solidarity, had brought the Communist government to its knees. Party and military leader,

General Wojeich Jaruzelski, had managed the democratic transition in 1989 from his post as President. He also sanctioned a 'big bang' approach to economic reform, counting on a Solidarity-led government's ability to win support for a rapid transition to a market economy. Solidarity's leader, Lech Walesa, won the first fully free Polish Presidential election in December 1990, but the massive economic reconstruction had still barely begun.

Whether ruled by Communists or not, Poland needs to be friendly with Russia because they both fear a resurgent Germany. But Poland has never known sustained democracy or rapid economic development, and without both, its revolution remains in doubt. It is true that there is no other direction to go but up and Poland has received massive Western aid, and yet the same has been said of the revolving military juntas of Latin America.

As its name implies, this slice off the Hapsburg empire was a *Czechoslovakia* manufactured country. The predominantly Protestant Czechs and the mainly Catholic Slovaks were merged after the First World War. The unhappy union was coveted and then conquered by Hitler's Germany, only to be cowed into a Communist coup in 1948 by Stalin. Yet Czechoslovakia is perhaps the most liberal and sophisticated of the East European states, with the closest thing to a democratic tradition and a basis for economic prosperity. With merely 15 million people, it likes to see itself as the Netherlands of Eastern Europe.

Its 'velvet revolution' was bloodless and even cultured. The selection of the dissident playwright, Vaclav Havel, as President was poetic justice for the savagery of the 1968 invasion of Czechoslovakia by a Soviet-led force. Havel quickly obtained Soviet agreement to withdraw its troops and he is most likely to lead his country into closer relations with, and eventually membership of, the EC. Unlike the Poles, the Czechoslovaks seem positively to relish Germany taking the country under its wing as the fastest means to wealth and stability.

Hungary never quite won its independence from the Hapsburg *Hungary* empire until 1918, and then quickly ended up under German influence. But Stalin eventually beat the openly independent instinct underground. In 1956, in the most brutal of the Russian invasions of its Warsaw Pact allies, an independence movement was crushed. Hungary under Janos Kadar was then allowed to tinker with reform rule by a Communist party. But despite a much freer lifestyle than anywhere else in the Soviet bloc, Hungary never quite found a way to mix Marx and the market.

Even before the Poles muddled their way to elections in June 1989, the Hungarians had set up the mechanism for the end of Communist rule. But it was not until elections in March and April 1990 that a Centre-Right government was safely elected. While democracy seemed reasonably well on course in a version of classic West European coalition politics, the economists could not quite decide on the best road to economic reform. The country had tinkered so much with various versions of socialism that it could see little coherent alternative to a Polish-type big bang way of forming a market economy. But even if Hungary wobbled economically, it certainly had moved swiftly to obtain Soviet agreement on troop withdrawals by July 1991. Hungary too looked to the EC as a way of perhaps earning a place such as Denmark in the Community, yet it had a long way to go.

Bulgaria and Romania

These southernmost outposts of the Warsaw Pact and CMEA have their own special history and problems (see section on Back to the Balkans). But with their election of successor parties to their old Communist rulers, and economies akin to that in the developing world, there can be little hope of transition to democratic state or market economies. With some 30% of the population of the newly liberated Eastern Europe, these two states are reminders of the difficulties ahead.

What is to be done

Obviously there is no single path to democracy nor to the market economy. Governments will be different, market reforms will find local roads and of course foreigners will treat each country differently. States on the perilous path to democracy have always needed external support and these six are already provoking different responses. Finance and advice is available to those most bold in market reform and most fair in forming new democratic institutions. The EC, with German leadership, looks set to support the revolutions and guide others, such as the United States and Japan, who are eyeing the opportunities.

But with the exception of the GDR, which West Germany swallowed whole, none of the remaining five is likely to present huge and immediate opportunities for foreign investment. Czechoslovakia and Hungary are the most likely to succeed, just as Bulgaria and Romania are the most likely to lapse into pre-war chaos. Perhaps the largest lesson to be unlearned from the era of the Warsaw Pact and CMEA is that these are not all of a piece – they are unique, in both their successes and failures.

Reading

Karen Dawisha, *Eastern Europe, Gorbachev and Reform* (Cambridge: Cambridge University Press, 1990).

'What is to be Done', *The Economist*, 13 January 1990.

J. Rollo, *The New Eastern Europe* (London: Frances Pinter, 1990).

K. Sword (ed), *The Times Guide to Eastern Europe* (London: Times Books, 1990).

Old and New Securities

Just as Europe seems to resolve one threat to its stability, new ones immediately arise. Even before the Second World War was won, Britain and the United States were manoeuvring to contain Russian power. In 1990, just as the East–West Cold War was ending, new worries about old insecurities arose. Europe has rarely been a peaceful place, and it may be that we will soon look back to the Cold War era as one of relative stability precisely because it seemed to suppress so many of the older European conflicts.

Building the alliance   In order to cope with what was perceived as an imminent Russian threat at the end of the Second World War, West Europeans undertook a strange exercise – organizing for war in time of peace.

In 1948, after the Soviet-inspired coup in Czechoslovakia, a treaty of West European Union was signed in Brussels by Britain, France, Belgium, the Netherlands and Luxembourg (Germany and Italy joined in 1955). Yet the West Europeans also understood that they were weaker militarily than the Soviet Union and that without the backing of United States' power they would always be at a military disadvantage. Therefore, on 4 April 1949, the foreign ministers of Belgium, Britain, Canada, Denmark, France, Iceland, Italy, Netherlands, Norway, Portugal and the United States signed the North Atlantic Treaty. Greece and Turkey joined in February 1952, Germany in May 1955 and Spain in May 1982.

Perception of a Soviet threat   The concept behind the alliance was to provide mutual assistance if any member should be attacked. This peacetime military alliance was a peculiar concept but then the state of Cold War was equally unusual. NATO's purpose was seen to be justified by Soviet preponderance in conventional weapons in Europe and by the series of post-war crises, such as the Berlin blockade (1948–9) and the Korean War (1950). In fact, it was only after Korea, and the realization that the division of Europe was permanent, that NATO emerged as a serious organization and western military forces were built up. With the lessening of East–West tension and the emerging confident nationalism of some NATO members, France withdrew from the integrated military command in 1966 and forced the headquarters to move from Fontainebleau to Brussels. Greece pulled out of the military command during 1974–80 because of the Cyprus conflict with its fellow NATO member, Turkey. The alliance held together remarkably well considering that it spans a series of proud states who, not too long ago, were at each others' throats. The essential glue was a shared perception of a Soviet threat to Western values and security.

But NATO was only as strong as the perception of a common interest in deterring a common threat. In 1989, when the East European states were each given their freedom to choose their own governments, they also chose to end their participation in their equivalent of NATO, the Warsaw Treaty Organization (established in 1955 but by 1991 its military role was terminated). As the Soviet Union began withdrawing its troops from Eastern Europe, East Germany joined West Germany, and the Soviet Union seemed so preoccupied with its own internal decay that no sensible NATO leader could claim the threat from the east still existed. So what was to become of NATO?

What happened to the threat?

NATO might, like the Warsaw Pact, just gradually fade away. As there was no NATO before the Second World War, who needs one now? But precisely because there was no organization for collective security in notoriously insecure Europe, the First World War was able to break out over the inconsequential Balkans. In the Second World War Hitler's Germany was able to trample all over the continent. Thus the new question for Europe was what form this organization for collective security should take.

A new NATO

The pessimists argued that without a clear sense of threat, no organization could be sustained in peacetime. What was most likely was a return to a version of great power politics, and in the 1990s this meant the five powers of Russia, Germany, France, Britain and the non-European exception, the United States. The optimists hoped that the arms control process could create a new version of a standing conference on European Security based on the Conference on Security and Cooperation in Europe (CSCE – see Negotiating Security, below). The realists in between clung on to NATO as at least an interim solution to European insecurity while the great powers managed the transition from the Cold War era. When the Russian empire seemed to be collapsing so fast, it seemed prudent to retain some way for the richer Europeans to ensure the resulting instability did not damage their own security.

The short-term agenda was the clearing up of the débris of the Cold War, including the transition to stable democracy in Eastern Europe and the emergence of a peacefully united Germany. NATO's role in these changes was passive but nevertheless important as a symbol of the success of the market economy of democratic states. As an anchor of the Western system, along with the EC, NATO helped ensure that the East Europeans and Germany did not seek unilateral solutions to their security. But in the medium term, and assuming the short-term remained relatively stable, it becomes more difficult to envisage how NATO can cope with the new, potential insecurities.

NATO as an anchor

Frontiers and states

The ending of a war usually results in changes of frontiers, thereby helping to sow the seeds of future conflicts. But the Cold War ended without border changes (apart from the takeover of East Germany by West Germany), and indeed it was crucial to stability in the 1990s that frontiers remain unchanged. Questions about the aspirations of Germany and Balkan states are dealt with in separate sections below, but there are other risks of conflict, some of which are old and some are merely new variants of old tensions. Most of the revived conflicts concern the dangerous process of picking up the pieces from the shattered Russian empire. Just as insecurity in the Balkans in the early 20th century was a cause of the First World War, so the boundaries of units in Europe are bound to change as the Russian empire shrivels.

Bother in the Baltic

Take the three Baltic republics of the Soviet Union (Lithuania, 3.6 million people of whom 9% are Russian, Latvia, 2.6 million people of whom 33% are Russian, and Estonia, 1.5 million people of whom 28% are Russian) for example, all of which were occupied by Russia as a result of the Nazi–Soviet Pact of 1939. None of these units has a history of sustained independence (or democracy), and all have large proportions of Russians in their present population. In the past this region has been the focus of rival Russian, German, Scandinavian and Polish empires, and the most recent period of Russian occupation resulted in millions of Russians settling in the area. With a combined population of barely 8 million, they might make an additional member of the Nordic states, but then the differences among these states would be no less great than they already are with Russia. With minority populations of Germans, Poles and Russians around the region, there is no perfect logic to any patchwork of frontiers. Formal independence for the Baltic republics might solve some problems, but it would create others.

Out of area operations

The Baltic question, as well as that concerning Germany and the Balkans, are the three major sets of insecurities in the near future. It is inconceivable that military force might be used by NATO in any of those conflicts, although a political organization committed to helping mend fences might have a limited role. But military force has been used by NATO, although not under NATO auspices, members in so-called 'out of area operations' in defence of what was said to be the interest of all NATO members. Can such operations continue, and can they even provide a rationale for NATO's military arm?

In NATO's 'good old days' before 1989, disputes about out of area operations were some of the most divisive. Britain and France failed to get American support in the 1956 Suez crisis and the United States failed to obtain allied support for the war in Vietnam in the 1960s. Britain did get some support for its Falklands War in 1982 and most countries who could, sent naval forces to protect

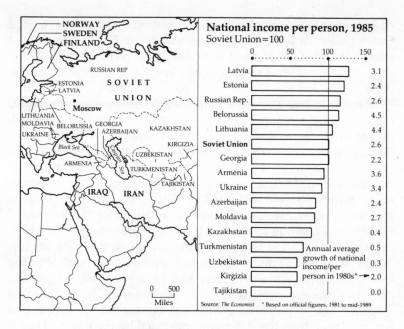

National income per person, 1985 Soviet Union=100	Annual average growth of national income/per person in 1980s*
Latvia	3.1
Estonia	2.4
Russian Rep.	2.6
Belorussia	4.5
Lithuania	4.4
Soviet Union	2.6
Georgia	2.2
Armenia	3.6
Ukraine	3.4
Azerbaijan	2.4
Moldavia	2.7
Kazakhstan	0.4
Turkmenistan	0.5
Uzbekistan	0.3
Kirgizia	2.0
Tajikistan	0.0

Source: *The Economist* * Based on official figures, 1981 to mid-1989

Population, 1987 (m)	
Soviet Union	281.7
Russian Republic	145.3
Ukraine	51.2
Uzbekistan	19.0
Kazakhstan	16.2
Belorussia	10.1
Azerbaijan	6.8
Georgia	5.3
Tajikistan	4.8
Moldavia	4.2
Kirgizia	4.1
Lithuania	3.6
Armenia	3.4
Turkmenistan	3.4
Latvia	2.6
Estonia	1.5

Source: National statistics

shipping in the last days of the Iran–Iraq War in the late 1980s. But many of these operations were justified in terms of sending a clear message of deterrence to the Soviet Union and none were officially undertaken by NATO.

The first test of NATO in the post-Cold War world came when Iraq invaded Kuwait in August 1990 and the United States asked its NATO allies to help defend Saudi Arabia and then expel Iraq. Unlike most of the United States' other 'allies', most NATO members sent forces to the Gulf, with Britain, followed by France, sending major contingents. NATO began breaking its official taboo

Responding to Iraqi aggression

against discussion of out-of-area operations and as the United States pulled its forces out of a demilitarizing Europe, they went straight to the Gulf to meet the new threat. When the Gulf War ended in early 1991, it soon became clear that not all the US troops deployed by Europe would return to their old roles.

Military cooperation   Assuming that at least a minimal role for NATO is envisaged, then the organization returns to its old, and still unresolved, debates over common equipment and strategy. There are also disagreements over who should command the troops and how much every member should pay. Many of the older debates about trusting the Americans will vanish as the United States is seen to be in Europe, albeit with smaller forces, for its own reasons, and not because American troops are required for the defence of Europeans unwilling to bear the burden of protecting themselves. However, the United States will continue to be the main nuclear power in NATO, if only as a way to keep Germany from wanting its own arsenal. Although there will be less questioning of the American nuclear guarantee for Europe, there will still be some who will see a potential Soviet nuclear threat to Europe that requires more than the deterrence provided by the limited French and British nuclear forces. It seems inevitable that NATO will reduce the numbers of battlefield nuclear weapons in Europe as it becomes harder to envisage any scenario for battle. But the need for theatre-range forces seems likely to remain, if only for minimum deterrence. Debates over the modernization and ownership of these weapons seem inevitable also.

NATO's future   As the EC looks set to expand, and the potential insecurities in Europe also look set to change, a decent case can be made for some organization committed to collective security. As NATO already exists, it makes some sense to transform it into a new organization for the new Europe. But if NATO should fail to change with the times, then it may soon become as much a part of the problem as a part of any solution to the new European insecurities.

Reading

B. Buzan *et al*, *The European Security Order Recast* (London: Pinter, 1990).

R.E. Hunter, 'The Future of European Security', *Washington Quarterly*, Fall 1990.

J. Sharp (ed), *Europe After an American Withdrawal* (Oxford: Oxford University Press, 1990).

G. Treverton, *Making the Alliance Work* (New York: Cornell University Press, 1985).

W. Wallace, *The Transformation of Western Europe* (London: Frances Pinter, 1990).

European Communities

Europeans have fought one another for so long that it both causes surprise and requires considerable patience when some Europeans decide to cooperate. In the first phase, West European democracies came together to build a better atmosphere for successful market economies. By the mid-1980s they had broadened their membership and committed themselves to a Single European Market by 1992. But before the exercise could be completed, the rival community of socialist states in Eastern Europe collapsed, leaving open the prospect of a wider European Community based on market economies and democratic political systems.

The shattering effects of the Second World War replaced a complex European balance of power with a Superpower division of Europe between East and West. West Europeans appreciated the need to recover swiftly from the war, and to combine forces against a very changed outside world. The first significant step in this direction came in May 1950, when the French Foreign Minister, Robert Schuman, formulated a plan to place French and German steel production under the control of an independent supranational authority. Belgium, Italy, Luxembourg and the Netherlands joined the plan and a treaty was signed in April 1951 in Paris establishing the European Coal and Steel Community (ECSC). *Recovering from the war*

Plans for broader political and economical cooperation soon ran up against a legacy of Europe's past – nationalism. The concept of a European Defence Community proved unworkable and the West Europeans settled for an alliance with the United States in NATO. But the idea of somewhat narrower cooperation did prove viable. The motive was not only economic reconstruction but also the need to transform the Federal Republic of Germany into a 'normal' state. The six countries in the ECSC agreed in 1955 to establish a European Economic Community and a European Atomic Energy Community. Treaties were signed in Rome in March 1957 and entered into effect in January 1958. The initial idea of the European Community (EC) was to establish a customs union and to coordinate economic policy. *The EC idea*

Early optimism about the EC soon faded and there were squabbles, particularly over competing farm products. But the EC could not have been all bad, because other states were still interested in taking part. Britain tried to join in 1961 and again in 1963 but was rebuffed by De Gaulle, who was suspicious of Britain's special *Expanding the Community* relationship with the United States. In January 1972 Britain, Denmark, Ireland and Norway were accepted into the EC as from January 1973, but a referendum in Norway rejected Community membership. Greece joined in January 1981 and Spain and Portugal in 1986.

The organization   The day-to-day operation of the EC is usually boring. But its organization does highlight the serious political problems that make real integration so difficult to achieve. The EC is led by a Commission of fourteen members, chosen for four years and headed by a President and Vice-President who serve two-year terms. But the real power, and the body which chooses the Commission, is the Council of Ministers. Each state's representatives speak for their national interests and the sum is supposed to be the EC interest. They vote in three ways: simple majority votes for minor issues, a qualified majority for semi-important subjects, with an unanimity rule on major issues. According to the Luxembourg Principle (1966), 'very important interests of one or more partner' have to be agreed by consensus, which has effectively given each member a veto. There is also a European Parliament, used so far mainly for consultation and advice on the budget. It is a vivid symbol of the slow but steady development of the European ideal.

Parliament   The Parliament can dismiss the Commission by a two-thirds majority and can reject the administrative budget by a similar vote, as it did in 1979. That year also saw the first direct elections to Parliament, giving it an increased sense of purpose albeit no additional power. In reality, power still lies with the Council and it alone can decide to grant the Parliament more power.

Guide to the best Europeans

	Implementation of 1992 measures	State aid to industry	Court rulings not implemented	Govt enthusiasm for:		Public response to: 'Is EC membership a good thing?'	Total (maximum 60 points)	Rank
				political reform	EMU			
France	7	5	7	6	9	5	39	1
Holland	6	8	7	5	4	8	38	2
Denmark	9	8	9	4	5	1	36	=3
Ireland	7	2	9	4	8	6	36	=3
Spain	4	4	9	6	8	5	36	=3
W. Germany	8	5	4	9	4	5	35	6
Belgium	3	3	4	9	9	6	34	=7
Luxembourg	5	2	9	4	7	7	34	=7
Britain	9	8	9	2	1	2	31	=9
Greece	3	5	3	8	5	7	31	=9
Italy	1	1	1	9	9	7	28	=11
Portugal	2	4	9	3	5	5	28	=11

Ranking based on figures from EC Commission, Eurobarometer public-opinion survey, and *The Economist* estimates of government attitudes

Formal state sovereignty remains paramount, although the real workings of the international market economy mean that corporations increasingly operate internationally, thereby becoming far more effective in undermining the decisions of governments.

As the real integration of market economies quietly set a new agenda, the EC eventually moved to build the common market that its name implied. A customs union has been in force since 1968, although some non-tariff barriers (such as health and technical standards) stand in the way. There is also, in theory, free movement of workers, although delays in harmonizing company law have impeded the process. A Common Agricultural Policy (CAP) was developed to ensure a fair standard for farmers by stabilizing markets, but it only resulted in huge over-production, creating wine lakes, butter mountains and higher prices. Reforms in February 1988 cut the subsidies, and in 1987 the EC set itself the far more ambitious task of formulating a real Single European Market (SEM) by 1992.

Wine lakes and butter mountains

The adoption of several measures for a SEM was intended to clear Europe of inequalities that hinder a genuine free market. Thus national governments agreed to enact laws that would allow capital, goods and people to move freely. With guidance from the European Court and the Council of Ministers, individual members are being dragged into the more competitive world of the largest market economy. Most of the regulations are designed to remove bureaucrats from the market place, although inevitably some governments are keen to regulate such complex matters as social policy.

Making a Single European Market

That other great capitalist market economy, the United States, has a Federal Bank and a common currency. The EC is moving increasingly quickly to that end. A European Monetary System was established in 1979 in order to keep currency fluctuation within certain boundaries and linked to a 'basket' of EC currencies called the ECU. This so-called currency snake, or Exchange Rate Mechanism, has had some success in ironing out short-term currency fluctuations and when the last major hold-out, Britain, joined the ERM in October 1990, the EC looked for ways to speed the pace towards a full EMU. The twelve EC members are also now creating a central bank (Eurofed), as the existing committee of central bank governors begin to recommend monetary policy, supervise banking and all with a growing permanent staff. Macroeconomic policy will be increasingly coordinated through more meetings of EC finance ministers. As the pace of change increased in 1990, rapid German reunification and the nearly-as-rapid collapse of the East European economies also spurred the EC to move even faster towards European Political Union. It certainly would

European Monetary Union (EMU)

have seemed strange if there were genuine monetary union without greater coordination of politics.

Fortress Europe   Not all Europeans, and most notably the British, have taken to the idea of losing sovereignty to the EC. Some members prefer to treat the EC as an *à la carte* menu, choosing the bits they prefer. But as the reality of the interdependent market economy becomes more clear, the integrative instincts of other EC members is strengthened. The outside world (especially the East Europeans) takes the EC more seriously, the more the EC itself speeds the pace of union. It was the Americans who first coined the phrase 'fortress Europe' to describe their fears of the EC's future, but as the SEM took shape, it has become increasingly clear that the United States is welcome as a more equal partner. As Washington has taken Brussels more seriously, so American fears have eased, and regular contacts have been formalized at the highest level. Japan soon took up the paranoia about a fortress Europe, but in the end it too has responded more constructively by increasing its own investment inside the EC in order to take advantage of the largest market economy.

EFTA and a   But the EC's largest trade partners are the six countries of
European   the European Free Trade Association (Austria, Finland, Iceland,
Economic Space   Norway, Sweden and Switzerland). In order to ease their worries about Project 1992, EFTA and the EC agreed in 1989 on the general outlines of a European Economic Area that would trade EFTA acceptance of basic freedoms (goods, services, capital, people) for access to the EC market and some influence in shaping EC policy. As the revolutions of 1989 in Eastern Europe looked like eventually leading to a change of membership in both EFTA and the EC, both sides saw increasing reason for cooperation as a way of managing the transition to markets and democracy in Europe. The more ambitious EFTA members, like Austria, seek full EC membership, and in the end EFTA may merely end up as a half-way house before joining the real European Community.

A Dying   The outside institution once considered the most important by
CMEA   the EC – the Council for Mutual Economic Assistance in Eastern Europe – is withering away. As the East Europeans marketize their economies, they hope to trade more with the EC than with the Soviet Union. But such a transition to real currencies, real prices and real goods and services can neither be swift nor simple. The EC has led in the creation of a European Bank for Reconstruction and Development in order to help speed the process. But whether it is through the strategy of the 'big bang' as now pursued in Poland, or more gentle changes as in Hungary, the reforms will mean the end of the CMEA as a manager of trade. As the EC gets deeper into its SEM, it will also eventually grow wider to encompass at least the most democratic and successful market

economies of the old CMEA. But if the EC's deepening means that it ignores the opportunities of widening, the resulting instability in Eastern Europe might threaten the future of the EC itself.

Reading

'Europe's Internal Market', *The Economist*, 8 July 1989 and 'An Expanding Universe', 7 July 1990.

G.C. Hufbauer (ed), *Europe 1992: An American Perspective* (Washington: Brookings, 1990).

P. Ludlow (ed), *The Annual Review of European Community Affairs, 1990* (London: Centre for European Policy Studies, 1991).

J. Rollo, *The New Eastern Europe* (London: Frances Pinter, 1990).

G. Smith, *Politics in Western Europe* (London: Heinemann, 1986).

W. Wallace, *The Transformation of Western Europe* (London: Frances Pinter, 1990).

W. Wallace (ed), *The Dynamics of European Integration* (London: Frances Pinter, 1990).

Negotiating Security

When wars end, a peace treaty is usually formulated. But the Cold War has always been peculiar, because although there were negotiations and treaties while the 'war was waged', it seems unlikely that any arms control in Europe can keep up with the fast pace of political change. The most important of the Cold War negotiations in Europe was the Conference on Security and Cooperation in Europe (CSCE) in Helsinki. All European states (except obscurantist Albania) attended, as did the United States and Canada. The conference concluded on 1 August 1975 with a Final Act, a peculiar piece of paper which was not a treaty but more like a fancy declaration. Thanks to the nimble minds of the Swiss, the conference had decided to divide the contentious issues into separate 'baskets'.

The first two baskets

Basket one dealt with matters of security. Thirty years after the Second World War, the Final Act reaffirmed the inviolability of European frontiers. Basket one also included measures to build confidence on both sides of Europe's divide despite the Cold War. These relatively unusual steps included prior notification of at least twenty-one days of military manoeuvres involving over 25,000 men and the exchange of observers for some manoeuvres.

The second basket dealt with measures to improve business contacts. While the Soviet bloc badly wanted these measures and the loans that came with them, the Western states were concerned that this was merely an attempt to avoid dealing with the EC and was designed to divide Western states by exploiting their competing economic interests.

Human rights in a basket

By far the most controversial basket, number three, included a restatement of basic human rights. But as a consequence, Helsinki monitoring groups sprung up in various East European states to report on violations of human rights. Charter 77 in Czechoslovakia was perhaps the most prominent such group.

Conflicting aspirations

The Soviet Union and its allies had seen the Helsinki conference as a way of enshrining their control over East Europe and obtaining recognition of parity in the era of East–West détente. Western governments were pleased with the confidence-building measures, resigned to the division of Europe and eventually pleasantly surprised to see an anodyne international declaration on human rights cause the Soviet bloc so much embarrassment. The Helsinki process continued with several 'follow-up' conferences but none was to be as successful as the first.

The Belgrade review conference, from October 1977 to March 1978, took place during the souring atmosphere when détente degenerated into polemics. Nothing of substance was achieved, except Western satisfaction at having kept the human rights spotlight on the Soviet bloc. The Madrid review conference (November 1980 to September 1983) took place after the Soviet invasion of Afghanistan and in the frigid atmosphere of the new Reagan administration and uncertainty over the Soviet leadership.

Review at Belgrade

The conference did produce a vacuous twenty-six-page document (compared with a two-page statement after Belgrade) mostly reaffirming the Helsinki principles. The West made no progress in its main objective of getting better protection for Helsinki monitoring groups. The meeting did take the 'daring' steps of condemning terrorism and reaffirming the rights of women. As it happened, Soviet officials were invited to most of the NATO manoeuvres but Moscow only allowed NATO to sit in on half the Soviet exercises. Agreement was also reached on the importance of economic cooperation but differences on trade sanctions after the Polish crisis made a mockery of most of the pious words.

Agreement at Madrid

Despite the foul East–West weather during the Madrid review, at least the conference did not collapse. In fact, for a time in the new chillier climate it was one of the few forums where the Superpowers were still prepared to shake hands and talk directly. In general, it was an exercise in outsitting the Soviet Union. But in the end there was a limit to Western pleasure in seeing the Soviet Union squirm and it was decided that the sterile slanging matches were not really in anyone's interest.

Outsitting the enemy

A separate conference on disarmament in Europe was set up to discuss the extension of zones of notification for troop manoeuvres and other confidence-building measures. It opened on 17 January 1984 in Stockholm and an agreement was concluded on 22 September 1986. In the only major East–West accord of the Reagan presidency it was agreed to stiffen the limp-wristed Helsinki provisions. Signators agreed to provide an annual calendar of planned military activity and even exercises with as few as 13,000 men have to be notified at least 42 days in advance. At Helsinki it was agreed that the zone covered by the agreement would extend only 155 miles from the frontier, now it was to stretch from the Atlantic to the Urals. What is more, observers must be invited to troop movements involving more than 17,000 soldiers and the Soviet Union accepted the principal of 'challenge inspections' as a means of verification. This sensible agreement, although long awaited, was the most far-reaching pact on confidence-building in the Cold War.

Success in Stockholm

On-site inspections of military activities conducted in 1989, as permitted by the Stockholm Document

Date	Inspecting state	Host state	Exercise name/area
4–14 Apr.	FRG	GDR	'Zyklus 89'
16–18 Apr.	Italy	USSR	Moscow Military District
28–30 May	USSR	Italy	'Dragon Hammer 89'
19–21 May	USA	GDR	. .
14–16 June	Canada	CSSR	Cheb–Jáchimov–Marianké Lázne
21–23 June	USSR	Denmark	'Avenue Express' 'Bikini 89'
11–13 Aug.	USA	USSR	Dubravka–Vishtitis–Vieshvile
19–21 Aug.	France	USSR	Dubrovo–Shatsk–Berezino–Ulla
13–15 Aug.	Italy	Bulgaria	'Mariza 89'
8–10 Sep.	GDR	FRG	'Caravan Guard 89'
4–6 Sep.	UK	GDR	Gardelegen–Magdeburg–Brandenburg
11–13 Sep.	USSR	FRG	'Offenes Visier'
17–19 Sep.	GDR	Belgium	'Plain Sailing 89'
23–25 Sep.	USSR	France	'Extel 1 Champagne 89'
30 Sep.-2 Oct.	FRG	CSSR	Cheb–Jáchymov–Marianské Lázné
18–20 Oct.	USSR	Turkey	'Mehmetcik 89'

Note: The first inspection in 1990 was made on 6–8 Jan. by the USSR in Belgium ('Reforger').

Annual number of military exercises notified in the annual calendars by NATO, WTO and NNA countries

Bloc	1987	1988	1989	1990	Total
NATO	17	13	11	10	51
WTO	25	22	17	7	71
NNA	5	3	3	4	15

Source: Compiled from *SIPRI Yearbooks 1987/8/9—1987*: appendix 10B; 1988: appendix 11A; 1989: appendix 11A, and the forecast of notifiable military activities for 1990.

Pointless MBFR talks

But if the CSCE process seemed protracted, it was strikingly efficient compared to the Mutual and Balanced Force Reduction (MBFR) talks begun in October 1973 and wrapped up without agreement before the revolutions in Eastern Europe in 1989. The aim of the MBFR talks was to agree real cuts instead of mere confidence-building measures. But in the end the negotiators were overtaken by events. The successor negotiations, under the auspices of the CSCE, were divided into two sections. The thirty-five nations of CSCE agreed to discuss confidence- and security-building measures, while agreeing on a second, smaller meeting on Conventional Forces in Europe (CFE) which began on 6 March 1989 and involved sixteen NATO states and seven Warsaw Pact states. But soon the negotiators found themselves scanning the front pages of their daily newspapers to find out the latest unilateral move of a democratizing East European state to reduce troop levels. The negotiators could also not keep up as Western governments also announced unilateral cuts of their own. Disarmament was no longer negotiated, at least not until the rapid political changes slowed down.

By the time of the 19–21 November 1990 CSCE meeting in Paris, the thirty-four heads of government (East Germany had been merged with the West) met for a grand celebration of the CFE agreement wherein massive cuts in all manner of conventional weapons were agreed (see chart). Both NATO and the Warsaw Pact were allowed to decide for themselves which states should have which weapons in which of the four zones in the treaty area. However the treaty contained a 'sufficiency rule' that prohibited any one country from fielding more than about two-thirds of its alliance allowance of any particular sort of equipment. The best bit of the treaty, apart from the reduction in numbers of weapons, was the scheme for close supervision and verification of the cuts. But parties were allowed to move as much equipment as they wished out of the region before the treaty was signed, and the Russians took the opportunity to move much equipment east of the Ural mountains to save it from having to be destroyed. Some American and British equipment, although counted in CFE totals, was moved out to the Gulf War zone. But in 1991, when more conservative voices asserted themselves in Moscow politics, it proved difficult to sort out last minute problems prior to ratification of the accord.

A CSCE and CFE Deal

The CSCE nations also agreed to set up a small secretariat in Prague, a Conflict Prevention Centre in Vienna and an office in Warsaw to gather information on elections. The secretariat will prepare yearly meetings of a ministerial council and there will also be a vaguely defined parliamentary wing called the Assembly of Europe. This modest bureaucracy-building falls far short of a serious collective security scheme for Europe but it does continue the valuable tradition of the CSCE in building confidence. The Crisis Prevention Centre will provide a 'military weather map' of troop deployments and the optimists hope that a mechanism for peacefully settling disputes will gradually emerge. The history of Europe suggests otherwise.

It is hard to see where the CSCE and CFE process can go from here. Europeans might want to extend CSCE-type confidence-building measures, although as the new concerns about insecurity focus on domestic unrest in the Soviet Union and Eastern Europe, or even wars further afield in the Gulf, it is hard to see such measures being of much use. Some have suggested that the CSCE process might take the place of NATO and the Warsaw Pact as a permanent organization of collective security, but there is little evidence that the CSCE nations are anywhere near a sufficiently common view of the nature of, and responses to, unrest in Eastern Europe to be able to create a meaningful organization. When the Soviet Union

Taking Arms Control Further?

WEAPONS	ALLIANCE/ COUNTRY	1988 LEVEL	MID-1990 LEVEL	TREATY LIMIT*
Tanks	NATO	22,000	22,000	20,000
	Warsaw Pact	60,000	41,000	20,000
	U.S. Forces	5,700	5,700	13,300
	Soviet Forces	46,000	25,000	13,300
Armored vehicles	NATO	27,000	27,000	30,000
	Warsaw Pact	63,000	52,000	30,000
	U.S. Forces	5,500	5,500	20,000
	Soviet Forces	45,000	32,000	20,000
Artillery pieces	NATO	21,000	21,000	20,000
	Warsaw Pact	61,000	49,000	20,000
	U.S. Forces	2,650	2,650	13,700
	Soviet Forces	47,000	33,000	13,700
Helicopters	NATO	2,000	No	2,000
	Warsaw Pact	3,000	specific	2,000
	U.S. Forces	700	figures	1,500
	Soviet Forces	2,800	available	1,500
Combat aircraft	NATO	6,300	No	6,800
	Warsaw Pact	14,000	specific	6,800
	U.S. Forces	800	figures	5,150
	Soviet Forces	11,000	available	5,150

*No single country can have more than about two-thirds of the alliance's total in most categories. Alliances have worked out distribution agreements among member countries. Treaty limit figures are maximums allowed by 1994; the actual figures could be lower.

Source: U.S. Delegation to negotiations on the Conventional Armed Forces in Europe Treaty

now calls for a Common European Home, it is best understood as a plea for the Europeanization of Russia rather than a genuine belief that all Europeans can agree on the future of their security. When the Europhoria of 1989–90 wears off, it will be seen that the negotiating record of CSCE, not to mention European history, certainly suggests that Europeans are far too fractious for permanent security from the Atlantic to the Urals.

Reading

B. Buzan *et al*, *The European Security Order Recast* (London: Pinter, 1990).

K. Dyson (ed), *European Détente* (London: Frances Pinter, 1986).

J. Sharp (ed), *Europe After an American Withdrawal* (Oxford: Oxford University Press, 1990).

J. Sizoo and R. Jurjens, *CSCE Decision-Making* (The Hague: Nijhoff, 1984).

J. Wyllie, *European Security in the Nuclear Age* (Oxford: Basil Blackwell, 1986).

A New German Problem?

It was an eminent Frenchman who said, 'I love Germany so much that I rejoice there are two of them'. The division of a country as proud and as powerful as pre-war Germany would have been a political obscenity were it not for the carnage caused between 1939 and 1945 by that very power and pride. Understandably, Germany's neighbours have had good reason to keep the country divided. But it was equally understandable that most Germans were not satisfied with a divided country, and because they were also the front line of the Cold War, they never completely lost the desire for German unity. When Russia finally let East Germans choose where they wished to live in 1989, the rush to reunification also redrew the map of Europe.

Dividing the Germans

At the Yalta Conference, in February 1945, Britain, the United States and the Soviet Union agreed to divide the control of the soon-to-be-defeated Germany and its capital Berlin into four zones for administrative purposes. France was given control of parts of the Anglo-American sectors, while the Soviet Union retained control of one-third of the country. Germany was to be ruled by an Allied Control Council, established by the Potsdam Conference in July–August 1945. Berlin, the German capital, was also placed under four-power control. Unfortunately, in a remarkable oversight, no formal provision was made for the three Western powers to gain access to their parts of Berlin marooned in the middle of the Soviet sector of Germany.

The Berlin blockade

The wartime alliance soon broke down along its natural East–West divide once the unifying cause of opposition to Nazi Germany had given way to practical disputes over reparations and the different political goals of what were, in essence, two opposing ideological systems. The Soviet Union began to hand power to German Communists in its zone, while Western powers began to support the creation of political parties in their areas. The failure to maintain a unified administration led the Western powers to foster democratic government in their sectors in 1948, and the Soviets walked out of the Allied Control Council in March. On 18 June the West introduced a currency reform which was followed by a Soviet blockade of the Western sectors of Berlin. The West began an airlift to transport supplies to West Berlin on 28 June and by November the two parts of the city were effectively divided into separate administrative zones. The blockade of Berlin was lifted on 12 May 1949, after the West had proved its resolve to maintain supplies to its sectors of Berlin.

On 8 May 1949 the Basic Law of the Federal Republic of Germany (West Germany) was approved by a parliamentary council. Although the ultimate goal of West Germany was a unified Germany, in the short term it settled for a separate entity. It also wanted its Basic Law to include Berlin but this the Western allies refused. The Federal Republic came into existence on 21 September 1949 but allied occupation zones only formally ended on 5 May 1955 when the sovereignty of the Federal Republic was established. However, all four powers retained ambiguous rights in Germany until such time as a formal peace treaty was signed.

Formalizing the split

The Eastern zone, the German Democratic Republic (GDR) was established on 7 October 1949 and it was immediately declared by the Western allies and West Germany to be 'without legal basis'. Henceforth, West Germany was to claim the right to speak for all Germany, East and West. In October 1954 West Germany joined NATO but the three Western powers remained in control of West Berlin. The GDR joined the Warsaw Pact on 13 May 1955.

In September 1955, the West German Chancellor, Konrad Adenauer, visited Moscow to establish diplomatic relations. The Soviet Union viewed the Federal Republic as 'part of Germany' according to the frontiers agreed at Potsdam in 1945. But West Germany insisted that the demarcation of borders still awaited a peace treaty.

Signs of détente

The existence of a democratic West Germany encouraged a flood of refugees from East to West (one-and-a-half million between 1950 and 1955) and implicitly threatened the stability of the GDR régime. In November 1958 the Soviet Union threatened to hand East Berlin over to the GDR and force the Western allies to negotiate with East Germany over access to West Berlin. But the Western allies held firmly to the concept of four-power administration. Both sides called up reservists in 1961, as the flood of refugees from the East became a torrent. By June 1961 over 2.6 million refugees had left the GDR since 1949, 300,000 of them since January 1960. The GDR's decision in 1960 to collectivize the remaining independent farms no doubt helped swell the exodus.

Refugees and crisis

The Soviet Union and East Germany clearly felt they had to stem the haemorrhage of their people, power and prestige. On 13 August 1961 the Soviet Union decided to close the East–West border in Berlin except for specified crossing points. On 17 August they erected the Berlin Wall, eventually to extend for 103 miles with an associated 'death strip', to keep people from escaping from East to West. Eleven thousand Western troops confronted the vastly superior Soviet conventional forces.

The Wall and the death strip

The two sides, armed with tanks, stood turret-to-turret in

Turret to turret

Berlin in one of the most dangerous post-war Superpower crises. But in October the Soviet Union withdrew its ultimatum on changing Berlin's status, recognizing once again that the West was prepared to defend its interests and hold the East–West line firmly in place. The Superpowers had stepped back from the brink of open conflict. It was, however, true that the West was unwilling to stop the Soviet Union and East Germany from cementing the division of the country and the capital. Although war had been avoided, the result was still a human disaster for those trapped in the East.

The divisions sink in Thus, defending the East–West line also meant defending a divided Germany – an ambiguity West Germany, with its constitutional commitment to reunification, always had difficulty in accepting. But with the rapid economic development in West Germany (and to a lesser extent in East Germany too) the effective division between the two Germanies became real enough. West Germany emerged as a pillar of the EC and orientated its economy westward.

Ostpolitik In 1969 the new West German Chancellor, Willy Brandt, had the remarkable political vision to recognize that it was in the interest of greater German unity to 'recognize realities in order to change them' and to establish closer relations with the East. That meant first and foremost with the Soviet Union. This policy of *Ostpolitik* (Eastern policy) began in earnest in October 1969 with the ultimate aim of increasing cooperation with the GDR and preventing the two Germanies moving farther apart. But for the Soviet Union and the GDR, the price for closer relations with West Germany was to be recognition of post-war boundaries, including the division of Europe that ran through Germany. On 12 August 1970 West Germany and the Soviet Union signed a treaty accepting the post-war frontiers as inviolable (though not immutable) including the Polish–German frontier along the Oder–Neisse rivers. The West German treaty with Poland, also in 1970, included a German statement that the unification of the two Germanies was not precluded.

Debates in Bonn When forced to confront the realities of a divided Europe and Germany, not surprisingly the West Germans paused for a vigorous and emotional debate of the issues. The two treaties were not approved by Parliament until the summer of 1972 (the Basic Treaty between the two German states was approved the following year) when the government clarified its continued desire for a unified Germany. In September 1973 the two Germanies joined the United Nations and in December West Germany signed a treaty with Czechoslovakia, thereby concluding this first formal round of *Ostpolitik*. The inviolability of frontiers was reaffirmed by the Helsinki Conference on Security and Cooperation in Europe in August

1975. But the Helsinki agreement also allowed 125,000 ethnic Germans to leave Poland for West Germany in the following four years. Up to that time some 471,000 ethnic Germans had already made the trek.

Relations between the two Germanies mirrored the general trend of East–West relations, only with a somewhat more cooperative gloss. Between 1974 and 1979 each set up a Permanent Representative Mission, but they were not called embassies because West Germany insisted that, though there were two German states, they were part of a single German nation. West German citizens found it easier to visit the GDR, although travel in the other direction remained restricted. In fact, by 1985, 74 people had died trying to cross the Berlin Wall and 110 had died on other stretches of the inter-German frontier. *Increasing tension*

In the colder days of the East–West Cold War in the 1980s, the continued existence of two German states seemed inevitable on both sides of the frontier. But as Mikhail Gorbachev lost control of his reform process at home, so he lost control of the GDR. When Gorbachev made clear that East Europeans were free to go their own way (the so-called Sinatra Doctrine – 'They do it their way'), he did not envisage that East Germany would choose immediately to join West Germany. In May 1989 the Hungarians dismantled barbed wire along their border with Austria allowing East Germans to trickle out and by August there was a flood of East German refugees heading West. East Germans who stayed at home marched in their hundreds of thousands for a democratic government and still the Soviet Union refused to stem the tide of protest. While celebrating the Fortieth anniversary of the GDR in Berlin on 7 October, Gorbachev made it plain he wanted to see sweeping reforms. But as the demonstrations grew larger and the new GDR government merely tinkered with reforms, the crisis continued to grow. On 9 November, the new régime even opened the Berlin Wall in a last desperate attempt to save the situation, but the demonstrators merely demanded full democracy. On 3 December they finally got their wish, and by then Communists had fallen from power nearly everywhere else in Eastern Europe. The Cold War could be said to have ended with the breaching of the Wall, and certainly the loss of the GDR was the fatal blow to the Russian empire in Eastern Europe. *The Wall comes down*

Elections in the GDR produced a Centre-Right government of parties closely aligned to those in West Germany and committed to reunification. Chancellor Kohl of West Germany set the pace of reunification by obtaining rapid approval for currency union on 1 July 1990 as a prelude to all-German elections by the end of the year. At every stage of these hectic months, Russia gradually gave grudging approval to German reunification and membership of *The rush to elections and unification*

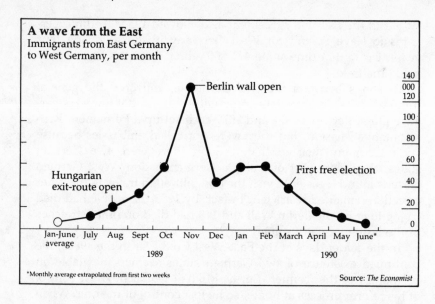

A wave from the East
Immigrants from East Germany
to West Germany, per month

Berlin wall open

Hungarian
exit-route open

First free election

Jan-June July Aug Sept Oct Nov Dec Jan Feb March April May June*
average

1989   1990

*Monthly average extrapolated from first two weeks

Source: *The Economist*

the new country in NATO. The German people were setting the
pace in such a rush that old worries about Germany began to
emerge from the political woodwork.

German
frontiers   In the 1970s West Germany had pledged itself to abide by the
post-war settlement frontiers, even though they left hundreds of
thousands of ethnic Germans in neighbouring countries. In 1990
both German states reaffirmed these commitments, but doubts
remained. Would a reunified Germany remain deaf to pleas from
ethnic Germans in Poland should a Polish government refuse
them rights to an education in German? Would Britain and France
refrain from having their say in defence of Polish sovereignty? The
scenario suddenly seemed reminiscent of the 1930s.

Of course, Germany is very different today from the way it
was in the 1930s. It is rich, democratic, and has a powerful stake
in the future stability of an EC-led Europe. Germany's leadership
instincts can be satisfied by its role in the EC and perhaps even
eventually an EC seat on the United Nations Security Council.
German prosperity is too dependent on the success of a closely
interdependent global market economy to risk throwing it all away
for a small number of long-lost compatriots. In any case, German
economic might can be expected to dominate and therefore influence its neighbours without resort to brute military force.

Making
two Germanies   Perhaps the most pressing German problem will be back at
into one   home, where 17 million East Germans have to be brought up to
the highest economic standards in the EC. It is already clear that
German (and hence European and OECD) inflation will rise as a
result of the costs of reunification. There have already been strikes

The Germanies Compared

Standard of Living Indicators	West	East
Household equipment 1988		
% of households with		
Car	97	52
Motorcycle	8	18
Deep freezer	77	43
Washing Machine	99	99
of which automatic	76	10
Television	98	96
of which colour	94	52
Telephone	98	7
Average living space for		
inhabitant per sq. metres	35.5	27.0
Health (1983)		
People per physician	431	472
People per hospital bed	89	97

Sources: Commerzbank, The Economist World in Figures

and major shifts of population in the former GDR as the shock therapy hits. East Germany is so badly polluted that just the cleaning bill will be mammoth. But West Germany will soon benefit from having new areas for investment and it certainly has a fine record in how to rebuild and even clean up its own country. The new Germans will work for less and therefore keep overall labour costs down, and they certainly ought to have an incentive to work harder. There is little hint of extreme German nationalism (e.g. from the Right-wing Republican party), especially as compared to the 19th century Bismarkian type of unification. In fact, reunification may be precisely what a prosperous forty year old needs to keep him young.

Reading

C. Bertram, 'The German Question', *Foreign Affairs*, Spring 1990.
The New Germany', *The Economist*, 30 June 1990.
F.S. Larrabee (ed), *The Two German States and European Security* (New York: St. Martin's Press, 1989).
E. Moreton (ed), *Germany Between East and West* (Cambridge: Cambridge University Press, 1987).
R. Morgan, 'Germany in Europe', *Washington Quarterly*, Autumn 1990.
A. Stent, *From Embargo to Ostpolitik* (Cambridge: Cambridge University Press, 1981).

Back to the Balkans

In the southeastern reaches of Europe, where the old Turkish Empire reached out and clashed with various Christian empires for centuries, lie the Balkan mountains in modern Bulgaria. Not far away lies Sarajevo in Yugoslavia – the flash point of the First World War. When historians of southern Europe think of the Balkans, they are reminded of war, instability and the developing world. Until 1989 all of the modern Balkans (roughly covering southern Hungary, Romania, Bulgaria, Albania and Yugoslavia) was under one form or another of Communism, but the revolutions in Eastern Europe are now threatening to return us to the uncertainty of old-style Balkan politics.

Few borders in the Balkans have any lengthy historical justification. Romania (independent since 1881) was on the winning side of the First World War and therefore won Transylvania from Hungary, along with its large Hungarian and German populations. Romania's demagogic politicians often saw agitation against these minorities as a quick route to popularity. But Transylvania has always been the most developed part of Romania and the 2 million Hungarians (25% of the population) have felt themselves to be subject to state-sanctioned pauperization. Under the Ceausescu Communist dictatorship, Romania continued the tradition of attacking ethnic Hungarians until they led the early stages of the revolt in 1989 that overthrew the Ceaucescu clan.

Hungary, as a Warsaw Pact ally of Romania, was not allowed to pursue the defence of its compatriots. But with the ending of Soviet control, and the election of ex-Communists to power in Romania and liberal democrats in Hungary, the basis for a new conflict is emerging. While Hungary is unlikely to contemplate the use of force against Romania, especially as it is focusing on domestic reconstruction, most of the tinder for future war is in place.

For all its mistreatment of Hungarians, Romania has also been abused by other neighbours. Bessarabia, part of the Danubian principality of Moldavia with a more than 85% Romanian population, was annexed by Russia in 1812, but lost to Romania in 1918. In 1940, squeezed between Germany and Russia, Romania lost Bessarabia to Russia, only briefly to regain it when taking advantage of the German invasion of Russia. But as Stalin's troops 'liberated' Romania in 1944, Bessarabia was taken back to form the largest part of the Moldavian republic of the Soviet Union. Two smaller parts were given to the Ukraine. In 1990, as various Soviet republics sought independence, Moldavia (now with 4 million people of whom only 12% are Russian) proclaimed its intention of joining with Romania, although the lower standard of living and greater political chaos across the frontier might well limit the speed of reunification. When the Russian minority in Romania declared its own 'independence' from Moldavia, the Moldavians treated them with the same harshness they themselves had received at the hands of the Russians in Moscow. The patchwork of nasty nationalism is merely re-emerging after decades under the cover of Russian imperialism.

Further around the Russian rim are the republics of Georgia (5 million people of whom 7% are Russian, 5% Azeris and 9% Armenians), Armenia (3.5 million people of whom 2% are Russian and 5% Azeris), and Azerbaijan (7 million people of whom 8% are Russian and 8% Armenians). The predominantly Christian republics of Armenia and Georgia have something in common with Russia, and all have deeper rivalries with Islamic neighbours in Azerbaijan and Turkey. In the case of Georgia, the persecution of Abkhazians as well as the inhabitants of South Ossetia has already led to much bloodshed and the use of Soviet troops to help keep the peace. The most serious separatist movement comes from the Azeris, but they have little support from states such as Turkey and Iran who have their own minorities to worry about. The real killing to date has involved the mainly Armenian enclave of Nagorny Karabakh in Azerbaijan and Armenian minorities in Baku, the capital of Azerbaijan. Soviet troops have been used in 1989 to restore order in a region where greater democracy seems to be unleashing xenophobic nationalism with little rational sense of how independence might be made viable. *The Caucasus*

At the furthest reaches of the Balkans lies Bulgaria. With some 10 million people it has long been the poorest of Russia's East European allies. In 1990 it even freely elected a government of ex-Communists. But the new freedoms have also allowed more open persecution of the 8% of the population who are Turkish and in 1989 some 100,000 fled across the border to Turkey. As a NATO member, Turkey has additional excuses to be a Bulgarian enemy. But it is surely bizarre that in 1989 Turkey sought Russian mediation in the dispute with Bulgaria. Of course Turkey has persecuted its own Kurdish minority and has long-standing disputes with Greece over Cyprus and intervening waters. The patchwork seems endlessly complex. *Bulgaria and the Turks*

Speaking of patchworks, nothing is quite so remarkable as Yugoslavia. This mosaic of people has also been described as a powder keg ready to explode. If we are lucky, the keg, unlike the Lebanon, will disintegrate before it has a chance to blow. So long as the place was a one-party state, it had some hope of being held together. But the coming of democracy has led the more prosperous areas of Croatia and Slovenia to elect non-Communist governments intent on seeking closer relations with Western- *Yugoslavia*

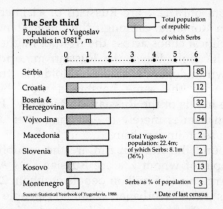

The Serb third
Population of Yugoslav republics in 1981*, m

Total population of republic
of which Serbs

Serbia		85
Croatia		12
Bosnia & Hercegovina		32
Vojvodina		54
Macedonia		2
Slovenia		2
Kosovo		13
Montenegro		3

Total Yugoslav population: 22.4m; of which Serbs: 8.1m (36%)

Serbs as % of population

Source: Statistical Yearbook of Yugoslavia, 1988   * Date of last census

oriented Hungary and Austria. Macedonia in the south has compatriots across the border in Bulgaria and Greece. Kosovo, 90% of
whose population is ethnic Albanian, is also seeking more autonomy. Serbia, the core of Yugoslavia, remains in ex-Communist
hands unwilling to give up power in the outlying regions. It is
supported by Romania which thereby hopes to inhibit the Hungarian claims in Transylvania.

Optimists hope a looser federation might just hold the Yugo-
mess together, but dreams of a Swiss model of unity merely seem
in keeping with the bizarre politics of the region. In 1991, the last
Communist state in Europe, Albania, a xenophobic country one-
third of whose compatriots live in Kosovo, actually more or less
freely elected a Communist party government. As with its Balkan
neighbours, a bit of democracy, when added to the ethnic powder-
keg was a dangerous concoction. Will the more sophisticated Europeans have the good sense to stay out of this mess that comprises
the Balkans?

Reading

A. Braun, *Small-State Security in the Balkans* (London: Macmillan,
1983).

D. Carlton and M. Schaerf (eds), *Southeastern Europe After Tito*
(London: Macmillan, 1983).

R.J. Crampton, *A Short History of Modern Bulgaria* (Cambridge:
Cambridge University Press, 1987).

A. Logoreci, *The Albanians* (London: 1977).

H. Lydall, *Yugoslavia in Crisis* (Oxford: Oxford University Press,
1989).

M. Shafir, *Romania* (London: Frances Pinter, 1985).

K. Sword (ed), *The Times Guide to Eastern Europe* (London: Times
Books, 1990).

Greece and Turkey

Before the end of the Cold War in Europe, the Greek–Turkey conflict between two NATO members looked much more peculiar. But now, when southeastern Europe looks like such a mosaic of murderous bands, somehow the conflict between Greece and Turkey makes more sense. As with all these complex cases, a glance at recent history is essential.

Following the dismemberment of the Ottoman Turkish Empire after the First World War, Greece in 1920–1 attempted to take by force the territory it was awarded under the 1920 Treaty of Sèvres (i.e. most of Thrace west of Istanbul, the islands of Imroz and Tenedos, and the Dodecanese, except for Rhodes as well as a mandated authority over Izmir). In the 1923 Treaty of Lausanne, Greece recognized Turkish sovereignty over the disputed territory, except the Dodecanese which was ceded to Italy, who had supported Turkey in the recent war. *Carving up the Ottoman Empire*

This conflict marked the end of the aspirations of greater Greece but it still left Greece in control of all major islands in the Aegean except Imroz and Tenedos. After the Second World War, defeated Italy ceded the Dodecanese to Greece. Officially, neither Turkey nor Greece challenges the present frontiers but they both dispute control of the Aegean continental shelf. There are modest hopes for exploiting minerals (especially oil) but, if Greece ever made its claimed 12 mile sea limit stick, Turkey's defence position would be untenable. Turkey is by far the more powerful of the two states militarily. Both spend roughly equal amounts on defence but Greece spends four times as much per capita and Turkey deploys three times as many soldiers. *Aegean rivalry*

Greece claims the seabed up to the median line between the islands it controls and the Turkish coast. Turkey refuses to entertain a ruling by the International Court of Justice on the dispute, claiming that the Aegean is a special case in international law because it is the natural extension of the Anatolian landmass – a novel argument, to say the least. Thus while not disputing sovereignty over the islands, Turkey claims half the Aegean continental shelf. Mineral prospecting has so far been carried out by international consortia. Yet Greek air traffic control has had responsibility for the airspace over the Aegean, except during 1974–80 when Turkey declared the zone to be dangerous and everyone steered clear. *The continental shelf*

In July 1976, Turkey attempted to carry out a seismic survey *Legal disputes*

159

of the seabed and Greece took the issue to the United Nations Security Council. The United Nations referred the issue to the International Court of Justice which refused the Greek demand for an injunction against Turkey. Turkey, in turn, accused Greece of illegal militarization of the Dodecanese (outlawed by the 1947 Paris Treaty that had given the islands to Greece) but the ensuing military tension was shortlived. The International Court refused to rule on the general issue of the seabed as Turkey refused to submit to its jurisdiction. Bilateral discussions continue but the issue has been consistently overshadowed in the past twenty years by events on nearby Cyprus.

The Cyprus problem   This strategically important island, 50 miles south of Turkey and 550 miles southeast of mainland Greece (and 180 miles from the nearest Greek island) has an 80% Greek population (mostly Christian) while most of the rest of the inhabitants are Turkish Muslims. Cyprus was under Ottoman rule from the 1570s to 1878, during which time most of the Turkish population arrived. At the 1878 Congress of Berlin, Britain was given the territory to administer under nominal Turkish sovereignty. Britain annexed the island in 1914 and it became a colony in 1925. The Greek population fostered the idea of *enosis* – union with Greece – and Turkey increased the pressure from the other side by speaking as the protector of the Turkish minority. A Greek-dominated administration was set up after Cyprus attained independence in 1960. The constitution guaranteed minority rights but the Greek Cypriot leader, Archbishop Makarios, eroded them. Britain maintained sovereignty over two bases (a total of 99 square miles at Akrotiri and Dhekelia) while both Greece and Turkey were allowed to station token forces on the island.

Turkish invasion   There were clashes between the two communities and, in 1964, the United Nations sent a peacekeeping force to the island. Talks remained deadlocked and, in December 1969, the Turkish Cypriots announced a plan to establish an autonomous administration for their part of the island. Separate elections were held in July 1970. On 15 July 1974, after wrangling within the Greek Cypriot community, Makarios was deposed by a pro-*enosis* group. Turkey and Makarios' supporters claimed Greece was about to take over the island and on 20 July Turkish troops landed 'at the invitation' of their Turkish brethren. Thirty thousand Turkish troops quickly defeated the Greek Cypriots and the United Nations Security Council called for talks. Britain arranged for negotiations at Geneva and a ceasefire was agreed on 30 July. But on 23 July the Greek military government fell and in the ensuing replacement of Greek Cypriot leaders, Turkey further expanded its hold on Cyprus.

After a new ceasefire on 16 August, Turkey controlled 37% of the land. One-third of the Cypriot population was made homeless, as Turkey encouraged a population shift across the 'Attila Line'. In February 1975, Turkey began to establish the Turkish Federated State as part of a putative federated Cyprus. Talks on a bicommunal state ensued, with the main disagreements being over how much land the Turkish area should include (Greek Cypriots offered 20%), security arrangements and Varosha (a Greek area of Famagusta now under Turkish control). Turkey demanded equality for the two areas, close ties for Turkish Cypriots to the mainland, and an alternating presidency.

Offers and counter-offers

On 15 November 1983 the Turkish area declared independence as the Turkish Republic of North Cyprus. It was condemned by the United Nations Security Council and recognized only by Turkey. Inter-communal talks continued with the first face-to-face meeting of leaders on 17 January 1985 under United Nations auspices. Turkey pressed its compatriots on the island for progress, as it wanted American military aid (which had been withheld, in part due to the Cyprus impasse). In November 1984 the Turks conceded that the President of Cyprus should be a Greek Cypriot and that Turks would control only 29% of the island. But in 1985 and 1986 both sides rejected United Nations plans. Turkey was upset that its troops would have to leave Cyprus, and Greece wanted Greek Cypriots to have freedom of movement and thus be able to dominate the island again. UN-backed talks in 1989 and 1990 also foundered on much the same issues.

Creeping progress

In comparison to nearby Lebanon or the Balkans, Cyprus was a relatively controlled and resolvable conflict. Refugees had already been housed in modern apartments and both Greece and Turkey kept a close eye on their Cypriot allies for fear of upsetting their more powerful allies in NATO. Some sort of federal state seemed possible but given the legacy of inter-communal violence, it was unlikely to be a stable structure.

Reading

J. Alford (ed), *Greece and Turkey* (London: Gower, 1984).

T. Coubumbis, *The United States, Greece and Turkey* (New York: Praeger, 1983).

R. Denktash, *The Cyprus Triangle* (London: George Allen & Unwin, 1982).

C. Hitchens, *Cyprus* (London: Quartet Books, 1984).

Insoluble Ireland

The Irish problem, like those in southeastern Europe, concerns two communities unable to share a territory peacefully. Curiously, in the new Europe with bigotry in its southern reaches, similar politics in the northwest makes a rotten kind of sense.

Ancient rivalries

Ireland evolved its Gaelic language and culture after the collapse of the Roman Empire. In 1170–2, neighbouring England grabbed control and forced the locals to accept a significant number of Anglo-Norman settlers. After 1607, some 170,000 Protestants (mostly lowland Scots) were settled by Britain in northern Ireland among the Catholic majority. The resulting Irish resistance was ruthlessly suppressed by Britain. Success for the Protestant cause was entrenched by the Battle of the Boyne (1690) and by 1700 the remaining Catholics in Ulster (now Northern Ireland) owned less than 15% of the land.

Famine and emigration

In 1801 the Act of the Union gave Ireland representation in the London Parliament but opposition to often brutal British rule continued. In 1846 the failure of the potato harvest led to mass famine and the death of an estimated 1 million out of 8 million people. Emigration resulted in a loss of a further 1.2 million people. Ireland was transformed from a land of tillage to a land of pasture and the British were seen as convenient culprits for all its ills. Opposition to British rule gathered pace and demands for Home Rule could no longer be ignored.

The evolution of Ulster

Yet Britain decided it could not simply dispose of the Irish problem as just another colonial embarrassment. As a result of rapid industrialization, closer links with Britain and its already largely Protestant character, the North of Ireland developed independently of the South and opposed Home Rule under Catholic control. In 1898 the Ulster Unionist party was formed as the main voice of the Protestants and in 1912 Sir Edward Carson established an armed opposition to Home Rule.

Irish Home Rule

The Irish Home Rule Bill was delayed by the First World War, although the Easter Uprising in 1916 in the South certainly kept the issue to the fore. The nationalist movement, led by Sinn Fein (established in 1905), pursued a dual policy of control of local government and guerrilla war against the British. In 1921, a treaty between British Prime Minister Lloyd George and Sinn Fein, to create the Irish Free State, was opposed by Sinn Fein leader Eamon de Valera because it did not include the six northernmost of the thirty-two counties. Between 1923 and 1927 rebellion was led by the Irish Republican Army (IRA), an extreme wing of Sinn Fein. The IRA cause collapsed when de Valera joined the democratic political process, and in December 1937, the fully independent state of Eire was established. On 18 April 1949 the Irish Republic was proclaimed and Eire left the Commonwealth. Northern Ireland remained an integral part of the United Kingdom.

In 1956 the IRA re-emerged in the North with a bombing campaign against British rule. The Irish government also wanted a united Ireland but to be achieved peacefully. However, the Protestant two-thirds of Ulster's 1.5 million people opposed union with Ireland's 3.2 million Catholics and preferred home rule from Belfast. The Protestants entrenched their domination of Northern Ireland's Catholic minority by rigging elections and restricting economic opportunities for Catholics. London grew increasingly exasperated with this Protestant violence and corruption and between 1965 and 1968 began to moderate Protestant rule and improve the position of Ulster's Catholics. But pressure from the extremes of the two communities led to a sharp increase in communal violence in 1969. As the local police failed to provide adequate protection for the Catholics, Britain sent troops to keep the peace and status quo. *Protestant bigotry in Ulster*

Inevitably, this policy of 'no surrender' came under increasing pressure. The IRA gained political support among Ulster Catholics and was declared illegal by the British. A breakaway Provisional IRA was established, a political wing continued, and a further split created the Irish National Liberation Army. All factions sought financial support from the South and from sympathizers in the United States. These groups fed on the real dissatisfaction of Catholics with social and economic discrimination in Ulster but the outlawed organizations soon resorted to indiscriminate violence. The strategy was to raise the cost of Britain's occupation and force a withdrawal of British troops. But the army responded with increasing pressure, resulting, for example, in the death of thirteen in Londonderry on 30 January 1972 (since known as Bloody Sunday). The violence spiralled out of control and two months later the Unionist government resigned and direct rule from London was imposed. Between 1969 and 1981, 1,213 civilians and 456 soldiers died, and by mid-1984 the total was 2,400 dead, including over 700 members of the security forces. By that time Britain was stationing over 11,000 troops in Ulster. *Escalating violence*

The core problem of how to guarantee Catholic rights remained. Britain suggested minority rights could be guaranteed within Britain, while Ireland claimed Protestant minority rights could be guaranteed in a united Ireland. Moderates on both sides hoped for some kind of federation. In the Anglo-Irish agreement at Sunningdale in December 1973, Britain accepted an 'Irish dimen- *Sunningdale* sion' to the Northern Ireland problem and a fourteen-member all-Ireland 'power-sharing executive' was established to further consultation. The South hoped this council would develop real powers and bring about genuine power-sharing. But Protestant 'loyalists' wrecked the agreement with a general strike in May 1974 which Britain refused to break with its troops. The status quo held and the cycle of violence spiralled upward.

The 1982 Assembly

In 1982, Britain proposed a seventy-eight-man Assembly to formulate a plan acceptable to both communities, but voting in October followed predictable communal lines. The Ulster Union-ists won most seats, Sinn Fein won five, and the moderate Catholic Social Democratic and Labour Party (SDLP) fourteen seats. The Catholic parties refused to take their seats and the killing con-tinued.

New Ireland Forum

The SDLP and the three main Irish parties in the South met in the New Ireland Forum in May 1983. Their report in May 1984 stressed the need for general consent to any settlement and the importance of maintaining separate traditions in a single state. Britain rejected the plan on the grounds that it violated the wishes of the Protestants to remain tied to Britain. London's policy remained consistently cautious. It encouraged Ireland to moderate its sectarian laws (rigid Catholic practices have been slowly moder-ated since 1959), tried to keep a semblance of peace in Ulster and, since both Ireland and Britain have joined the EC, tried to encour-age greater cooperation between North and South (including in the security sphere).

Progress in 1985

Britain's basically passive approach was finally abandoned on 15 November 1985. The British and Irish Prime Ministers signed a formal, binding agreement in which both recognized Dublin's 'legitimate interest' in the North but also that Northern Ireland remains a part of the United Kingdom. An inter-governmental conference was set up to coordinate responses to terrorism and to promote cooperation. The ambitious hope was that, as at Sunning-dale, eventually the moderates in both camps would see a common interest in real cooperation. Needless to say, the bigots in Catholic and Protestant camps tried to destroy the agreement, but for the time being the reforming centre was holding. The combination of Protestant intransigence and an IRA bomb in Brighton in 1984 that almost killed the Thatcher cabinet, gave the moderates the best chance they had had in decades.

The core problem

However, the essential problem – which community would be a minority – lay unresolved. Although extremism in both camps often makes it difficult to see, there appears to be a gradual swing in favour of a federated Ireland. The more optimistic hoped that in the climate of greater European integration through the EC, the concept of federation would become more acceptable. It was, like the expectations for the EC itself, a very long-term plan.

Reading

P. Arthur and K. Jeffrey, *Northern Ireland Since 1968* (Oxford: Basil Blackwell, 1988).

T.P. Coogan, *The IRA* (London: Collins, 1987).

R.H. Hull, *The Irish Triangle* (Princeton: Princeton University Press, 1976).

K. Kelly, *The Longest War* (London: Dingle, 1982).

J. McGarry and B. O'Leary (eds), *The Future of Northern Ireland* (Oxford: Oxford University Press, 1990).

J. Whyte, *Interpreting Northern Ireland* (Oxford: Oxford University Press, 1990).

5

EAST ASIA AND THE PACIFIC

Japan and the United States

The world's two largest economies are supposed to be allies. Indeed Japan and the United States are so interdependent that the effective economic, military and even cultural distances across the Pacific have shrunk as the two countries grow closer together after having been at war in the early 1940s. But forty-five years on, with the decline of their mutual enemy – the Soviet Union and its ideology of Communism – the glue of the US–Japan alliance seems to be melting.

Opening Japan

On 8 July 1853, Commodore Perry of the US navy sailed his squadron of 'black ships' into Tokyo bay to force Japan to open its doors to foreigners. With expanding American (and European) economic interests in the Pacific, the capitalist economies found it intolerable that Japan was a closed market and society. But the ensuing modernization of Japan in the Meiji Restoration soon became the most rapid rise to great power status ever seen. By the end of the century, Japan had become a major international trader, and also a major imperial power, taking territory in Korea and China. This was not quite what Commodore Perry and the United States had expected.

Japan's Co-Prosperity Sphere

Once awakened, Japan merely mimicked the great power practices it saw around its shores. If everyone else could have empires, then so could Japan. Because Japan's neighbours were especially vulnerable, and by the early 20th century the European powers were losing their imperial drive, Japan became the main imperial power in East Asia. In the 1930s, when Germany was challenging many of the same older powers, Japan joined a *de facto* alliance with Nazi Germany and reordered the East Asian balance of power. Yet without its colonies, Japan was a vulnerable island and so the lure of imperialism seemed even more attractive. By 1940, when Germany smashed the European home bases of the colonial powers with holdings in East Asia, Japan swiftly moved to pick up the pieces. But as the United States joined Britain in taking on German power, Japan was foolish enough to attack America's main Pacific outpost – Pearl Harbour. A surprised and furious United States was now in the war, and determined to make Japan pay for its impudence.

Nuclear Weapons and Nuclear Deterrence

The United States invented the atomic bomb for use against Germany, but by the time it was ready, Germany was defeated and only Japan was still fighting. Thus the only use of an atomic weapon in war was against Hiroshima and Nagasaki in August

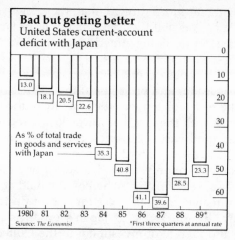

Bad but getting better
United States current-account
deficit with Japan

As % of total trade
in goods and services
with Japan — 35.3

13.0
18.1
20.5
22.6
40.8
41.1
39.6
28.5
23.3

1980 81 82 83 84 85 86 87 88 89*
Source: *The Economist*   *First three quarters at annual rate

The flood, kind of
Stock of Japanese direct investment
in United States

As % of total foreign
investment — 12.9

16.2
12.2
10.5
9.7
8.3
7.8
7.1
5.7

1980 81 82 83 84 85 86 87 88
Source: *The Economist*

1945. With the war ended, the United States soon set about rebuilding Japan with a Peace Constitution that restricted the type of military force Japan could maintain. But with the outbreak of the Korean War in 1950, Washington also came to recognize that it needed Japan as an ally against the new Soviet threat and by 1954 a mutual assistance pact was signed which formally tied Japan into the United States' alliance structure. The problem was obvious: if Japan could not defend itself, then it had to rely on United States deterrence, and without a multilateral alliance like NATO, Japan would always feel inferior and frustrated.

In 1960 the security treaty was renegotiated and the United States gradually returned Japanese territory. But American bases remained and played a crucial role in the Vietnam War. With the determination of the Nixon administration of the 1970s to get all its Asian allies to bear more of their own defence burden, Japan was encouraged to spend more on defence, especially as its econ-

Renegotiating
security

omy was growing far more strongly than the ailing American one. The United States was still the basic guarantor of Japanese security, but in an age of declining American power and rising resentment of Japanese economic success.

Japan's economic miracle

And yet the Japanese economic miracle was a tribute to the United States as leader and protector of the alliance of free market economies. The real problem was the inability of the United States to come to terms with the fact that it was losing relative economic power to Japan (and East Asian NICs in general) and to the West Europeans. The growing interdependence of these three legs of the global market economy created a series of Mutual Assured Destruction (MAD) relationships whereby it would be MAD for any one party to threaten economic war for fear of destroying everyone's economy. By the 1980s, as Japan's products became more sophisticated and its rate of investment in the United States (and then Europe) grew, the United States was forced also to recognize the MAD logic that made the United States dependent on its allies. This was a difficult lesson for a once-proud Superpower that had also lost a war in Vietnam.

Trade tension

By the early 1980s the United States was doing more trade across the Pacific than it did with Western Europe. As Americans, and especially the world's sixth largest economy in California, began musing about the Pacific Century and the reorientation of United States policy in that direction, Americans also came to recognize that the Japanese economy was very different from its own or even those in Europe. Japan had a more command economy with a higher savings rate and more sophisticated cultural barriers to imports. As the trade deficit with Japan peaked at nearly $60 billion in 1987, the calls for a trade war with Japan grew louder.

Japan as a threat

But Japan was still an ally against Communism. With the retreat of American military power in East Asia, Japan was a crucial engine for growth of other market economies in the region and economic prosperity was seen as the best bulwark against Communist revolution. In the 1980s Japan even played the leading role in bringing China into the international market economy. But in 1989 a number of key strategic changes took place. China's televised massacre in Peking's Tiananmen Square in June left many Americans less interested in supporting China. And then the revolutions in Eastern Europe later in the year turned American attention back to Europe and sharply reduced the perception of a Soviet threat. Subsequently, an opinion poll in January 1990 showed a sharp rise in the American perception of Japan as a threat – not because of anything Japan had recently done, but more because older threats had faded.

The get-tough-with-Japan brigade filled American bookshelves with analyses of why Japan had to be given shock therapy before its trade balance would change and how the Japanese economy was more command- than market-driven. There was even a whiff of racism in these suggestions, especially as Europeans with even larger combined trade surpluses were getting away without much criticism. Japanese investment surged as a way to reduce the trade balance and provide more employment in the United States. But Americans then complained about foreign ownership, even though the Europeans had long owned far more of the United States, just as Americans had invested in Europe and East Asia in previous decades.

While Americans spoke of Japan as only responding to shock therapy, it was clear that too sharp a shock would be more catastrophic than therapeutic to all concerned. Some Japanese rose to American levels of xenophobia by suggesting Japan had some other alternative to interdependence. Yet the reality was that a deal had to be struck. As Japan's yen rose in the late 1980s, the trade surplus was reduced. Louder American complaints about Japanese trade practices led to negotiations about the Structural Impediments Initiative (SII) and in 1990 Japan agreed to increase domestic spending in order to suck in more imports. It also looked set to open its rice market to foreigners and reduce the absurd subsidies paid to local producers. The United States began to take steps to reduce its budget deficit, thereby reducing interest rates and making American companies more competitive. In any case, the vastly more complex international market economy ensured that American multinationals were moving into East Asia in search of better manufacturing conditions while Japanese firms bought into the American market in order to make themselves less visible as a source of imports into the United States.

Shock therapy

This mix of market forces and shock therapy seemed to be working, but the longer term tasks concerned psychological adjustments in the United States and Japan. Americans had to come to terms with interdependence and the loss of control that entailed. Japan and Western Europe were merely doing what the Americans had done to them for decades. But Japan also had to open up its economy, and concentrate more on domestic growth than export growth. Both countries had to improve relations with the Soviet Union and Japan in particular would have to adjust to a more complex military environment. With less American protection, and American frustration that Japan was unwilling to send troops to held defend common interests in the Gulf in 1990, Japan was being pushed into rethinking its approach to military security. Both countries would also have to take the New Europe more seriously, for only with a more equal balance of the three legs of the international market economy would the undue pressure be taken off the US–Japan leg.

Reading

The Atlantic Council, *The United States and Japan* (New York: University Press of America, 1990).

B. Emmott, *The Sun Also Sets* (London: Simon and Schuster, 1989).

E. Lincoln, *Japan's Unequal Trade* (Washington: Brookings, 1990).

C. Prestowitz, *Trading Places* (New York: Basic Books, 1988).

G. Segal, *Rethinking the Pacific* (Oxford: Oxford University Press, 1990).

K. van Wolferen, *The Enigma of Japanese Power* (London: Macmillan, 1989).

China and the Soviet Union

China and the Soviet Union were once dreaded by the West as a monolithic Communist bloc and hence the greatest threat to Western security. But with the Sino–Soviet schism the Communist bloc was dealt its most devastating blow. The transformation of China from Soviet ally to Soviet enemy was, at least until 1989, the single most important shift in the strategic balance since 1945. But just as the image of a monolithic Sino–Soviet bloc was false, so the image of China as a useful Western weapon against the Soviet Union was dangerous. China's emergence as a genuinely independent force in the 1980s was yet further evidence of the new multi-power balance of power.

The relevant roots of Sino–Soviet relations go back to the 17th and 18th centuries when an expanding Russian Empire across most of northern Asia collided with a declining Chinese Empire barely able to meet the challenge. By the 19th century the Chinese Empire was in decay and Russian settlers pushed across to the Pacific (and built Vladivostok). In a series of 'unequal treaties' (e.g. Aigun 1858 and Beijing 1860) Russia grabbed territory that China had once claimed. The new border largely followed the line of the upper Amur (Heilongjiang) river and its tributary the Ussuri river. *Unequal treaties*

After the 1917 Russian revolution, the Soviet Union gradually reasserted control of its Asian territories. However, China's nationalist revolution in 1911 merely led to the warlords splitting China and allowing further Soviet penetration. In 1924 an 'independent' state of Mongolia was established but under Soviet domination. In 1927 the Chinese Communist Party was formed and in its early years was led by Soviet agents from one setback to another. When Mao Zedong took control of the movement and established a base at Yanan, the leadership and ideology of Chinese Communism took on a Chinese form. Following the defeat of Japan in 1945, Mao's forces routed the American-supported nationalist régime of Chiang Kai-shek. Communist victory in the civil war (1949) was achieved largely without Soviet help. *The Chinese Revolution*

The ties of a common ideology, and a common enemy in the United States, led Moscow and Beijing to sign (on 14 February 1950) a thirty-year friendship pact. China entered the Korean War in October and, with heavy Soviet support, fought American troops to a stalemate. Soviet aid to China extended well beyond military equipment and included a 'Soviet model' for Chinese economic and social life. However, this close cooperation began *1950 friendship pact* to break down because of shifts in the domestic politics of both countries. In 1956, Khrushchev initiated a program of de-Stalinization and important ideological reform in the Communist bloc, without consulting China.

Failure of the Soviet model

More importantly, China found the Soviet model of economic development and industrialization unsuited to China's poor peasant conditions and began to search for a more 'Third World' model of development. The resulting Great Leap Forward in China in 1958 was an economic fiasco, leading to as many as 20 million deaths from starvation in 1960–1. The Soviet Union was unwilling to aid China because of its refusal to toe the new ideological line and also because of a series of disputes between the two countries on foreign policy.

The split goes public

Khrushchev was increasingly engaged in détente with the United States (1959 at Camp David), and opposed China's wish to support a more active revolutionary line in the Third World. In the dispute between India and China in 1962, the Soviet Union failed to provide the comradely support China expected. In July 1963, the Sino–Soviet split became public when the two Superpowers and Britain signed the partial nuclear test ban treaty. China wanted its own nuclear weapons and saw the test ban pact as an attempt by the Soviet Union and the West to relegate China to the permanent status of a second class power.

Talk of 'united action'

This Sino–Soviet split has been the most devastating setback suffered by the Soviet Union since 1945. The Soviet Union now had to worry about the possibility of a two-front war and the United States benefited from the deep ideological split in the enemy camp. Attempts were made to patch up the Sino–Soviet dispute in 1964, after the fall of Khrushchev and the first Chinese nuclear test in October. But neither side was prepared to moderate its basic principles. Even during the Vietnam War, both sides refused to engage in 'united action' against the United States, although in practical terms they competed for Vietnam's favour with aid. In political terms the split reached its worst point when in March 1966 China severed inter-party ties. China's radical experiments during the Cultural Revolution took it further away from the Soviet ideological orbit than ever before.

To the brink of war

In military terms, the split was deepest following the Soviet invasion of Czechoslovakia and the declaration of the Brezhnev doctrine of limited sovereignty for Communist states in 1968. China feared a Soviet attack and, in March 1969, tried to demonstrate to Moscow, along the Ussuri frontier, that China would be a tougher nut to crack than Czechoslovakia. But in the second of two border clashes in March, Soviet troops trounced the Chinese, inflicting hundreds of casualties. By October, Soviet nuclear threats during the course of 1969 had forced China to negotiate on reducing tension. The specific territorial dispute over Damansky (Zhenbao) island (China claims the border runs through the centre of the river channel which places the island on China's side) was inconsequential. But the island did emerge as a symbol of Chinese independence and of the Soviet desire to impose its order of events along the frontier.

In part because of a heightened sense of Soviet threat, China improved relations with the United States in the 1970s. Moscow's paranoia went into overdrive – fearing a triple alliance in the East: the Chinese masses, Japanese technology and American power and wealth. The death of Mao in September 1976 at first did not bring any swift changes in Beijing's policy. But from 1978 China began to open its doors to foreign trade and contracts. Sino–Soviet relations remained cool because of the Soviet-backed Vietnamese invasion of Cambodia, the Sino–Vietnamese border war and the Soviet invasion of Afghanistan.

China opens doors

While Moscow had built up its armed forces along the Sino–Soviet frontier to deter a Chinese attack, major changes were underway in Chinese policy. The new Reagan administration's support for Taiwan angered China and forced it to reassess the global balance and its closer relations with the United States. But most important, political and economic reforms at home led China to abandon Maoist radical politics and shift towards a more orthodox, if reform-minded, socialism that the Soviet Union found largely acceptable. China's foreign policy began to change in 1981–2, with signs that China now viewed the Soviet threat as less pressing. Because Moscow was seen to be bogged down in Afghanistan, trapped uncomfortably into costly support for Vietnam and under pressure from America's rearmament under Reagan, China could now negotiate without a sense of inferiority. Brezhnev's speech at Tashkent in March 1982 recognized China as a socialist state and on 5 October 1982 'consultations' opened at the deputy-foreign minister level.

Towards Sino–Soviet détente

Sino–Soviet relations improved in fits and starts through the period of transition in the Kremlin from Brezhnev through Andropov and Chernenko to Gorbachev. Trade and cultural relations led the way, with a major trade agreement signed in Moscow in July 1985. By 1986 China had become the Soviet Union's second largest trading partner in the Pacific (after Japan). China's more independent foreign policy gradually encouraged the Soviet Union in 1986 to make concessions on the definition of the river frontier and formal talks were opened to delineate the border. China and the Soviet Union both made *de facto* arms reductions along the frontier and formal talks on cuts and confidence-building measures opened in 1989. Most importantly, in May 1989 Mikhail Gorbachev came to China for the first Sino-Soviet summit in thirty years.

Developing détente

Clearly, Sino–Soviet relations were warmer than at any time since the early 1950s. But even though both sides no longer spoke of each other as a threat, there were important problems. Just as they both seemed to be growing closer on the matter of reforming their ideology, China suffered major unrest in May and June 1989, culminating in the Beijing massacre of 3–4 June. This heavy price paid for the continuation of Communist Party rule, made it more clear to Mikhail Gorbachev that Communism could not be maintained in Eastern Europe at the point of a bayonet. The revolutions in Eastern Europe in the last six months of 1989, and the major changes in the Soviet Union itself, showed the widening gap between former comrades. China and the Soviet Union would now get along because they shared economic and even military interests in East Asia. But the days of ideological comradeship were over, and they could get down to treating each other as good old-fashioned great power rivals with a sometimes-common interest in a complex regional balance of power.

Reading

O.E. Clubb, *China and Russia* (New York: Columbia University Press, 1971).

J. Gittings, *Survey of the Sino–Soviet Dispute* (London: Oxford University Press, 1969).

G. Segal, *Defending China* (London: Oxford University Press, 1985).

G. Segal, 'Sino–Soviet Relations After Mao', *Adelphi Papers* No. 202 (London: 1985).

G. Segal, *The Soviet Union and the Pacific* (Boston: Unwin/Hyman, 1990).

The Koreas

As the Cold War fades into history, the most dangerous remnant is to be found on the Korean peninsula. The Korean people were divided between Communist north and capitalist south, but as that other great divided country – Germany – finds unity in the post-Cold War world, Koreans are once again looking at their predicament. But the virulence of the Korean conflict is also the result of the peculiar politics of the two states, their unreliable leaders, and the intense interests of nearby Japan, looming China and Russia, and a concerned United States. The mix is unstable.

The Korean peninsula had been annexed by Japan in 1910 but *Cold War comes* the wartime allies agreed in Cairo in 1943 that the United States *to Korea* and Soviet Union would divide the area at the 38th parallel, pending the transition to independence. In December 1945 the Superpowers and Britain agreed on a five-year trusteeship under four-power control (i.e. including China). But all sides failed to agree on a national government and, in February 1946, the Soviet Union set up a provisional Communist government in the North. Further talks failed and a provisional legislature was established in the southern part of the peninsula (which had two-thirds of the population). Against a background of deepening Cold War in Europe, the Soviet Union denied entry into the North to a United Nations supervisory commission to organize free elections throughout Korea.

Elections in the South, in May 1948, led to the establishment *The outbreak of* of the Republic of Korea in August. In the North, Soviet forces *war* left in December 1948, having established the People's Democratic Republic of Korea (PDRK). United States forces departed in mid-1949. But in June 1950, the PDRK attacked the South, apparently with prior Soviet knowledge but not necessarily with Moscow's approval of the timing. The United States arranged for the United Nations to authorize a military force under General MacArthur to push back PDRK forces. After MacArthur's drive north to the Yalu river, China entered the war in support of the Communist North and fought United Nations forces to a stalemate roughly along the 38th parallel. Both sides settled down to a murderous war of attrition which ended only with an armistice in July 1953. Until the Iran–Iraq War in 1980, this was the bloodiest post-1945 conflict with Chinese casualties said to be about one million.

Neither North nor South Korea abandoned aspirations of vic- *Fading hopes of* tory and unification but both were constrained by great power *unification* allies more concerned with controlling the risks of conflict. In the period (up to the early 1970s) when China was less worried about such crisis-management, Beijing emerged as North Korea's closest ally. But, especially after the Sino–Soviet split, Moscow competed for influence by providing arms to the Kim Il Sung régime. The United States, concerned about the dangers of war damaging its key Asian ally, Japan, encouraged South Korea to concentrate on economic development. With strong American support, heavy Japanese investment and strong-arm military rule in Seoul, the South Korean economy began to boom. Part of the United States' motive in engaging in détente with China in the early 1970s was to control the risks of war in Korea. But the two Koreas had not abandoned hopes of unification and for different, but similar, reasons feared a great power deal was being done over their heads.

High risk-controlled conflict   On 4 July 1972 both Koreas agreed to the principle of 'peaceful unification of the fatherland' and representatives met at Panmunjom, the seat of the joint military armistice commission set up in 1953. But talks were suspended in 1973 and tension remained unresolved. North Korea demanded a withdrawal of all foreign troops from Korea; the United States maintained some 40,000 troops in the South, though all Chinese troops had been pulled out in 1958. A series of military incidents, at sea and over tunnels under the demilitarized zone, especially in 1974–5, were clear signs that the risks of war remained high. As if to underline the venom of the conflict, in August 1976 two United States officers at Panmunjom were axed to death by North Koreans.

War of words   In February–March 1979 new 'talks about talks' broke down. But in January 1980 the North, for the first time, accepted the South Korean régime as an established government rather than just a United States puppet. Yet further talks were ruined by distrust and occasional naval incidents. The vitriolic war of words and the cruel military incidents between the two Koreas contrasted with the concern of the great powers to avoid a war that might escalate if one ally seemed in danger of defeat. Bouts of political turbulence in the South were matched by rigid one-party rule in the North. Martial law was declared in South Korea in May 1980 after students rioted in support of demands for political reform.

Pressures for détente   But there was little real change either on the local or international front. China and South Korea increased their 'unofficial' contacts in 1984, as China sought to safeguard its growing hidden trade with the South and to convince the North of the need to open a real dialogue and reduce tension. But at the highest level, for example when Premier Zhao met President Reagan in January 1984, China continued to convey the North Korean line that talks should be held between the North, the Americans and the South.

South Korea continued to insist on simple bilateral talks, and the Reagan administration was inclined to be less critical of its Korean ally, especially on issues of domestic reform, than President Carter had been.

North–South talks achieved little of substance. The inflated   *Bombs and talks*
expectations for Korean détente were demonstrated by the North's outrageous bomb attack on the South's cabinet in Rangoon (Burma) in October 1983, when several ministers were killed. In November 1987, the North was responsible for the death of more than one hundred people on a South Korean civil aircraft over Thailand. Yet, in September 1984 the North sent aid to flood victims in the South and trade talks began at Panmunjom in November. Various other negotiations continued, including those on family reunification, sports cooperation and military disengagement. Although the scope and frequency of the discussions were unprecedented, there was little sign that either side was doing much more than posturing. Minor agreements on family reunification were reached in August 1985 but some ten million people remain separated from their families.

The South feared the North was trying to create the illusion of   *Essential*
progress so as to divide South Korea from the United States. The   *deadlock*
North continued to demand that United States forces pull out but the South insisted that was only possible *after* the threat from the North was eliminated. Neither side seemed genuinely interested in compromise but pressure from the Superpowers, China and Japan kept both sides never very far from the negotiating table.

While neither side has a clear military advantage, the North   *Olympic games*
must be concerned that the booming South Korean economy will inevitably make South Korea's defence burden less heavy to bear. As the hosts for the 1988 Olympic games, the South gained international prestige while the North stagnated. More than forty years of division have also encouraged the two societies to grow apart and certainly the standard of living in the South is obviously outpacing that in the North.

So long as Kim Il Sung was alive, any major breakthrough   *Pressure for*
seemed unlikely. But as the events on the other side of the Com-   *détente*
munist world in 1989 demonstrated, changes in the external environment can have a major impact. By the late 1980s the Soviet Union was engaged in reform and pressing all its allies to do the same. Moscow also improved relations with South Korea in an effort to join the booming Pacific economy. In September 1990 South Korea and the Soviet Union established diplomatic relations and in December the South Korean President visited Moscow. China, which had first improved trade relations with South Korea in the mid-1980s, was reluctant to move so fast on diplomatic relations, but it too was telling North Korea to open a dialogue

Marriage Lines

	South Korea	North Korea	West Germany	East Germany
Population 1989 m	42.4	22.4	62.0	16.4
GNP per head 1989 $	4,500	400	19,300	4,500
Labour force in agriculture % latest	20	35	5	11
Total trade 1989 $ billion	110	5*	610	28
% of total trade with socialist countries 1989	3	71*	5	56
Defence budget as % of GNP latest estimate	5	30	3	8
Passenger cars per '000 population latest	27	1†	450	220
T.V. sets per '000 population latest	170	10†	360	360

Sources: World Bank, FAO, IMF, IISI, PlanEcon, OECD, Commerzbank, UK Dept of Transport.
Economist estimates   * 1988   † rough estimate

with the South. Indeed the two Koreas inched closer to a summit of their own in 1990. The Prime Ministers from North and South met in South Korea in September, but as the Korean proverb has it, 'At a highly publicized party, there is often not much to eat'. These talks, as indeed did further rounds in October and December, resulted in no significant agreement, although clearly it was better that the two sides were finally talking at nearly the highest level. But on balance, the best bet is that this Palestine of East Asia will remain as dangerous as its namesake, at least until the old guard leadership in North Korea passes from the scene. Then watch for major reforms in this, the most important region in East Asia.

Reading

W. Barnds, *The Two Koreas in East Asian Affairs* (New York: New York University Press, 1976).

B. Bridges, *Korea and the West* (London: Chatham House Papers no. 33, 1986).

G. Henderson, *Korea* (Cambridge, Mass.: Harvard University Press, 1968).

D.S. Lewis (ed), *Korea: Enduring Division* (London: Longman, 1988).

G. Segal, *Rethinking the Pacific* (Oxford: Oxford University Press, 1990).

F. Weinstein and F. Kamiya, *The Security of Korea* (Boulder, Colorado: Westview Press, 1980).

Prospects for Hong Kong

Few international problems are as peculiar or as tragic as the fate of Hong Kong. In 1997, this wealthy bastion of the capitalist system, skyscrapers, prostitutes and all, will be handed over to the rulers of one of Communism's poorest states, China. Negotiators have framed a complex agreement in the hope that this accident of history has a profitable transition between economic and social systems. But few realists, and Hong Kong is a supremely realistic city, can have much confidence that, even with a great deal of goodwill, one country (China), can manage two systems (capitalist and communist) at the same time.

The unnatural future facing Hong Kong can only be under- *The fruits of* stood with reference to its turbulent past. In the Treaty of Nanjing, *gun-boat* 29 August 1842, Hong Kong island was ceded to Britain by China. *diplomacy* In the 1860 Treaty of Tianjin, Kowloon was also ceded and in 1898 the 365 square miles of New Territories were leased for 99 years, rent-free. China's new Communist rulers in 1949 did not recognize these 'unequal treaties'. But unlike other, similar cases of inequality (for example along the Sino–Soviet border) in the Hong Kong case, China felt it could get back more than just the leased territory (the lease is scheduled to expire in 1997). China controlled the water and electricity supply to Hong Kong and the neighbouring Portuguese colony of Macau. With the return of the New Territories alone, the position of Hong Kong island and Kowloon would become even more precarious.

Unfortunately for China, the nearly 6 million people of Hong *Reluctant* Kong, 98% of whom are Chinese, do not wish to become part of *Hong Kong* the mainland's political system. Roughly half the population has either already fled from China since 1949 or is comprized of the families of those who did. Since 1949, Hong Kong has evolved a free-wheeling capitalist economy. It cast off its past as merely an entrepôt for the China trade and looked outward for markets for its light industrial goods (22% of the GDP) and financial services (20% of GDP).

Since 1949, China has been remarkably tolerant of this capitalist *Hong Kong's* enclave on its fringe; and for good economic reasons. Until the *benefit for* mid-1980s China had not been a great trading nation (about 5% *China* of its GDP was dependent on foreign trade), it earned between a quarter and a third of its foreign currency in Hong Kong, a third of which comes from the sale of food and water to Hong Kong in return for foreign currency. In 1986, Hong Kong took a quarter of

China's exports but almost a half of that total was re-exported, suggesting Hong Kong was returning to the role of entrepôt.

The Hong Kong 'school'

China also benefits in less tangible ways from Hong Kong. Since Beijing's new opening to the West in 1978, Hong Kong has served as a 'school' for China to learn about foreign banking and international trade practices. By maintaining a good atmosphere and stability in Hong Kong, China helps encourage foreign investment in its own new Special Economic Zones, just across the frontier from Hong Kong. Overseas Chinese and Westerners can observe China at close quarters and gain confidence in doing business with the Communist régime. Also, by encouraging a positive, cooperative climate in Hong Kong, China sends clear signals to resistant Taiwan that reunion with the mainland need not be too painful.

Reaching an agreement

By and large China has helped maintain stability in Hong Kong. Except for a brief spell, when the radicalism of the Cultural Revolution spilled over into the colony in 1967, China has taken care to reassure investors. But as 1997 approached, investors were concerned about the shortness of property leases in the New Territories. Negotiations between China and Britain began in the early 1980s and got off on the wrong foot when a jingoistic British Prime Minister, fresh from the Falklands triumph, indicated she was not willing to transfer sovereignty of Hong Kong to China. But Britain soon capitulated over sovereignty and, on 19 December 1984, Prime Minister Thatcher signed an agreement for the transition of the entire territory to Chinese rule in 1997.

The terms

According to the agreement, China is to assume sovereignty on 1 July 1997 and Hong Kong will become a special administrative region of China under the Beijing government. This falls short of full autonomous status. Yet Hong Kong will be allowed to raise its own taxes and control revenue. Public order will be under Hong Kong control but defence and foreign affairs will be the responsibility of China.

Restricted democracy

A locally elected legislature will replace the presently non-elected legislative council. But local democracy will be severely circumscribed by a Chinese-appointed chief executive, who will in turn appoint chief civil servants. The current social and economic system will be retained for fifty years after 1997 but it may well not include such 'social' characteristics as prostitution and the secret societies that have flourished in the Hong Kong underworld. Hong Kong will issue its own travel documents but residents will be Chinese nationals. It will remain a free port with its own shipping and airlines. The Hong Kong dollar will remain convertible and the colony will remain a foreign exchange centre. Under the name 'Hong Kong, China' it will be able to sign economic and cultural agreements with other states and organizations. Finally, a joint liaison group has been set up to supervise and smooth the transfer to 1997.

Britain claims the agreement is the best it could have obtained. But there can be no escape from the conclusion that London capitulated to Chinese demands and the deal still transfers Hong Kong to Chinese control against the wishes of most of its people. There are serious doubts, too, about whether the agreement will work. Can a China that is still unsure of its own minor flirtations with capitalist methods, cope with the free-market capitalism of Hong Kong? China claims that under 'one country, two systems', such adjustment is possible. But that is a slogan, not a policy. Can China live with such a wide gap in per capita annual income between Hong Kong ($8,000) and the mainland ($400)? The creation of special economic zones just inside China may help blur the lines but the gaps between systems are still huge.

One country – two systems

Can China itself be counted upon to remain politically and economically stable through 1997 and the fifty years beyond? Past fluctuations in Chinese policy are scarcely reassuring, even if written off as a period of 'revolutionary adjustment'. The Beijing massacre in June 1989 suggests that the much sought-after stability is not at hand. Can a Chinese government used to slow decision-making adjust to the three-to-five-year business cycles of modern Hong Kong? Only, it seems, if it really does allow Hong Kong to get on with its business without interference. Can a Communist government, with a tradition of ministerial finger-poking into all aspects of the economy and society, avoid intervening to alleviate the harsher consequences of Hong Kong capitalism (not only gambling and prostitution, but also poverty and crime)? Clearly Hong Kong is in for some changes but it as yet unclear how much this will affect confidence in Hong Kong's economic future.

Counting on Chinese stability

The previous time China took over a major capitalist city – Shanghai in 1949 – promises of an orderly and peaceful transition to socialism were disregarded. Hong Kong is a different case, if only because China has changed and now has a strong economic stake of its own in stability. Yet, investors are bound to ask whether investment under these uncertain conditions is as sensible as, say, investment in Singapore, where the future of capitalism seems more secure. In the aftermath of the Beijing massacre, confidence in Hong Kong took a bad knock. The Basic Law – a *de facto* constitution for Hong Kong – was published by China in 1990 and seemed to have harsher than expected conditions about those who 'subvert' the Communist system on the mainland from Hong Kong.

The Shanghai model

The sapping of confidence led to an increase in the number of emigrants from Hong Kong, said to be 50,000 in 1989 and 60,000 in 1990. Britain designed a package that included the promise of

Emigration

the right of abode in the UK for some 200,000 people in the hope that key residents would stay in the colony and not flee in search of a foreign passport. Although the vast majority of the refugees from Communism are stuck in Hong Kong, the rich and ambitious middle class are buying passports and homes abroad, mostly in Canada, Australia and the United States. The creation of this 'goodbye culture' is only the start of what will be this century's best qualified and talented flow of refugees – yacht people rather than boat people.

Reading

J. Morris, *Xianggiang* (London: Penguin, 1989).
F. Patrikeeff, *Mouldering Pearl* (London: George Philips 1989).
K. Rafferty, *City on the Rocks* (London: Viking, 1989).
G. Segal (ed), *Chinese Politics and Foreign Policy Reform* (London: Kegan Paul International, 1990).
D. Wilson, *Hong Kong, Hong Kong* (London: Collins, 1990).

Taiwan and other Disputed Islands

After years of making the headlines for its wars, in the past decade East Asia has become such an economic success story that the tendency is to overlook the still simmering problems that might lead to war. The oldest problem is the dispute over the status of one of the most successful of the Newly Industrialized Countries, Taiwan, but nearby a number of other territorial problems remain unresolved.

The island of Taiwan lies 145 kilometres off the coast of mainland China. Of Taiwan's 19 million people, less than 20% are recent arrivals (since 1949) from the mainland and barely 300,000 are aboriginal. The original tribes of Malay origin were swamped by massive settlement of Chinese from the mainland in the 14th century. A brief spell of Dutch and Spanish settlement in the 17th century was ended by Chinese conquest in 1661. Taiwan remained under Chinese imperial rule until 1895, when it was ceded to Japan. More than two hundred years of heavy Chinese immigration left its stamp on the island, which has had a Chinese majority since 1800.

China grabs control

With Japan's defeat in 1945, Taiwan returned to mainland control. But in early 1949 the remnants of the United States-supported Chinese régime of Chiang Kai-shek, defeated by the Communists in the civil war, retreated to Taiwan. The population in 1950 increased from 6.8 million to 7.5 million, not including the 600,000 military personnel. Chiang had dreams of using Taiwan as a base for recapturing the mainland. His parliament even included 'representatives' of mainland provinces. But with massive American military and economic aid, Taiwan began to look away from China for survival. Economic reforms were pursued on Taiwan, many of which, if they had been introduced earlier on the mainland, might have kept Chiang from having to flee in the first place.

Chiang escapes to Taiwan

Taiwan's conflict with the mainland flared into disputes over offshore islands such as Quemoy and Matsu in 1954–5, 1958, and 1962. The United States used its fleet and even threatened the use of its nuclear weapons, not only to restrain China from seizing Taiwan but also to restrain Chiang from attacking the mainland. Sporadic and idiosyncratic shelling of Chinese and Taiwanese outposts, sometimes only on even days, continued into the 1970s. But, more often than not, the shells contained propaganda leaflets rather than explosives. The United States, in part because of domestic pressure from the anti-Communist 'Taiwan lobby' at home,

Crises over offshore islands

pursued a 'two-China' policy, recognizing the Taiwan régime as the legitimate voice of the Chinese people.

The US discovers China   In 1971, Washington opened a secret dialogue with the Communists in an attempt to bring mainland China into the mainstream of world politics, and in part to exploit China's anti-Soviet inclinations. In October 1971, Taiwan was ousted from the United Nations and China took its place as one of the permanent members of the UN Security Council. In 1972, President Nixon visited China and, in the Shanghai communiqué released during the visit, recognized that there was only one China. In January 1979 America and China normalized relations; the two countries exchanged ambassadors and the United States promised gradually to reduce arms sales to Taiwan. The United States withdrew its ambassador from Taiwan but put in its place a non-governmental mission (called the American Institute) which carried out almost all normal ambassadorial functions and had full diplomatic privileges. The United States did terminate its 1954 mutual defence pact with Taiwan and agreed to withdraw all military personnel in four months. By 1984 only twenty-three states still recognized Taiwan.

The booming economy   Although Taiwan was losing the diplomatic battle with China, its economic ties with the outside world continued to expand. With a booming economy based on trade, it far out-distanced the mainland as a trading nation, ranking as the United States' fourth-largest trading partner. Taiwan also began to groom a younger generation of leaders (Chiang died in 1975) and gave a greater voice to those Chinese Taiwanese who had settled on the island before 1949.

China comes a' courting   China became concerned that time was not on its side and its diplomatic victories were not necessarily bringing Taiwan any closer to unification with the mainland. In October 1981, Beijing proposed that Taiwan become a special administrative region of China with a high degree of autonomy, including its own armed forces and independent economic and social status. In 1984, after China's deal with Britain over Hong Kong, Beijing argued that the concept of 'one country, two systems' was applicable to Taiwan as well.

Hong Kong factor   Taiwan anxiously watched the Hong Kong negotiations. Hong Kong was Taiwan's third largest export market and a trans-shipment point for hidden trade with the mainland. But so long as the economic gap between the mainland and Taiwan continued to widen, as it has been doing, the notion of 'one country, two systems' held little attraction to Taiwan. Taipei was also encouraged by the advent of the Reagan administration which had pursued Sino–American détente less single-mindedly than previous administrations.

Offshore reefs   Unfortunately for Taiwan, the Reagan administration did agree, in August 1982, to reduce its arms sales to Taipei and in May 1984 the President visited China. Taiwan then showed a mite more flexibility by attending the 1984 Olympics as 'China, Taipei'. The old points of dispute, such as the offshore islands, no longer loomed large. China ceased shelling Quemoy and Matsu on 1 January 1979. But with the decline in military tension and the rise in economic cooperation, it remained unclear whether Taiwan would be prepared to be integrated with the mainland or was in fact on its way to proper independence.

However, disputes sharpened over the Senkaku (Diaoyu) islands between Taiwan and Japan. Although claimed by both Taiwan and China, Japan obtained them under the terms of a 1971 treaty with the United States. In August 1978 China agreed to set aside the issue for the time being but disputes resurfaced from time to time. *Senkaku or Diaoyutai*

In October 1990, following reports that Japan would officially recognize a lighthouse erected in 1978 by Japanese nationalists, unofficial Taiwanese groups (including journalists) tried to land on the island to claim Chinese sovereignty. Although the Japanese repelled the visitors and the issue died down, it was notable that China and Taiwan were on the same side of a dispute, both having vital trading relations with Japan. Conflict may also flare again if offshore oil reserves are found and the expanding Chinese navy is used to pursue China's territorial claims as it was against Vietnam in the dispute over the Paracels in 1974.

In March 1988, when the Soviet Union was improving relations with China and therefore unwilling to protect Vietnam from China, Beijing sent its forces into the more southern part of the South China Sea to take some of the Spratly islands from Vietnam. While China was developing its longer-range naval forces, Taiwan sat on its own share of the Spratly islands and watched where China would strike next. Skirmishes between unloved Vietnam and China continued in 1989–90, but the Southeast Asian states such as Malaysia and the Philippines began to feel that their islands in the region were to be next on China's list. *Spratlys in contention*

China claims the entire South China Sea as its own and with the retreat of the Superpowers from the region, there are few powers able to stop China from eventually taking what it wants. Both Japan and India have expressed increasing interest in the region and both are worried about China's apparent determination to acquire an aircraft carrier in order to pursue its claims. A regional arms race, and a complex one at that, appears increasingly likely as the Superpower overlay is lifted. As in Europe, there are all kinds of nasty conflicts just waiting to see the light of day.

One of the oldest territorial dispute in the region results from the Soviet occupation of four islands (one is an island group) in *Contending for the Kuriles* the Kurile chain which Japan refers to as its Northern Territories. Soviet occupation began after the Second World War but in 1956, in an aborted deal, Moscow promised to return the southernmost island group (the Habomais) and Shikotan island. It was not until the late 1980s that the two sides resumed formal talks on the territorial issue, but the matter is now complicated by whether the government of the Soviet Union or Russia is in charge of the islands.

The elusive prize   But Taiwan itself is the main Chinese prize. Periodic defections of individuals to one or the other side merely indicate that the issue has not died. In April 1985, China's party leader, Hu Yaobang, reminded Taiwan that China had still not renounced the use of force to reunify Taiwan. He suggested that a declaration of independence by Taiwan (and ironically an abandonment of Taiwan's claim to speak for the entire mainland) might well trigger a Chinese response in aid of 'patriotic' forces in Taiwan. For the time being China lacked the military power to seize Taiwan but its navy is the fastest growing service of its armed forces. The United States would be faced with a tough choice if an independent Taiwan requested recognition. In the meantime, China seems prepared to hope that a successful transition to Chinese sovereignty in Hong Kong will ease Taiwanese fears. But Taiwan is economically more important than Hong Kong and has the potential (if nuclear armed) to deter most threats and remain independent. The China–Taiwan saga is far from over.

Reading

Chi-kin Lo, *China's Policy Towards Territorial Disputes* (London: Routledge, 1988).

S. Long, *Taiwan* (London: Macmillan, 1991).

J. Pollack, *Strategic Cooperation* (Santa Monica: Rand, 1984).

G. Segal, *Rethinking the Pacific* (Oxford: Oxford University Press, 1990).

G. Segal (ed), *Political and Economic Encyclopaedia of the Pacific* (London: Longman, 1989).

M. Yahuda, *China's Foreign Policy after Mao* (London: Macmillan, 1983).

Indochina and the Great Powers

The most sustained and severe conflicts since 1945 have taken place in some of the poorest parts of Southeast Asia. The prize can hardly be worth the millions of deaths and the dangers of a wider, great power confrontation. The conflicts have undergone a bewildering number of changes but at every stage has drawn the attention of local and outside powers. In recent years the hostilities have been confined to more controlled skirmishes but this unhappy part of the globe is still far from at peace.

Cambodia, Laos and Vietnam had all been independent kingdoms until the second half of the 19th century when they fell under French colonial rule. But during the Japanese occupation (1940–5) national independence movements developed in all three countries. In Vietnam the movement was led by a dynamic Communist, Ho Chi Minh. Phase one of the modern war in Southeast Asia was underway in earnest. With the return of French colonial rule in 1945, the Soviet Union and China both supported rebel movements in Vietnam and Laos. In accordance with the Geneva agreement of 1954, France agreed to pull out, Vietnam was temporarily divided into North and South, and Cambodia's independence was recognized. *France quits Indo-China*

As the Sino–Soviet split intensified, Communism's two great powers competed in their support for revolutionary movements. At the same time, the United States took up the French 'responsibilities' in Southeast Asia by supporting an independent South Vietnam. In the American view, unless support were lent to pro-Western forces in Southeast Asia, the states of the area would fall to the Communists like a row of tottering dominoes. Phase two (the American phase) of Southeast Asian conflict had begun. Eventually the United States sent more than 500,000 troops to fight Soviet- and Chinese-aided North Vietnamese infiltrators and South Vietnamese Communists. The war spilled over into Laos and Cambodia as the Communists used both countries for sanctuary and supply routes, which in turn drew United States air strikes and incursions. The Communists' Tet offensive in 1968 convinced many already sceptical Americans that the war was not being won and the United States began a protracted and painful withdrawal. *The American phase*

In March 1970 the nominally independent ruler of Cambodia, Prince Sihanouk, was ousted by a pro-American military coup. Sihanouk joined forces with the Communist Khmer Rouge guerrillas. But by far the most important strategic shift was the Ameri- *The dominoes fall* can rapprochement with China and the East–West détente in the early 1970s. The United States' aim was to sever the local Communists in South Vietnam from their outside support, while American troops pulled out. However, the local parties, backed by military support from North Vietnam, were strong enough to establish, by April 1975, Communist régimes in Vietnam, Laos and Cambodia. Three dominoes had fallen but, unfortunately for the much trampled people of the area, the Communist triumph did not mean the end of war.

The Cambodian genocide   The régimes in Vietnam and Laos were more closely aligned with the Soviet Union, which had provided the bulk of the aid during the Vietnam War. But the Khmer Rouge, who feared traditional Vietnamese domination, were more closely aligned with China. Cambodia was renamed Kampuchea in June 1976, and the Khmer Rouge, under the leadership of Pol Pot, began a brutal course of land and thought reform. Several million Cambodians died in the upheavals, in what ranks as the most obscene case of genocide since Hitler's concentration camps.

The inter-communist phase   Pol Pot also led Cambodia into border skirmishes with Vietnam in pursuit of ancient territorial rivalries. Phase three of modern Southeast Asian conflict broke out into the open. China was unable or unwilling to halt Pol Pot's prodding of Vietnam and on 25 December 1978 Vietnam invaded Cambodia and installed a puppet régime under Heng Samrin on 11 January 1979. The new Cambodian régime only obtained limited recognition (mainly from the Soviet bloc) but the war established Vietnam as the regional military powerhouse.

Rivalries and boat people   China not only saw its Cambodian ally trounced but it also looked on Vietnam as a challenge to China's dominance in the region and as a tool in the Soviet strategy of encirclement of China. After Vietnam began a collectivization scheme in March 1976, hundreds of thousands of ethnic-Chinese fled, many by sea as 'boat people'. In May 1978 China cancelled its aid projects in Vietnam and border clashes along their 1,200 kilometre frontier were reported. Talks on a wide range of matters, which began in October 1977, broke down in the summer of 1978. In June, Vietnam joined CMEA and on 3 November signed a friendship treaty with the Soviet Union.

Teaching Vietnam a lesson   The Chinese were clearly running out of patience with Vietnam and, while the Vietnamese were trouncing Pol Pot, agreed to normalize relations with the United States in January 1979. An 'educational' foreign policy was embarked upon, to 'teach Vietnam a lesson' that it could not use military force at will in what China saw as its sphere of influence. Deng Xiaoping visited the United States in January 1979 and made clear his intention to strike at Vietnam. On 17 February Chinese troops attacked Vietnam but their advance soon became bogged down. On 5 March Beijing announced it would withdraw (after some 20,000 Chinese had been killed) and all Chinese troops had left Vietnamese territory by 16 March. In fact, it was China that was 'taught a lesson'.

Sino-Vietnamese talks opened on 18 April 1978, but no progress was made. Border incidents continued after 1979, sometimes reportedly producing casualties in the hundreds. But China's main purpose in keeping up the military pressure at the border was to tie down Vietnamese forces in the North and force Vietnam to spend increasing resources on its armies in the hope that it would be forced to withdraw from Cambodia. But Vietnam, bolstered by Soviet aid, showed no signs of caving in to Chinese pressure. The Soviet Union found Vietnam to be a costly economic burden but, in exchange, acquired basing rights at Da Nang and Cam Ran bay. Yet in late 1986 the Soviet Union, anxious for détente with China and better relations with ASEAN states, helped to engineer a change in Vietnam's leadership and opened the door for political reform and détente. *Vietnam holds firm*

As reforms developed in Soviet foreign and domestic policy, the pressure grew for Vietnam to improve relations with China and withdraw from Cambodia. But apart from the traditional problems of national rivalries between China and Vietnam, there was also the problem that the Cambodian parties did not want to be shoved into a compromise. On 22 June 1982 the disparate groups fighting the Vietnamese-backed régime in Cambodia formed a notionally united government-in-exile, including the Khmer Rouge, with Prince Sihanouk as President and former Premier Son Sann as Prime Minister. The government-in-exile held the Cambodian seat at the UN, so Vietnam and the Phnom Penh régime were not keen on UN involvement in a settlement. Vietnam refused to withdraw from Cambodia as long as its favoured government was not stable. But military successes in 1985, coupled with pressure to quit from the Soviet Union, led Vietnam to withdraw all but some advisers by September 1989. *Great power pressures*

Indeed Vietnam seemed increasingly anxious for a deal with China and negotiations in 1989–90 were at an increasingly higher level. As the Superpower Cold War ended, Moscow and Washington worked more closely on the Cambodian problem and on 28 August 1990 a deal was struck between the UN Security Council's five permanent members. At the heart of the plan was the creation of a Supreme National Council for Cambodia (6 from the Phnom Penh government and 6 from the resistance) which would take Cambodia's UN seat. The Council would in turn hand over the administration of Cambodia to the UN which would supervise a cease-fire and arrange free elections. *Slow-moving détente*

The fighting   But the fighting has not ended. The local parties still dither
continues   over membership of the Council, the size of the UN administration,
and the method of election. With distractions in the Gulf conflict,
the great powers had more pressing matters on their mind. The
cynics suggested that so long as the verdict of the battlefield was
inconclusive, and some parties still saw some purpose in fighting
on with support from willing great powers, the combat would
continue. China and Vietnam might be able to settle the matter
between themselves, but both had ageing leaders uncertain about
the path of their domestic policies. Meanwhile, the killing continued in Cambodia.

Reading

N. Chanda, *Brother Enemy* (New York: Harcourt Brace Jovanovich,
    1986).
J. Harrison, *The Endless War* (New York: Free Press, 1982).
S. Karnow, *Vietnam* (New York: Viking, 1983).
G. Segal, *Rethinking the Pacific* (Oxford: Oxford University Press,
    1990).
M. Vickery, *Kampuchea* (London: Pinter, 1986).
D. Wurfel and B. Burton (eds), *The Political Economy of Foreign
    Policy in Southeast Asia* (London: Macmillan, 1990).

Bases and Other Grand Strategies

In the good old days of Superpower rivalry, the United States and the Soviet Union sought bases around the world and then manoeuvred in order to keep open access to their further reaches of empire. In East Asia the United States had bases in the Philippines and the Soviet Union reached down the coast from its home ports to Vietnam. Both Superpowers sought access around to the Indian Ocean. Local powers were ambivalent about all the attention. On the one hand, they had an excuse for not settling their own problems and could play off one Superpower against the other in order to get more aid. But on the other hand, they often lost control of their own destiny and failed to undertake necessary domestic reforms.

The United States seized the Spanish colony of the Philippines in 1898. In 1953 the United States granted the Philippines internal self-government and, after the Japanese occupation in the Second World War, full independence in 1946. Its population of 50 million is 90% Christian and 7% Muslim. It has since been ruled by a succession of Presidents who served the interests of a small land-owning class and, for the most part, the United States. Land reform was consistently blocked. *Coming to the Philippines*

In November 1965 President Marcos was elected, and stimulated rapid economic growth. But by 1969, growth stalled and domestic unrest began to threaten stability. Guerrilla activity in the North was led by the New People's Army (the armed wing of the outlawed Communist party), and in the South by a Muslim separatist group, the Moro National Liberation Front. In September 1972, before completing the maximum two terms of office, Marcos declared martial law. A 'referendum' confirmed Marcos in power, while the United States looked on uneasily. *Marcos' successes*

As the United States withdrew from Vietnam in the 1970s, offshore bases such as those in the Philippines assumed far greater strategic importance. The air and naval bases at Clark field and Subic bay are America's largest outside the United States. But Marcos had no need of direct American military support and seemed to have the guerrillas under control. Negotiations with the MNLF in December 1976 produced a ceasefire, after Marcos agreed to set up an autonomous region for the Muslims. But a referendum in the provinces concerned, rejected the plan and, although the civil war continued, the MNLF ceased to be a threat to the régime. *US bases and guerrillas*

193

The NPA
challenge

The real challenge came from the Communist NPA. According to a United States study, this 20,000 strong Marxist movement controlled 20% of the villages and its guerrilla activities led to the death of some 3,000 people in 1984 alone. The armed forces, numbering 200,000, were unable to get the upper hand in the war against the guerrillas in the north and east of Mindanao. But the United States was genuinely divided on the best response to the NPA threat. Most observers agreed that real economic reform would break its back but some in the United States saw the NPA as Philippine Sandinistas and concluded that Washington should bolster the Marcos régime.

The other Shah

But the challenge to Marcos that really caught American attention was the political one in Manila. In August 1983, opposition leader Benigno Aquino was shot dead on his return from exile in the United States. The United States began to distance itself from the Marcos régime. It feared being stuck with 'another Shah' – a deposed ruler, as in Iran, upon whom the United States had built its policies for regional order. Washington seemed to settle for the soft option – signing an agreement that extended its basing rights in the Philippines until 1991, in exchange for political and economic aid of $900 million. It was estimated that a relocation of the bases would cost $8 billion.

Crony
capitalism

By now Marcos certainly needed all the help he could get. The war with the NPA had undermined economic confidence and reduced the flow of investment. The high growth rates of the 1970s had been unequally distributed, leaving the Philippines with the greatest inequality of wealth of any Asian state. Its average calorific intake per person was also the lowest in Asia. The collapse of world sugar prices and the tough policies demanded by the IMF in exchange for new loans to prop up the economy put strong pressure on Marcos to reform. But his 'crony capitalism' seemed corrupt enough to be beyond change.

Washington's
choices

The Reagan administration was keen to maintain its bases. The Soviet Pacific fleet was growing fast and was now operating out of bases, across from the Philippines, in Vietnam. The question was whether to support the 'safer' opponents of Marcos, in the hope of maintaining a more stable friendly régime, or to stick with Marcos and 'ride out the storm'. Similar debates in the United States, before the Shah of Iran fell, had landed Washington with a hostile Muslim fundamentalist régime. Therefore, with some reluctance, the United States chivied Marcos into calling an early Presidential election in February 1986. Marcos counted on a divided opposition and his usual skills in rigging the vote. But, at the prodding of the Catholic Church, the opposition coalesced behind Aquino's widow, Corazon.

International observers and the Philippine Church monitored the election and declared the predictable Marcos victory to be a fraud. Popular discontent brought the country to a standstill and when leading members of the armed forces and the Marcos cabinet defected, the masses filled the streets and convinced Marcos that he could not use force to crush his opponents. The United States then gave Marcos that extra shove into retirement (in the United States) and Corazon Aquino took power on 25 February 1986. *People's power triumphs*

The euphoria that swept the Philippines soon gave way to a realization that at best they were likely to get mild reform. Corazon Aquino was no revolutionary and her fragile coalition was challenged by her ambitious defence minister Enrile on the Right, and the NPA rebels on the Left. While the American government clearly wished Aquino to prosper, there were vultures in the Philippines waiting for her to stumble. International bankers looked favourably on Aquino's desire to obtain easier terms for the foreign debt of more than $27 billion (of which 40% was owed to American banks). But by early 1987, and despite an overwhelming vote in favour of a new constitution, a ceasefire with the NPA broke down. A series of coup attempts followed with one in 1989 only put down with the assistance of American aircraft in the Philippines. The Aquino government was in trouble. *The formidable task ahead*

The usual trick for leaders of the Philippines is to ask the Americans for more money for their bases, and talks in 1990 about the future of the bases pursued just this line. But in the new era of Superpower détente, the United States Congress was not prepared to stump up more money and the bases were far less useful than before. The idea of relocating the American facilities to Guam was not nearly as absurd as once thought. Singapore offered to host other 'facilities' and talks were underway to see how American forces could be spread out around the region. Cuts in American deployments were announced and the thought of losing the Philippines bases was now neither as unbelievable nor as much of a nightmare for American strategic planners. *Base talks*

For much of the late 1980s the Soviet Union had offered to trade a retreat from bases in Vietnam for an American withdrawal from the Philippines. The deal was never sensible, largely because despite all the American scaremongering, the bases in Vietnam were always far less important. But by 1990 the Soviet Union announced it would be leaving its bases anyway as it concentrated on its home ports in the Northwest Pacific. Out-of-home-area operations by the Soviet navy were down by 30% and falling and some eighty ships have recently been retired from this, the largest of the Soviet fleets. *Russian retreat*

The implications for the region were far from all rosy. Vietnam and the Philippines could no longer drag much more aid out of their patrons. Local states were now more vulnerable to the actions of China, or even of Japan and India, in the South China Sea for example. Some even suggested the age of Superpower involvement was a far more comfortable time, for at least it stopped the more restless local states from sorting out long-standing grievance by more violent means.

Reading

R. Bonner, *Waltzing with a Dictator* (London: Macmillan, 1987).

R. Broad, *Unequal Alliances* (Berkeley: University of California Press, 1988).

F. Greene, *The Philippine Bases* (New York: Council on Foreign Relations, 1988).

S. Karnow, *In Our Image* (New York: Random House, 1989).

G. Segal, *Rethinking the Pacific* (Oxford: Oxford University Press, 1990).

Association of South-East Asian Nations

ASEAN, like most loose associations, needs a good enemy in order to hang together. Although it has survived radical changes of direction and endured military confrontations within the organization, the threat of peace in Indochina looks likely to cause the biggest crisis that ASEAN has yet seen.

An important source of Southeast Asian disunity is the unequal impact of external powers. Before 1939 Thailand was the only independent Southeast Asian state. The rest suffered under various types of colonial rule. But with the breakdown of that colonial rule and the coming of the East–West Cold War to Asia, Thailand, the Philippines, Australia, Britain, France, New Zealand, Pakistan and the United States agreed to form the Southeast Asian Treaty Organization (SEATO). It was designed to provide for mutual defence or concerted action if Cambodia, Laos or South Vietnam were attacked. Some SEATO members did fight alongside the United States in the Vietnam War but the military victory of the Communists in Vietnam, Laos and Cambodia in 1975 spelt the death of the organization.

The impact of outsiders

The absence of any strong sense of regional identity in Southeast Asia is largely the result of long-standing cultural differences between the various peoples. In recent decades, this has been exacerbated by the deep divide between Communist and non-Communist régimes. In July 1961, the Philippines, Thailand and Malaysia formed the Association of Southeast Asia (ASA) in order to promote economic and social cooperation. But even between these non-Communist régimes there were deep differences. The Philippines and Malaysia fell out over the former's claim, in June 1962, to Sabah province in North Borneo, which joined the Malaysian federation in September 1963. Also in 1963, oil-rich Brunei decided not to join the federation and relations with Malaysia were strained until the early 1970s. Malaysia and Singapore fell out over communal and economic policies in the federation, and in 1965 Singapore pulled out.

Divided by interests

The idea of ASA was revitalized by Thai mediation in a dispute between Indonesia and Malaysia in 1966 and by the fall of the radical Indonesian leader Sukarno in 1967. On 8 August 1967, Indonesia, Malaysia, Singapore, the Philippines, and Thailand met in Bangkok to form ASEAN (Brunei joined in 1984 and Papua New Guinea is an observer). This non-military organization clearly had a pro-Western tilt, as both the Philippines and Thailand retained

Forming ASEAN

197

their close military ties to the United States. ASEAN was essentially
an organization intended to promote economic and social growth
in states outside the war zone in Cambodia, Laos and Vietnam.
But until that war ended, ASEAN was little more than a name,
holding its first summit only in February 1976 in Bali. In the
meantime, its member states bickered among themselves, for
example over Sabah.

Seeing different
threats

With the withdrawal of most United States forces from the
Asian mainland in the 1970s, some ASEAN states thought that the
organization ought to concern itself more with defence issues.
However, the 1971 ASEAN proposal of a 'zone of peace' remained
merely rhetoric, as the states could not agree on how to react to
the coming Communist victories in Southeast Asia. Some, such
as Thailand, emphasized the Soviet threat, while others, such as
Indonesia, emphasized the dangers of Chinese power. In the end,
ASEAN tacitly relied on the counter-balancing powers of China,
the United States, the Soviet Union and Vietnam to ensure their
independence.

Economic co-
operation

With security taken care of in other ways, ASEAN states turned
their attention to economic issues, especially those raised by
Japan's rapid economic growth. The economies of most member
states were prospering because of the new markets in Japan and
the impact of Japanese investment. Taking the European community as the example, Singapore led the way in urging greater
economic cooperation. Trade talks in the 1970s with the United
States, Japan and the EC were intended to help cement these
relations. The sudden oil price rises in the 1970s drove ASEAN
further towards economic cooperation, although some of its members were oil exporters and thus had different economic interests
than the oil importers. However, ASEAN cooperation, was a long
way from that of the EC.

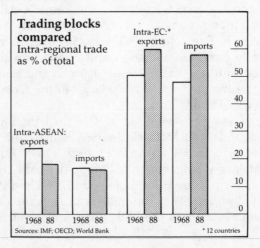

Trading blocks compared
Intra-regional trade as % of total

Intra-EC:* exports   imports

Intra-ASEAN: exports   imports

1968 88   1968 88   1968 88   1968 88
Sources: IMF; OECD; World Bank   * 12 countries

Among ASEAN's achievements was an agreement with Japan *Gradual*
(which accounts for 22% of ASEAN trade) on development aid for *progress*
specific large-scale projects and a February 1977 agreement on
preferential trading and industrial cooperation. But in a July 1985
meeting to discuss further coordination of policy all that could be
agreed was a common recognition of domestic driving licences
and cooperation on nature conservation. Further integration was
likely to be even slower and, by 1985 inter-ASEAN trade remained
only 20% of the group's total trade (inter-EC trade is 56%). Singapore is the major beneficiary of inter-ASEAN trade and is a strong
supporter of a more integrated organization. ASEAN is Japan's
second-largest trading partner, the world's second-largest grouping of market economies and has a population of 280 million
(equal to that of Latin America) but still seems incapable of serious
cooperation.

The organization's most immediate problem is that it has few *The Vietnam*
clear objectives in a region beset with intricate problems. The flood *problem*
of refugees to ASEAN states from Vietnam, the 1978 Vietnamese
invasion of Cambodia and the 1979 Sino–Vietnamese War all confronted it with tough choices. In keeping with its pro-Western
orientation and its desire to concentrate on economic growth in a
peaceful environment, ASEAN chose the path of least resistance
and decided to lie low. When ASEAN tried to be more dynamic in
organizing a Vietnamese withdrawal from Cambodia, Indonesia,
Malaysia and Thailand went their own ways at various times. In
1985 and again in 1987 ASEAN was helpful in arranging talks but
in the end it was Soviet pressure on Vietnam that had the greatest
impact there.

In another sense, it is an achievement merely to keep an organ- *Keeping*
ization like ASEAN together. When the organization cannot even *ASEAN*
hold a summit in one country (the Philippines) because another *together*
(Malaysia) is unhappy about just being there, ASEAN obviously has
deep rifts. That it even managed to hold a summit in the Philippines in 1987 at all was touted as a great achievement. An organization that supports the idea of a zone of peace and a nuclear free
zone when one of its members, the Philippines, is host to two
vital American military bases, suggests hypocrisy. But the trend
towards integration and cooperation, however slow, is evident.
An end to serious military conflict in the area might help ASEAN
unite but it will not solve all its deep-rooted problems and may
well make its members less worried about disagreeing in public.
However, by comparison with other regional groupings such as
the OAU in Africa and the OAS in the Americas, ASEAN, which
combines reasonably similar political and economic systems,
stands a better chance of success.

Reading

A. Broinowski, *ASEAN: Into the 1990s* (London: Macmillan, 1990).

D. Crow, *The ASEAN States* (New York: Praeger, 1983).

A. Jorgensen-Dahl, *Regional Organization and Order in South-East Asia* (London: Macmillan, 1982).

M. Leifer, *ASEAN and the Security of Southeast Asia* (London: Routledge, 1989).

G. Segal, *Rethinking the Pacific* (Oxford: Oxford University Press, 1990).

D. Wurfel and B. Burton (eds), *The Political Economy of Foreign Policy in Southeast Asia* (London: Macmillan, 1990).

Paradise in the South Pacific

The Pacific is a travel agent's dream and a strategist's nightmare. Dotted across the Pacific are a number of islands of varying size and importance. But with the attention of the world beginning to turn towards the Pacific as the growth area of the 21st century, the fate of these islands may be of increasing strategic concern. Undoubtedly, there is an expanse of water to be muddied by great and small powers alike.

The islands fall into three broad groups; the Melanesian people *Island groups* occupy the larger islands in the Southwest Pacific, the Polynesians live on islands from Hawaii to Easter Island in the Southeast and to New Zealand in the Southwest; and Micronesia lies to the north and west of Melanesia, in the Central and Western Pacific. Almost all the islands have been given independence (mostly by Britain and France) except for some 'accidents of geography'. Britain still controls the Pitcairn Islands (4.5 square miles of territory with a population of fifty-nine, using New Zealand currency). France still holds Wallis and Futuna and the United States has incorporated Hawaii as one of the fifty American states. New Zealand controls the internally self-governing islands of Tokelau, Niue and the Cook Islands. Australia holds Norfolk Island, France holds French Polynesia and New Caledonia, and the United States holds the Caroline, Marshall and North Mariana islands, Guam and American Samoa, which all have similar self-governing status.

In 1980 the British–French condominium of New Hebrides *Revolt in* attained independence as Vanuatu. Its elected government was *Vanuatu* headed by English-speaking Melanesians. French-speakers on part of the group, Espiritu Santo Island, attempted to secede but Vanuatu called in troops from Papua New Guinea to suppress the revolt. It is interesting that Papua New Guinea appears as a major power to most of its neighbours to the east, but cannot defend its own frontier with far larger Indonesia to the west.

The Indonesian territory bordering Papua New Guinea, Irian *Unrest in Irian* Jaya, is not naturally a part of Indonesia (its people are Melanesian) *Jaya* but the United Nations refused the territory independence in 1963 and an opposition movement continues to operate. Indonesia has moved 300,000 Javanese into the area to change the population balance and has given them the best land. Some 10,000 Melanesians have fled to under-populated Papua New Guinea, carrying with them stories of atrocities. In Fiji in 1987, a coup by Melanesians was undertaken because the Indians imported by Britain in

201

colonial days won a democratic election. The problems of racism were clearly not confined to black–white conflict.

Trouble in Tahiti

The most recent and serious violence has taken place in several of France's self-governing territories. French Polynesia, an overseas territory of France (4,200 square kilometres), has a population of some 170,000 on 6 island groups. The French have carried out nuclear tests on the nearby Mururoa atoll since 1966. When testing was above-ground, there was widespread concern about the effects of fall-out. With more recent attempts by states of the region, especially New Zealand, to have the area designated a nuclear free zone, criticism of France for testing weapons in the Pacific that it is unwilling to test at home, has increased.

New Caledonia divided

France also has a problem with its Melanesian territory of New Caledonia (19,103 sq kilometres with a population of 150,000). It is divided between 43% Melanesians (Kanaks), 37% Europeans (many hard-bitten exiles from former French colonial struggles), 12% Wallisians and Tahitians, and 8% assorted other Asians. In 1974 there were violent demonstrations against France and a general strike to gain local control of nickel mines was defeated. The territory is the world's third largest producer of nickel but the market collapsed in 1973. The Kanaks increasingly demanded independence but the conservative governing groups refused. France pressed for a gradual move to independence but the Kanaks were outnumbered in their own land.

Kanak complaints

In December 1981 France formulated a new plan for greater equality and decided to rule by decree so as to help the Kanaks get organized. The Kanak Front Independiste boycotted the new assembly, claiming that France had failed to set a timetable for independence. France attempted to mollify the Melanesians by having the franchise extended only to Kanaks and those with at least one parent born in the territory. Kanak and French settler-militants murdered each other while France and its 6,000 troops procrastinated. In the gerrymandered elections in September 1985 Kanaks won control of three of the four regions, including the vast majority of the mineral and agricultural land. But anti-independence parties polled nearly twice as many votes and had a twelve-seat majority in the new forty-six-seat territorial congress. But a referendum in September 1987, boycotted by the Kanaks, voted by 98% (on a 59% turnout) to remain part of France.

The South Pacific Forum

Because of the diversity of the states in the Pacific, the huge distances and sparse population (the largest island, Fiji, has 650,000 people), attempts at forming an effective regional political organization have been frustrated. In 1971 most of the islands and Australia and New Zealand combined to form the South Pacific Forum. The SPF helped arrange a trade agreement, Sparteca, in January 1981 but Australia and New Zealand have mostly ignored their island neighbours and even refused to open their markets to the tiny economies of the scattered islands. The SPF has fourteen members and mainly concentrates on promoting tourism and developing peripheral aspects of trade. Yet the Pacific/Oceania states may have the potential for future growth. Even tiny islands can control large areas of sea with mineral and fishing rights. For example, in June 1984, the Solomon islands seized a United States-owned ship for violating its claimed 200 miles sea limit.

In the late 1980s the new problem was with drift-net fishing, especially by Japan, Taiwan and South Korea, which was rapidly depleting fish stocks. The tiny and poor island states were unable to enforce a ban, even if one could have been agreed.

The intensity and importance of such disputes does seem to be growing, as the Law of the Sea gains adherents and the region increases in strategic and economic importance. In 1984, the United States found itself embroiled in a squabble with its ANZUS allies (New Zealand and Australia) over New Zealand's decision not to allow nuclear-armed American ships in its waters. The United States contended that ANZUS needed to remain a nuclear alliance in face of the growing Soviet threat in the Pacific. New Zealand countered that there was no threat in the area that required nuclear weapons for deterrence. *Squabbling over ANZUS*

Since 1982 the tiny, but strategically-located, American-administered island of Palau (in the West Pacific north of Indonesia, with a population of 12,000) held up an agreement for a 'compact of free association' because the United States wanted to base nuclear materials on Palau. In the mid-1980s the United States had clearly begun to pay far more attention to the strategic importance of its Micronesian holdings, both as bases for use against the Soviet Union and for testing of strategic missiles (e.g. on Kwajalein). But since the Soviet Union has not been terribly concerned with Pacific/Oceania except for its potential as a partner in processing fish and the Cold War rationale for military deployment has been undermined, the Pacific may yet live up to its name. *Even Palau counts*

Reading

G. Naldi, 'Self determination in the South Pacific', *The World Today*, August 1985.

The Far East and Australasia, 1989–90 (London: Europa, 1990).

G. Segal (ed), *Political and Economic Encyclopaedia of the Pacific* (London: Longman, 1989).

Towards a Pacific Century?

Futurology is a dangerous game, but it does not seem unreasonable to dream of the 21st century as the 'Pacific century' – just as the 19th century was the age of Europe and the 20th century was the age of the Superpowers. Of course, while it is undoubtedly true that growth in many Pacific states' economies has been prodigious, it is far less certain that this growth will carry on at the same pace into the next century. In any case, the coming of the Pacific century has already been much heralded, even as long ago as the late-19th century when the Russian and American empires reached the Pacific. Nevertheless, despite having played host to the most devastating post-war military conflicts (e.g. Korea and Vietnam), the region has enjoyed an economic boom.

Defining the Pacific area is not easy. It is often taken to mean *Defining the* the Asian Pacific, excluding the Superpowers, Canada, Australia *Pacific* and New Zealand. Yet the Asian Pacific has several tiers. There is China, with a huge population but which is essentially a poor, developing, great power. There is Japan which has by far the most developed economy and would be a possible great power were it not for its tiny military force and its serious vulnerability to blockade. The so-called newly industrialized countries (NICs), including South Korea, Taiwan, Hong Kong and Singapore, are at the core of hopes for the Pacific century. There are also proto-NICs such as Thailand, Indonesia, Malaysia and the Philippines, all with largely market economies but all developing more slowly than the 'big tiger and the four tiger cubs' (Japan and the NICs). Finally, there are the centrally-planned Communist states of Vietnam, Laos, Cambodia and North Korea, all but the last of which are the poorest states in the region.

In total, the Asian Pacific accounts for some 17% of world GNP, *The Pacific* while North America and Europe each account for 20–25%. The *boom* three groupings are expected to be roughly equal by the year 2000. If the Pacific areas of the non-Asian Pacific states are included (such as the Superpowers and Canada) the Pacific jumps to a commanding 33% of total world GNP. The per capita GNP of this non-Communist Asian Pacific is $7,000, ahead of the Soviet Union and Eastern Europe but behind Western Europe and North America. By the year 2000 the per capita GNP of Japan will be higher than all but two West European states and the NICs will have a higher per capita GNP rate than half the states of Western Europe. In 1900, fifteen of the world's twenty-five largest cities were in

Europe, five in America and five in Asia, but by the year 2000, ten will be in the Asian Pacific. However, the Asian Pacific has not been as important for overall world trade, accounting for only 14% in 1983 (of which 8% is Japan's trade) compared with 14% for the United States and 32% for the EC.

Interventionist governments   Clearly the region is riding an economic boom, even at a time when other developed economies are stagnating. There are at least six characteristics which help explain this pattern of growth. First, it is based mostly on a high level of government intervention in key sectors of the economy (the big exception here is Hong Kong). In Japan, the Ministry of International Trade and Industry has served as midwife at the birth of high-growth industries and supervised the rapid winding down of dying ones. Similar intervention is evident in South Korea. But in both countries, below this level of state intervention in larger industries, many smaller enterprises are allowed *greater* freedom than in developed Western economies. In Taiwan the relative independence of the smaller industries is greater still. But all the economies have basic features of an interventionist policy – some type of incomes policy and a leading role for major cartels.

Education, birth control and investment   Second, there is high government investment in education. In Japan 40% of school leavers go to university, 20% in Taiwan, 10% in Singapore (compared with 10% in Britain). Third, all these states have managed to control birth rates. Without such control, economic growth is merely swallowed up in feeding more and more mouths, as in Catholic Latin America. Fourth, all the states have relatively high rates of savings, providing easy and inexpensive investment for future growth.

Consensus politics   Fifth, most states can be characterized as mildly authoritarian, state-run mixed-economies. Even in Japan, government changes are between factions of a single party. The state rules through a generalist bureaucracy, not the sort of tiny élites that brought many Third World states to independence and grief. Competitive capitalism exists within this system but mostly at the local level and smaller scale enterprises. Consensus politics are said to be based on an authoritarian political culture, but the consensus is often more apparent than real. However the culture does seem to encourage work discipline, attention to detail, family values, frugality, simplicity and diligence.

Economics in command   Sixth, most states tend to go for 'economics in command' rather than politics in command. Under mildly authoritarian rule, pragmatic politics are pursued, not the wasteful, polarized exercises of many Latin American states. With economics in command, nationalism is often not as strident and emotional, as is the case in the Middle East.

Yet, even if all these factors explain the past growth, the future *Storing up* may well be less successful. Values can change as societies and *problems* economies change. For example, the Japanese savings rate is declining and there are signs that the famed work ethic is fading in some sectors. Nor can new dangers of military conflict be entirely ruled out. The uncertain future of Hong Kong, Chinese pressure on Taiwan, a future war in Korea or factional politics in China or Korea, may upset stability. It may also be optimistic to assume that the proto-NICs will be able to follow the tigers from export-led growth based on labour-intensive manufactured goods such as textiles, to more skill- and capital-intensive exports such as electronics.

What happens when these economies, so heavily dependent on *The problem of* export-led growth, find their markets closed, say in the United *adjustment* States, or if the developed economies stagnate and can afford few imports? Some of these problems are already evident in the slow-down in the NICs' growth rates. Witness Singapore's problems of adjustment as its ship-repair and oil-rig industry dies, or Japan's as its heavy industry weakens in the face of South Korean competi-tion and a revalued Yen.

What is more, the small population of many NICs makes it *Declining* difficult for them to be self-sufficient. A declining rate of popu- *growth* lation growth means the tax base will narrow, requiring higher taxes to support rising demands for social security. These are of course problems of growth well known in developed economies and support the thesis that the NICs are merely catching up with developed states' problems.

The Pacific will clearly be a region to watch well into the next *New political* century. Yet the Pacific states do face real problems and it is *vocabulary* difficult to suggest any over-arching lessons that can be drawn from an area as diverse and as changing as the Asian Pacific. Although Asian Pacific states are not suffering from familiar Third World development problems, they are not simply embryonic Western economies preparing to burst into life. Perhaps what is required is a new political vocabulary for states where wealth is created with relative social and economic control and cohesion, and limited political diversity, albeit with wider choice for the individual on the personal level. As they look towards the 21st century, the cautious people of the Pacific might do well to recall the Chinese curse: 'May you live in interesting times'.

Reading

M.T. Dalby and M.I. Logan, *The Brittle Rim* (New York: Viking, 1989).

P. Drysdale, *International Economic Pluralism* (Boston: Allen and Unwin, 1988).

R. Elegant, *Pacific Destiny* (New York: Viking, 1990).

S.B. Linder, *The Pacific Century* (Stanford: Stanford University Press, 1986).

G. Segal, *Rethinking the Pacific* (Oxford: Oxford University Press, 1990).

G. Segal (ed), *Political and Economic Encyclopaedia of the Pacific* (London: Longman, 1989).

S. Winchester, *The Pacific* (London: Hutchinson, 1991).

6
SOUTH ASIA

Reshaping Central Asia

In the vast space between the Caspian Sea and Burma lies Central Asia, a poorly defined area of various Islamic peoples. It was part of the ancient Silk Route linking Imperial Rome and China and it was the battleground of Russian and British forces engaged in the Great Game of the 19th century when two expanding empires manoeuvred for supremacy. In modern times it was forgotten by strategists until the Soviet Union invaded Afghanistan in December 1979 and a decade later, despite a Soviet withdrawal, from Afghanistan, the Central Asian republics of the Soviet Union showed signs of shaking the regional balance of power.

The Afghan Débacle Afghanistan has always been a mess of warring factions. But its rulers have recognized the need to retain independence by remaining friendly with Russia while on decent terms with other neighbours. But when a radical, Marxist régime came to power in a coup in 1978 its policies alienated the people, eventually dragging the Soviet Union deeper into the mire of local politics. The Soviet invasion in 1979 was the last of a series of attempts by the Soviet Union to get a more predictable ruler in place.

But the use of Soviet troops was no solution. Even with some 115,000 soliders engaged at any one time, the Afghan rebels could not be subdued. Pakistan provided sanctuary for many of the 5 million refugees created by the war and arms supplies came from the West, Islamic states, and China via the Pakistan frontier. With the Soviet Union unwilling to escalate confrontation across the frontier and determined to fight a limited war as the Americans did in Vietnam, the cause was hopeless. The Gorbachev administration sought various face-saving solutions but in the end agreed at a conference in Geneva in April 1988 to withdraw by 15 February 1989.

In search of an Afghan deal But the war carried on, costing the Russians $300 million a month in supplies and the Afghan people thousands of dead. The Superpowers negotiated in 1990 about ways of bringing their allies to their own negotiating table, but the fighting continued. The Soviet-installed government of President Najibullah controlled Kabul and most major towns while the divided mujaheddin rebels roamed in the rest of the country. In November 1990 some rebel leaders met Najibullah and the exiled king Zahir Shah (ousted in the 1973 coup) and reached an agreement for a transition to an election if the king could arrange full mujaheddin support. But many rebels were Islamic fundamentalists and were aligning with

Pakistan which did not favour the return of the king. The Soviet Union continued to provide massive aid to the Najibullah régime, ironically at the same time as the Soviet Union received even larger aid from the developed capitalist world. But Moscow's calculation was based in part on the premise that effective resistance to Muslim rebels in Afghanistan might also help deter those Muslims within the Soviet Union who contemplated their own fight for independence.

The Afghan War, more than any other single event, demon-strated the weakness and limitations of Soviet power. It also dem-onstrated to the Islamic populations within the Soviet Union that Soviet troops could be beaten and that Soviet Asians need not necessarily remain part of the Russian empire. Right around the western and southern rim of the Soviet Union, the message went out that independence was possible. As the Baltic republics tested the limits of Russian tolerance in 1989–90, the resistance within Soviet Central Asia began to grow.

Rebels within the Soviet Union

The five Soviet Central Asian Republics do not form a coherent group. By far the largest is the breadbasket of Kazakhstan with 16 million people, 40% of whom are Russian. Although Kazakhs comprise about 40% of the population, these once-nomadic people have barely settled into the 20th century. The largest population group are the Uzbeks, most of whom live in Uzbekistan (19 million of whom 69% are Uzbek) and are 'represented' by a nationalist movement called Birlik. By contrast there is the much smaller group of Turkmens of Turkmenia (population 5 million, of whom 10% are Russian, 28% Uzbek, 62% Turkmen). Clearly the problem of ethnic fragmentation is complex. The Central Asian republic of Kirgizia has 4 million people, of whom 26% are Russian, 12% Uzbek and 48% Kirgiz. They did not come under Russian rule until 1927 and there are still close to 1 million Kirgiz across the frontier in China. The fifth Central Asian republic, Tadzhikistan, has a population of 5 million, of whom 10% are Russian, 28% Uzbek and 60% Tadzhik. In clashes in June 1990 between Kirgiz and Uzbeks in the Kirgiz city of Osh, 116 people died. Just across the frontier in China are the 5 million Uighurs in Xinjiang, with another 300,000 compatriots scattered around Soviet Central Asia. Some 50 Uighurs were killed in rioting near Kashgar in Xinjiang in April 1990.

Republics on the move

The location of the populations of Central Asia bear the scars of botched imperial boundary-making. With people straddling arti-ficial frontiers and rivalries extending back centuries to their ori-gins as warring Central Asian Khanates (descendants mainly of the Mongol conquest), there is no sense in which the Central Asian republics can emerge as a coherent unit. Should they desire independence from Russia, they are just as likely to war among

People and frontiers

themselves as with neighbours such as China, Pakistan, Afghanistan and Iran, all of whom have overlaps of population.

The potential for new international crises is as vast as the mosaic of peoples. If Pakistan should seek friends in the new Central Asia, will India sit idly by? Surely Iran would pursue its own interests. The best guess is that there may well be a bunch of Afghanistans in the making. The challenge to the more developed parts of Eurasia will be whether they will have the good sense to stay out of this cauldron. They all might wish the Russian empire the best of health, at least in this part of the world.

Reading

G. Arney, *Afghanistan* (London: Mandarin, 1990).

G. Fuller, 'The Emergence of Central Asia', *Foreign Policy*, Spring 1990.

M. Hauner, *What is Asia to Us?* (Boston: Unwin/Hyman, 1990).

P. Hopkirk, *The Great Game* (London: John Murray, 1990).

A. Saikal and W. Maley, *The Soviet Withdrawal from Afghanistan* (Cambridge: Cambridge University Press, 1989).

An Indian Superpower?

Consider the map of South Asia, with India at its core. Is there any country around its rim that has not had a military conflict with India? The root of the problem is that India has never liked the fact that Britain divided the South Asian empire in the 1940s. What is more, like China, India is a poor great power with nuclear weapons and domestic problems.

The roots of regional conflict are buried deep in history. As independence from Britain approached in the 1940s, the Muslim minority in the colony agitated for a state independent of the Hindu majority. As a result of increasing violence, the Muslim groups forced Britain to grant an independent Muslim Pakistan. The partition of India and Pakistan in 1947 was protracted and violent. The provinces of Punjab and Bengal had roughly equal Muslim and Hindu populations and, in the ensuing division of the territory and 'exchange' of population, hundreds of thousands died in communal violence. In total, partition resulted in over half a million deaths. Eight million Muslims fled to Pakistan and a roughly equal number of Hindus and Sikhs fled to India. Yet over 40 million Muslims (11% of the population) remained in India and 10 million Hindus (3% of the population) remained in Pakistan. Pakistan itself was divided into two parts by 1,000 miles of Indian territory. Both East and West Pakistan held roughly equal halves of the population but the Bengalis in the east received less attention from the government which was based in the west. *Britain carves up the sub-continent*

Kashmir, a Hindu-ruled but predominantly Muslim province bordering India, Pakistan and China, was the location of the first of a string of crises in India–Pakistan relations. The Hindu ruler was slow to make up his mind whether to join India or Pakistan at independence and prodded by the Pakistan government, Pathan tribesmen invaded Kashmir, forcing the ruler to ask for Indian aid. After a brief war, Pakistan held the smaller area to the north and west while India took the rest. The United Nations arranged a ceasefire and the placement of observers along the frontier. *Conflict in Kashmir*

With the passage of time, the two South Asian states drifted further apart. While India tinkered with democratic government, Pakistan regularly slipped in and out of military rule. India emerged as a major leader of the Non-aligned Movement while trying to reorder events in its own sphere of influence in South Asia. In 1965 Indian and Pakistani forces clashed over the partially- *More conflict in the 1960s* demarcated Rann of Kutch salt marsh in Sind province. The dispute was eventually settled by arbitration in 1968.

Kashmir – 1965   Also in 1965, India attempted to integrate Kashmir more completely into India. After a brief war in August, a United Nations ceasefire was agreed and more truce observers sent. The United States verbally supported Pakistan, a fellow member of CENTO. The Soviet Union had 'tilted' to India's side in an attempt to win friends by balancing American support for Pakistan. China, which had recently split with the Soviet Union, supported Pakistan by threatening India with hostilities along a second front in 1965. But it was the Soviet Union which earned the most credit from the events. It arranged an Indo-Pakistan settlement of sorts in 1966 at a conference held in Tashkent under the watchful gaze of Soviet Premier Kosygin. A more complete settlement was reached in 1972 although tensions have occasionally erupted.

Pakistan represses East Pakistan   By far the bloodiest India–Pakistan clash came in 1971 as mounting Bengali dissatisfaction in East Pakistan erupted into violence. West Pakistan tried to repress Bengali demands for greater self-government and millions fled across the border to their brethren in India. In the midst of this mounting tension, India and the Soviet Union signed a treaty of friendship in August. The United States remained silent about Pakistani atrocities in Bengal, in part because Pakistan was a key conduit for still secret and delicate Sino–American contacts.

India liberates east Pakistan   India took advantage of the opportunity to dismember Pakistan by launching a twelve-day war in December against Pakistani forces in the east. The independent state of Bangladesh was created. Yet Bangladesh did not turn out to be a passive Indian puppet. A military coup in 1975 brought to power a more independent régime although domestic instability in this impoverished state continued. There was conflict with India over the waters of the Ganges and Brahmaputra rivers, the possession of newly-formed islands in the Bay of Bengal, border demarcation east of Chittagong and refugees who fled into the Indian province of Assam from Bangladesh. In 1983 the latter issue flared into conflict within India as Bengali refugees were attacked by mostly Hindu Assamese, resulting in some 5,000 deaths that year. In August 1985, India upset Bangladesh by barring all Bangladeshi immigrants to Assam since 1965 from voting in elections. All immigrants since 1971 were to be deported.

Kashmir again   Previous settlements of the Kashmir issue involved the renunciation of the use of force in the dispute but good intentions did not survive the cartographic imprecision which left the boundary unclear. In the late 1980s India and Pakistan exchanged fire 18,000 feet up on the Siachin glacier. Initial agreement was reached in 1989 in this heated Cold War but conflict continued into 1990 when the more important conflict over Kashmir proper surfaced again. A smouldering secessionist movement led by Muslim fundamentalists in Indian Kashmir flared into a popular uprising in January when fifty people were killed by police firing on demonstrators in Srinagar. Tension was high by April when India accused Pakistan of supporting the rebels and both sides shuffled their troops about in public. The Superpowers counselled restraint and refused to support a new conflict in this age of East–West détente.

India has clearly been the dominant power in South Asia since the 1971 war. But after the Soviet invasion of Afghanistan, Pakistan drew closer to the United States, leading to further Soviet rearmament of India. Pakistan stepped up its search for an atomic bomb, with finance from the Islamic world, in part in response to India's nuclear test in 1974. So far, both India and Pakistan have remained ambiguous about their nuclear capability, which under the circumstances helps limit a potential nuclear arms race. But Pakistan well knows that as it has been regularly defeated on the battlefield, it feels that perhaps only nuclear weapons will keep India at bay. *Nuclear dangers*

Nuclear weapons aside, the real threats to regional security come from the patchwork of ethnic groups that make up the region. In 1966 India divided its portion of the Punjab into three parts: a Hindu portion (Harayana), the Himalayan foothills which stretched to Himachal Pradesh and the residual territory of Punjab dominated by Sikhs. The 20 million Sikhs (2.5% of the population but 15% of the armed forces) have a militaristic tradition but, with a per capita income 50% higher than the national average, are relatively prosperous. They have traditionally lived on the margins of Hindu and Muslim groups, as they originally formed themselves into a separate group in an attempt to reconcile the two. They chose to remain in India after partition but felt aggrieved that they were granted so little regional autonomy. The central Indian government, fearing the knock-on effect of granting Sikh autonomy, took a hard line while trying to placate this important minority (in 1982 a Sikh was appointed President). *The Sikhs*

Sikh extremists, some of whom obtained support from nearby Pakistan, demanded an independent Sikh state of Khalistan. Fighting between Hindus and Sikhs worsened in 1983 and militants seized the Sikh's holiest shrine, the Golden Temple at Amritsar. In June 1984, the Indian army stormed the temple. Violence and inter-communal killing increased and the Sikh community became increasingly dissatisfied. On 31 October, Premier Indira Gandhi was assassinated by Sikh members of her bodyguard. The fiercest communal bloodshed since 1947 ensued, with 2,000 Sikhs killed and 30,000 made homeless in Delhi alone. *Fighting for Khalistan*

And yet despite all the communal violence, there are some *SAARC* moves towards more controlled conflict. In 1980, Bangladesh began moves which resulted in the South Asian Association for Regional Cooperation (SAARC). It was launched on 7–8 December 1985 in Dhaka, Bangladesh, with a meeting of the heads of government of the seven members (Bangladesh, Bhutan, India, Maldives, Nepal, Pakistan, Sri Lanka) representing over one billion people. SAARC is thus the world's largest (and poorest) regional organization, in a region where it is difficult to telephone or fly between capitals and where member states have recently waged bloody war. Initially, SAARC envisages cooperation on such basic issues as agriculture, rural development, drug trafficking and terrorism, but much-needed population control is ruled out because it is considered 'un-Islamic'. Bilateral issues have also been ruled beyond SAARC's agenda – and a good thing too for the fragile unity. Of course, such shying away from basic issues suggests SAARC is likely to remain yet another Third World forum for bombast and bureaucrats.

With declining Superpower activity in the Indian Ocean, India is more free to flex its muscles in the region. With crude pressure on Nepal over a trade dispute in 1989–90, an invasion of Sri Lanka and even the Maldives in the previous two years, and naval operations approaching the reaches of Southeast Asia, there seems to be little to stop India from increasing its influence. Only geography seems to be a cause for complacency, because once it reaches East or West Asia, India begins running into powers more of its own size.

Reading

M. Ayoob, 'India in South Asia', *World Policy Journal*, Winter 89–90.
W. Barnds, *India, Pakistan and the Great Powers* (New York: Praeger, 1972).
B. Buzan and G. Rizvi, *South Asian Insecurity and the Great Powers* (London: Macmillan, 1986).
Z. Khalizad, *Security in Southern Asia* (London: Gower, 1984).
C.K. Tiwari, *Security in South Asia* (New York: University Press of America, 1989).

Sri Lanka

Sri Lanka, the tropical Indian Ocean island at the southeast tip of India, was called Serendip by its early Arab visitors, and Paradise by many who followed. But all has not been well in paradise in recent years. Bloody civil war between Tamil separatists and the Sinhalese majority has sucked in neighbouring India.

Ceylon, renamed Sri Lanka in 1972, obtained independence from Britain in February 1948. About 80% of the population of 15 million are Sinhalese, some of whom see as their mission the creation of a pure Buddhist state on the island. They therefore oppose the approximate 20% of the population that is Tamil, a darker skinned, mostly Hindu people, 70% of whom are descended from Tamils who crossed the water from India some 1,000 years ago. Other Tamils were brought in by the British in the 19th century, in large part to work on tea plantations. Many are still virtually stateless. India, 35 miles away across the Palk Straits, contains most of the 40 million Tamil brethren, primarily in Tamil Nadu state. Sri Lanka's Tamils live mainly in the north and east of the island. *The Tamil minority*

The Tamil minority had adapted better to British colonial rule, learning English and prospering in education and business. With independence, came a Sinhalese desire to dominate and in 1956 the government insisted on greater use of the Sinhalese language to undermine Tamil power. The United National Party (UNP) ruled from 1950–6, in 1960 and from 1965–70 and was relatively more sympathetic to Tamil minority rights. But the Sri Lanka Freedom Party (SLFP), which introduced changes in 1956, was more concerned with enhancing national Sinhala tradition, entrenching Sinhalese as the official language and Buddhism as the official religion. In 1971 there was a non-sectarian uprising of Left-wing forces against a SLFP-led Left-wing coalition. A state of emergency was declared but the trouble was unrelated to communal tension. *Party politics*

However, from 1972 the SLFP began extending Sinhalese domination and in 1976 the Tamil United Liberation Front (TULF) was formed from various Tamil parties. The TULF called for the creation of Elam, a separate Tamil state in north and east Sri Lanka. When the UNP returned to power in July 1977, led by Junius Jayewardene, Sinhalese chauvinism was still supported by powerful elements in his cabinet. The government made concessions, especially in recognizing Tamil as an official language, but the TULF refused to *Elam and Tamil violence*

217

enter into talks on a coalition government for fear of reprisals, this time from Tamil extremists.

Tamil Tigers and communal violence

A referendum in December 1982 agreed to prolong the life of the current parliament. On a 77% turnout, 55% voted in favour but the Tamils were strongly opposed. In ensuing local elections the UNP won a sweeping victory except in Tamil areas, where the TULF did well. Polarization of the two communities seemed to be growing. It was therefore not surprising that in May 1983 yet another state of emergency was declared to control vicious inter-communal violence. Growing Tamil terrorism drew heavy-handed responses from the security forces, egged on by Sinhalese extremist factions in the government. Some 600 people died and over 135,000 Tamils fled Sinhalese areas in the rioting. Tamil terrorists, led primarily by the Tamil Tigers, numbered several thousand and were trained in bases in Tamil Nadu. As the defence burden grew, the once-booming economy staggered into recession and tourists took their much-needed foreign currency elsewhere.

Tamil Nadu support

The central Indian government did not support the dismemberment of Sri Lanka, although the regional Tamil Nadu authorities were openly sympathetic to the rebels. But as the political communities in Sri Lanka grew further apart, the Indian government found itself uncomfortably trying to sit on two stools at once. By 1985 some 100,000 Tamil refugees had fled Sri Lanka for India, and by 1987 in total some 300,000 had fled. Delhi became increasingly worried at signs that outside influences were at work in an area it viewed as within India's sphere of influence.

Bhutan talks

In 1985, following the murder of the Indian Prime Minister, Mrs Gandhi, and the continuing violence in Sri Lanka, India under Rajiv Gandhi took a more determined part in urging inter-communal talks. Both sides met in Bhutan under the watchful gaze of the Indians. By 1986 the talks broke down and India began 'leaning on' Sri Lanka for more concessions.

Violence from the extremes

In January 1987 the Tamil Tigers consolidated their grasp on the north and agreed to an autonomous Tamil region rather than full independence. But the Jayewardene government was only prepared to create such a zone in the north, not in the east where the Tamils did not quite constitute a majority. India grew impatient with both sides, especially as the ground for compromise still appeared clear. On 29 July, India and Sri Lanka signed an agreement that gave the Tamils local control of the north and a chance to have the same in the east – all in exchange for an end to the warfare. India sent in up to 20,000 'peacekeepers' to crush Tamil Tiger opposition, but the fighting was more violent and prolonged than expected.

Peacekeepers

In the six years since 1983, more than 17,000 people died in

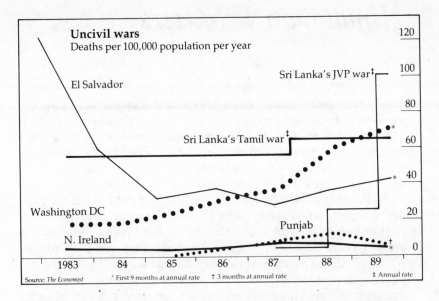

Uncivil wars
Deaths per 100,000 population per year

El Salvador

Sri Lanka's JVP war†

Sri Lanka's Tamil war†

Washington DC

Punjab

N. Ireland

1983 84 85 86 87 88 89

120
100
80
60
40
20
0

Source: *The Economist*   * First 9 months at annual rate   † 3 months at annual rate   ‡ Annual rate

the battles with the Tamils, and the Indians were able merely to bottle up the Tigers in the northern jungles. Sri Lanka's new President, Ranasinghe Premadasa, reached an agreement with the Tamil Tigers in April 1989 that would allow for an Indian withdrawal. By the end of March 1990 the Indians were gone (suffering 1,300 dead and 3,000 wounded), leaving the locals to battle it out. The Tigers first took on their main rival, the pro-Indian Tamils who won the local elections promised in the 1987 accord. At the same time, the government took on the extreme Sinhalese nationalists, the JVP, in 1989–90, killing more than 16,000 in the process. By mid-1990 the Tigers and the government resumed their direct confrontation, with the government soon stalled in its offensive. With the war costing $1 million a week and the economy in trouble, paradise is not all it was cracked up to be.

Reading

C. Manogaran, *Ethnic Conflict and Reconciliation in Sri Lanka* (Hawaii: University of Hawaii Press, 1987).

J. Manor (ed), *Sri Lanka in Change and Crisis* (London: Croom Helm, 1984).

M. Ram, *Sri Lanka* (London: Penguin, 1989).

K.M. de Silva, *A History of Sri Lanka* (Oxford: Oxford University Press, 1981).

Himalayan Frontiers

Asia's two great states, India and China, have massive, poor, peasant populations and face many common problems. But both offer different political and economic solutions and therefore represent competing paths to modernization. Predictably, these two Asian states became rivals for leadership of the decolonized states and came to blows over their own lengthy frontier.

Five principles of peaceful co-existence

India gained its independence in 1947 and the People's Republic of China was established in 1949. Between 1949 and 1955 relations were overwhelmingly cordial, as both young régimes (but ancient cultures) sought friends wherever they could be found. Although China in 1950 consolidated control over Tibet (a neighbouring territory which many Indians viewed as independent), the atmosphere was characterized by the 'five principles of peaceful coexistence'. These bland principles of inter-state friendship were agreed by Premier Zhou Enlai and Premier Nehru in 1954 and both then took the lead in having them adopted at the meeting of non-aligned states in Bandung in 1955.

The 1959 Tibet uprising

But the more natural rivalry of these two great statesmen emerged later in the 1950s. China's split with the Soviet Union led Beijing to call for more and faster revolutionary change in the developing world, which was out of step with the gradualist approach of Nehru. The Soviet Union improved its relations with India while Sino–Soviet relations deteriorated. In 1959 a Tibetan uprising, brutally suppressed by the Chinese, was then followed by Sino–Indian border clashes.

The eastern border

The dispute between China and India about their 2,500 mile-long frontier can be divided into three distinct sections. In the eastern, 700-mile section, where Tibet borders Arunachal Pradesh, the frontier has always been uncertain and the nomadic population paid it little heed. At the 1913–4 Simla conference the British drew a line (the McMahon line) which China never accepted. Despite a number of small border incidents in the 1950s, it was the 1959 Tibet uprising that first made both India and China acutely conscious of the ill-defined frontier. The Nehru–Zhou talks in 1960 were inconclusive and, after other diplomatic exchanges, India opted for a 'forward policy' in the frontier area which put its troops across the line claimed by China. In November 1962 the Chinese trounced the Indians in a brief border war, but quickly withdrew to a line mostly north of the McMahon line. Although little progress has been made in resolving the border conflict, there have

also been a few border clashes. In October 1975 four Indian soldiers were killed in an incident but essentially the 1962 war provided the answer to which great Asian state was more powerful.

In the second, central section of the frontier, where Tibet bor- *The central*
ders on Bhutan, Sikkim (an Indian state since 1975), Nepal, and *sector*
the Indian states of Uttar Pradesh and Himachal Pradesh, there
have been no serious disputes. The third sector in the West, where
Kashmir borders on Tibet and Xinjiang, has seen some problems
in its eastern portion. India claims the crest of the Kuenlun range
(including the Aksai Chin) although all this territory has been
under Chinese control since 1950. China claims the crest of the
Karakoram range as the frontier and uses the Aksai Chin as a
crucial link between Tibet and Xinjiang. It was in this region that
the 1959 clash took place and after victory in the 1962 war China
pulled back to just behind the positions it claimed. There were
minor incidents in this area during the 1965 India–Pakistan conflict, in which China supported Pakistan.

In March 1963 Pakistan and China agreed to a demarcation of *China and*
the Xinjiang–Kashmir frontier, even though India, which contests *Pakistan*
Pakistan's claim to that part of Kashmir, protested that Pakistan
had no frontier with China. Two all-weather roads linking China
and Pakistan were opened, the first in 1968 at Mintaka Pass and
the second at the Khunjerab pass in 1978. Indian objections have
been ignored.

India's increasingly close ties to the Soviet Union after the *India and the*
Sino–Soviet split were of great concern to a China which feared *Soviet Union*
Soviet encirclement. In the 1971 India–Pakistan war, China was
unable to support Pakistan because the Soviet Union threatened
China from the north. In the 1970s, India was the key to Soviet
attempts to organize an Asian Collective Security scheme aimed
against China.

The Soviet invasion of Afghanistan in 1979 and China's aban- *The impact of*
donment of extreme anti-Sovietism encouraged both Delhi and *Afghanistan*
Beijing to explore the possibility of improving their bilateral
relations. Preliminary talks opened in December 1981 and in 1982
China indicated that it was prepared to be conciliatory. Chinese
leaders suggested a deal whereby territory in the Eastern sector
of the border could be traded for the more strategic Western sector.
India was unwilling to make such a swap but in October 1983
China agreed to a sector-by-sector analysis of the frontier, while
continuing to expect a final deal that would trade territory in the
east for territory in the west. Talks continue with little sign of a
formal agreement. In 1986, for the first time in more than a decade,
border skirmishes were reported, but they apparently did not
constitute a worsening of relations, only the petty politics of Indian
politicians. In October 1987, Tibetans on the Chinese side of the

Tibetans protest border with India rioted in protest at Chinese suppression of their identity, but India was careful not to exploit the unrest or link it to border tension earlier that year. In the meantime, mutual trade increased, especially after an August 1984 agreement that replaced the ad hoc arrangements in effect since trade was resumed in 1979. The Indian Prime Minister visited China in December 1988 and direct trade on land was resumed in 1991.

Towards détente   By the late 1980s, Sino–Indian relations have again emphasized the five principles of peaceful co-existence. Yet true cooperation between these two states is difficult to envisage. The Soviet Union will always be more useful to India than China, if only because Moscow serves as an anti-China counterweight. Pakistan will similarly rely on China to help it live securely between India and the Soviet Union and Afghanistan. Nevertheless, both India and China have plenty of pressing domestic problems to take their minds off their Third World rivalry. In the next phase of their relations, when both giant peasant states have had a chance to test their rival development strategies, we may see a new, more dangerous round of foreign policy rivalry.

Reading

T. George *et al*, *Security in Southern Asia* (London: Gower, 1984).

J. Rowland, *A History of Sino–Indian Relations* (New York: Van Nostrand, 1967).

G. Segal, *Defending China* (London: Oxford University Press, 1985).

A. Whiting, *The Chinese Calculus of Deterrence* (Ann Arbour: University of Michigan Press, 1975).

7

THE AMERICAS

Quebec, Canada and the USA

Canada, the world's second largest country, is best known for its cold fronts and ice hockey stars; it is equally well known (somewhat tongue-in-cheek) as one of the most boring, yet prosperous countries. For the United States, it is comforting to know that, unlike other great powers which have unstable or covetous neighbours, they can rest secure in their home base. But can they? If Canada were to collapse into a mess of feuding provinces, would the United States want a few extra states in the union?

The origins of Canada   In the 17th and 18th centuries, when the British empire was extending across vast parts of the globe, the mostly empty territory of modern-day Canada was the nearest space to fill. Scattered Indian and Inuit populations were easily subdued, but Britain's European rival, France, was not so easily pushed off the North American map. Most of the French settlement was in New France, more or less the territory of the modern Canadian province of Quebec. On 13 September 1759, British troops under the command of General Wolfe captured Quebec and the territory was handed over to Britain in the Treaty of Paris in 1763. But the French settlers remained a distinct society and in 1774 the Quebec Act recognized that the French-speaking people had the right to exercise their own customs, laws and religions. With the former British colonies to the south gaining their independence as the United States of America, the remaining British holdings to the north began shaping a distinct identity. In 1841 the French-speaking colony was politically united with English-speaking Ontario (called Upper and Lower Canada) as other British colonies were established across North America.

The British North America Act in 1867 united the four colonies of Quebec, Ontario, Nova Scotia and New Brunswick, and although *de facto* home rule was established, the British monarch remained sovereign. In the ensuing years Canada incorporated a string of other British colonies along the USA's northern border. It was not until the British House of Commons approved the Statute of Westminister in 1931 that legal limitations on the legislative autonomy of the parliament in Ottawa were lifted. In 1949, Newfoundland joined Canada as the tenth province.

Federalism and French identity   Canada developed in a far looser federal system than the United States. The provinces retained greater autonomy and the sense of loyalty to the central government in Ottawa was often tenuous. Connecting lines of rail, road and then air, communications were strung across the vast land, but geography often combined with history to make the Union uncertain. Although there never was a civil war as endured by the United States, the identity of French-Canadians was always much more distinct than that of the south in the USA. With a much smaller Canadian population strung out along the border with the United States, there was a tendency to develop close links across the frontier as much as east or west to other parts of Canada. While there were various periods of tension along the USA–Canada border, there has been well over a century of peace largely because Canadians always recognized the United States as the dominant power. Yet Canadians were also proud of their stronger connections with Britain, or in the case of French-Canadians, their separateness from everyone else on the continent.

Frustration for the Québecois was accentuated by the fact that even in the federal structure of Canada, they were ultimately ruled by English power in one form or another. Certainly the main economic power was American and the ruling élite in Quebec may have been French, but they worked closely with the English powers around it. Quebec was also dominated by its backward-looking Catholic Church which connived in the frustration of a confident French political culture.

In the 1960s, with decolonization underway around the world and a sense of radical politics of protest in the developed world, the Québecois began to find their own voice. During a visit to Canada in 1967 as part of the centenary celebrations, French President De Gaulle declared his support in Montreal for a 'free Quebec'. A separatist movement developed, complete with some extremist elements who used bombs and kidnapping to get their case heard. While the USA was more used to a violent streak in politics, Canadians prided themselves on a far more civilized approach to political disputes. Thus it was a French-Canadian prime minister, Pierre Trudeau, who declared a state of emergency in 1970 when a particularly nasty series of kidnappings led some to believe that there was a serious threat to the federation, or at least to the law and order within it. Before then, Trudeau had led a sweeping set of reforms which righted many of the wrongs felt by the French by entrenching bilingualism and biculturalism in an effort to create French confidence in the federal structure. Yet many Québecois were encouraged merely to believe that much more could be obtained, while some English-speaking parts objected to the special treatment of a minority population.

A sense of separate identity

As law and order was restored and the sense of fear faded, the legal Parti Québecois emerged as a major political force. In an effort to forestall the opposition, the provincial Liberal party (Trudeau ran a Liberal government in Ottawa) passed Bill 22 which

Voting against a split

made French the sole official language of the province and attempted to undercut the right to use English in education and trade. As English-speakers left the province in droves, the French could feel some confidence that their campaign to preserve their special identity was working, albeit at some economic cost. In this new confident mood, the people of Quebec elected the Parti Québecois in November 1976, albeit with only 41% of the vote. New laws such as Bill 101 further entrenched French predominance in such symbolic ways as public signs, although the reality of economic power was a Quebec playing its part in the complex, American-dominated interdependence of North America.

A referendum in May 1980 saw a decisive vote (60%) against separatism by a people pleased to have gained new rights and pride, but fearful of the economic impact of a fully independent state. In 1985 the Liberals returned to power in Quebec, although their brothers at the federal level were replaced by the Conservative Party, but led by a native-Quebecker, Brian Mulroney.

Meech Lake   The later years of the Trudeau government had resulted in a constitutional conference that led to Britain passing the Canada Act of 8 March 1982, giving Canadians the right to change their own constitution. Along with a charter of rights and freedoms, the Act affirmed bilingualism and biculturalism. Mulroney brought Quebec more formally into the constitutional process of hammering out an agreement at Meech Lake. This promised reforms to the constitution that would recognize Quebec as a distinct society within the Canadian federation. Other reforms gave the provinces more power, for example over immigration.

But the Meech Lake accord also required each provincial parliament to pass the deal unchanged. By the time of the deadline in June 1990, Newfoundland and Manitoba failed to do so and the accord died. But contrary to many dire warnings, the Canadian dollar held firm and Montrealers did not run riot. Canada is far too nice for such a thing.

Redrawing the map?   Many Québecois now feel rejected by the rest of Canada but they seem divided about whether the best response would be separatism. At a time when the EC is building a closer union, and Canada and the United States have negotiated a free trade agreement, the economic logic is certainly far more towards a looser federal system within a closely intertwined market economy. If the worst were to happen, then it is certainly possible to envisage various parts of Canada becoming independent, or even seeking statehood in the USA. Of course, this new reality would also leave a distinct French society in North America, making its living in the emerging, North America-wide market economy. Either way, the result is 6 million French speakers in Quebec, with

Montreal as the world's second largest French-speaking city in the world, and certainly the most lively town in North America.

Reading

R. Bothwell *et al*, *Canada since 1945* (Toronto: University of Toronto Press, 1989).

D. Clift, *Quebec and Nationalism in Crisis* (Montreal: McGill-Queens University Press, 1982).

J. Fitzmaurice, *Quebec and Canada* (London: C. Hurst, 1985).

A. O. Hero and L. Balthazar, *Contemporary Quebec and the United States* (Boston: University Press of America, 1988).

K. McNaught, *The Pelican History of Canada* (New York: Viking Penguin, 1985).

Panama and the Canal

Whomever was responsible for the geography of the Americas seemed to have forgotten to make a canal across the thin ribbon dividing North and South America. Therefore it was only sensible for geopoliticians to think they could correct the mistake by building one themselves. The problem was that the politics of such construction became messy, and have remained that way ever since.

Making Panama

The present state of Panama, with its 2.5 million people, was the creation of the United States. In 1903 the USA negotiated a treaty with the Colombian government which controlled the territory whereby the United States would obtain the canal concession for $10 million along with a 100-year lease on a 1,432 square kilometre strip known as the Canal Zone. But the Colombian Congress opposed the idea and the United States then supported a revolt in Panama, leading to a declaration of independence. A similar deal was then negotiated with the Panamanians, including the right of United States intervention to protect the canal.

Controlling riotous politics

Panamanian politics have always been turbulent, but the first major upset came with a coup in 1941. Elections in 1968 were soon overturned by yet another coup, this time led by Colonel Omar Torrijos Herrera. Under Torrijos there was a period of stability as the government adopted a broadly Left-wing stance in foreign policy and undertook significant agrarian reform. Torrijos, with strong support from other Latin American leaders, cajoled the United States into renegotiating the terms under which the canal was operated. Talks opened in 1973, were broken off in 1976 but resumed in 1977 by the recently elected President Carter. In September, two draft treaties were signed.

Canal treaties

Under one treaty the Canal Zone was abolished although 40% of the land was to remain under United States control until the end of 1999. Panama also gained control of eleven of fourteen United States bases in the Zone and the Panama Canal Company was replaced by a nine-member Panama Canal Commission on which the USA was to retain a majority until 1989. The second treaty made Panama and the United States jointly responsible for guaranteeing the canal's permanent neutrality. The United States Senate gave the USA the right to deploy troops if the canal were closed or if access was restricted. The treaties finally came into effect in October 1979.

In July 1981 General Torrijos was killed in an air crash and

General Manuel Noriega Morena soon took effective control of the armed forces (called the National Guard). But the United States, which had once used Noriega for CIA operations, grew increasingly frustrated with his dealings with drugs, trade with Cuba and a murderous domestic political record. As relations deteriorated, aid from the United States was suspended and opposition forces were funded and organized by the USA. In the run-up to the change in control of the canal in 1989, the United States was especially anxious that the government in Panama be to its liking. As a result of the sometimes ludicrous sabre-rattling in 1989, Noriega eventually declared that a state of war existed between Panama and the United States. For Washington under the new Bush administration, this was a heaven-sent opportunity to demonstrate that the United States would use force in its own 'backyard' to defend what the USA saw as its vital interests. Even though 1989 was the year of Soviet retreat from its empire in Europe, the United States demonstrated it was not prepared to give up its international role.

With the excuse now provided, and after an election in May 1989 was overturned by Noriega's thugs, the United States had more excuses than it needed to send in its troops. On 20 December 1989 the United States operation began and, after an embarrassing delay, Noriega was captured so that he could stand trial in the USA on drugs charges. But peace and quiet was not at hand as the United States soon became embroiled in the usual mess of Panamanian politics. Aid was resumed, but the domestic situation remained very fragile.

Even as United States troops pulled out of Panama, they remained in the Canal Zone. Howard Air base is one of the largest in the hemisphere and there are some 13,000 United States troops in the Zone. The reality was that at least for another decade the United States would remain in control. It was unlikely that Panamanian politics would become any more stable, or the country more prosperous. Under such uncertain circumstances, will Washington still be happy to pull out its troops at the end of 1999? Eight years is a long time in politics, but it is probably a safe bet that the United States will be garrisoning the Canal Zone well after all Soviet troops are out of Eastern Europe.

Still guarding the canal

Reading

W. Jordan, *Panama Odyssey* (Austin: University of Texas Press, 1984).

R. Looney, *The Economic Development of Panama* (New York: Praeger, 1976).

Cuba and the Caribbean

Apart from Mexico directly across the border to the south, the United States' closest and most prickly southern neighbour is Cuba. The United States still maintains a naval base at Guantanamo as a result of a 1903 lease granted by Cuba – the only American base on Communist territory. The 1956–9 Cuban civil war was won by Fidel Castro's forces, but his close alignment with the Soviet bloc and the extent of his radicalism was in part a response to United States pressure. The botched American attempt to help Cubans depose Castro at the Bay of Pigs invasion in April 1961 merely drove the Cuban leader further into Soviet arms. The embrace was tightened in 1962 when the Soviet Union attempted to establish a missile base in Cuba. Castro tried to challenge the United States, and wriggle away from Moscow, by supporting revolutionary adventurism, first in Latin America and then in Africa in the 1970s. Peace feelers extended to Castro by President Carter were withdrawn by the Reagan administration which saw Cuba as a radical Soviet agent trying to cause revolutionary havoc in the United States' tidy backyard. Washington reacted particularly angrily to what it saw as Castro's active involvement in the events in Nicaragua.

Revolutions in retreat

By 1989 the victory by Left-wingers in Nicaragua began to look increasingly strained and the burdens of Cuba's imperial operations in Angola were also taking their toll. But the death of Communist régimes in Eastern Europe in 1989 was the final blow. The loss of trade partners, the collapse of the CMEA trading system that was so vital to Cuban trade, and the ending of aid from fellow socialist states, all increased the pressure for reform in Cuba. The Soviet Union, which provided $5 billion in aid, also looked set to cut back its help as its own economy went from bad to disastrous. Western states were unwilling to assist the Soviet Union unless Soviet aid to the unreformed Cuba was terminated.

And yet Cuba, which unlike the East European comrades had created its own revolution, was unwilling to abandon Communist party rule. While the Cuban economy staggered on, there was a clear sense of decay and waiting before the inevitable succession took place. In preparation for that day, the United States began broadcasting Western-style news and popular culture in the hope of laying the groundwork for revolution as was done in Europe. The defeat of the Nicaraguan comrades in a free election in 1990 meant merely that Castro was more isolated than ever. The revolutionary tide had crested.

Cuba and then Nicaragua were always the socialist exceptions in a region that grew used to the United States' willingness to use force to defend interests as defined in Washington. The events in Panama were also evidence of this trend. In 1983 the United States also sent troops into Grenada in the Caribbean in order to remove a Left-wing régime. Guatemala was restrained from seizing British-controlled Honduras by American pressure. When the territory became Belize on independence in September 1981, Britain left a military force to deter the Guatemalan dictatorship. Other conflicts in the region have included the territorial dispute between Colombia and Nicaragua over islands in the Caribbean, and the tension between El Salvador and Honduras over their common frontier (the so-called Football War of 1969 was supposedly sparked off by a soccer match). But most attention has focused on the more significant struggles over the fate of Cuba, Panama and the Central American conflicts in El Salvador and Nicaragua.

The United States as policeman

A somewhat more encouraging development was the establishment of the Caribbean Community and Common Market including thirteen tiny island states, but not Cuba. Its aim is to enhance economic integration in the region, but these states are so fragile and poor that less than 10% of their imports have come from intra-regional trade. With even this paltry rate falling, the organization is characterized by fine resolutions but little effective action. The group was also badly split over the United States invasion of Grenada and was powerless to sort out the chaos surrounding an attempted coup in Trinidad and Tobago in July 1990.

CARICOM

Thus by the early 1990s American dominance in its backyard seemed more secure than ever. With a combination of brute force, economic dominance and political machinations, no sustained opposition has been able to develop. With even the fate of Cuba now in the balance, the USA can be satisfied that while the Soviet Union is clearly in retreat, the same cannot be said for the power that flows from Washington.

Reading

J.I. Dominguez and R. Hernandez, *US-Cuban Relations in the 1990s* (Boulder: Westview, 1989).

G. Fauriol, *Foreign Policy Behaviour of Caribbean States* (New York: University Press of America, 1984).

J. Heine and L. Monigat (eds), *The Caribbean and World Politics* (New York: Holmes and Meir, 1988).

H. Thomas, *Cuba* (London: Eyre and Spottiswode, 1971).

Nicaragua and El Salvador

For much of the 1980s it seemed as if the United States was mesmerized by events in Nicaragua and El Salvador. In the much calmer days of 1990, when Communism seemed to be in retreat in Europe, Asia and the Americas, the fuss over Central America seemed particularly exaggerated. But for those who still saw Communism as a threat, the very fact that the United States sent such a strong message of a willingness to confront the rival ideology in its southern reaches was part of the reason for the collapse of Communism. For others, the problems were always far more about the roots of poverty and the failure of the United States to offer more enlightened leadership.

In 1979, the Right-wing dictatorship of the Somoza family in *Nicaragua in* Nicaragua was deposed after a bloody civil war (resulting in at *turmoil* least 50,000 deaths). The Left-wing Sandinista guerrillas assumed power but quickly began to fritter away popular goodwill by silencing critics and delaying elections. Widespread nationalization contributed to a worsening economic situation. With American support, Somoza supporters (known as the Contras) began military operations against the Nicaraguan régime from bases in Honduras. The war escalated in 1982, with deaths running at a rate of up to sixty per month.

Both sides began as they meant to go on – often murdering *The Contras* indiscriminately and under incompetent military command. In March the Sandinistas declared a state of emergency and hasty attempts to integrate the 120,000-strong English-speaking Indian population drove even more to join the Contras. The United States under President Reagan froze the remainder of a $75 million aid package to Nicaragua which had been agreed by Carter and increased aid to the Contras' Nicaraguan Democratic Front (FDN) via the CIA. The United States also supported the tiny rebel groups along the southern border with Costa Rica but they constituted a small fraction of the Contra strength (said to total 15,000 in 1987 against a Nicaraguan army of 110,000).

The holding of joint United States–Honduras military exercises *The Contadora* in 1982–3 and the arrival of 1,000 American advisers in Honduras *process* were both intended to step up the pressure on Nicaragua. The Sandinistas had, in their time, also operated from Honduras but the return to democracy in Honduras in 1982 made the government worry for its own stability as the guerrilla war intensified across its borders. Inside Nicaragua, the régime came under

233

increasing pressure and began to totter. In 1983, a peace plan of the Contadora states (Colombia, Mexico, Panama and Venezuela) was accepted by the Sandinistas and elections were promised by 1985.

The Reagan hard line

After Congress cut off aid to the Contras in June 1984, the Reagan administration softened its hard line and opened talks with the Sandinistas. The negotiations were never seriously pursued by the United States in the run-up to America's own presidential election in November and were finally broken off (in June 1985). In July 1984, Nicaragua accepted a plan drawn up by the Contadora group calling for the withdrawal of all foreign military advisers in the area and the removal of all foreign bases. The United States declined to support the plan, or a revised one in September, claiming the forthcoming Nicaraguan election would be a fraud. The relatively free elections of 4 November 1984 resulted in victory for the régime but, under American prodding, they had been boycotted by the major opposition parties.

Reagan plays his cards

The second Reagan administration placed its cards more openly on the table and spoke more clearly of the need to remove the Sandinistas from power. Congress did not support that aim, but nor was it prepared to tolerate 'non-alignment' by the states of Central America. In 1985 'non-military' aid was restored to the Contras. In October 1985, the Sandinista régime extended the three-year-old state of emergency and suspended a wide range of civil liberties. The threat of an American invasion, and its attacks on the Nicaraguan régime, helped unify the Sandinistas and frustrate President Reagan. With the Contadora process stalled, the Costa Rican President Oscar Arias cajoled five Central American leaders into signing a peace plan in August 1987. For his efforts leading to direct talks in all the main conflicts of the region, Arias won the 1987 Nobel Peace Prize. But the plan relied on simultaneous progress in a number of linked conflicts – a near impossible task.

Arias peace plan

Elections and after

Like other socialist states, Nicaragua found the new environment in 1989 much less favourable. Reforms in the Soviet Union and the collapse of Communism in Eastern Europe meant far more pressure for free elections. Soviet aid was being reduced and in the atmosphere of Superpower détente, Moscow wanted no wrangling from uneasy allies in Central America. The elections that were held on 25 February 1990 in Nicaragua were supervised by a team of international observers and resulted in a clear defeat for the Sandinista régime. In the following delicate months the armed forces were transformed and the Contras disarmed. The new government of Violeta Chamorro was deeply divided now that the reason for creating a common cause was gone, but still the civil war seems to have ended, for the time being. The real test – genuine domestic reform – was still to come.

The sudden victory for the United States' line in Nicaragua came as a jolt to all Central Americans. As the pace of history rolled out from Europe where Communism was in retreat, revolutionary movements elsewhere in Central America counted the costs. Part of the reason for the tough American line in Nicaragua was the belief that without Sandinista support for Left-wing rebels, the régime in nearby El Salvador would be far more stable.

The link to El Salvador

The roots of contemporary rivalries in El Salvador run back to the 19th century. The sharp polarization into Left and Right in the 1970s led the Left to wage a guerrilla war and by 1980 the rebels controlled vast areas of the countryside. The United States supported the more Centrist government of President Duarte against the extremes both of Right and Left. Under the Reagan administration, the United States seemed primarily concerned with defeating what it viewed as Soviet, Cuban and Nicaraguan-supported rebels in El Salvador. In the three years to 1982, over 35,000 deaths were reported in the war in El Salvador.

The United States and the OAS supported elections in March 1982 which were boycotted by the Left wing. In January 1984, a United States report (by Henry Kissinger) proposed heavy aid to Duarte. However, Right-wing death squads continued to operate freely and the United States threatened to stop its $200 million aid package unless Duarte could demonstrate he was effectively in charge. Duarte won presidential elections in May 1984 but the poll was also boycotted by the Left. The two sides met for inconclusive talks in October, with the church as mediator. Duarte offered only an amnesty while the rebels wanted a new constitution, with new elections at the end of the reform process.

Duarte and death squads

Unlike Nicaragua, in El Salvador there did seem to be some room for a political compromise. Duarte was genuinely caught between two extremes and hoped to entice the social democratic wing of the rebels to compromise with his government. Total rebel strength in 1985 was about 9,000 (against an army of 40,000) and the rebels controlled about one-third of the country. Counter-insurgency sweeps had become more efficient but a military solution was not in sight. Only when the Nicaraguan supporters of the radical Left were defeated in 1990 did a real ray of hope emerge for serious talks, if not outright capitulation by the Left. Early in 1990 the United Nations sent Alvaro de Soto to negotiate between the government of President Alfredo Cristiani (Duarte had died of cancer) and the Farabundo Marti National Liberation Front (FMLN), but a deal was elusive. By early 1991, some 70,000 people had died in the past eleven years of civil war. The FMLN were reluctant to lay down their arms and the government was finding

Room for compromise

it hard even to agree to try to curb the army's power and bring it under the rule of law. The real need for reforms in El Salvador remained, but because the army believed that the worst threats to its power had passed with the retreat of Communism, it was reluctant to allow a deal to be struck.

Reading

J.A. Booth and T.W. Walker, *Understanding Central America* (Boulder: Westview, 1989).

P. Davis, *Where is Nicaragua?* (New York: Simon and Schuster, 1987).

G. DiPalma, *The Central American Impasse* (London: Croom Helm, 1986).

J. Dunkerley, *Power in the Isthmus* (New York: Verso, 1988).

N. Hamilton *et al* (eds), *Crisis in Central America* (Boulder: Westview, 1988).

South American Squabbles

Why is South America, unlike much of the rest of the developing world, so relatively peaceful? Like North America, it had the 'advantage' of being dominated by only two major European imperial powers (Spain and Portugal). But, for a combination of geographical, cultural and historical reasons, South America divided into a number of competing states while North America remained relatively united. Yet, despite the variety of independent states, in comparison to other parts of the developing world South America has fewer states and is extraordinarily peaceful.

Unlike the African experience, few South American conflicts can be blamed on colonial powers. Because of its relatively long period of independence from colonial rule, the continent's conflicts have had time to take on distinctly nationalist character. But, equally unlike Africa, the local conflicts are often strongly influenced by the looming backyard Superpower, the United States.

Don't blame the imperialists

A prime example of a relatively mature and controlled South American conflict can be found at the very foot of the continent. Since the 19th century, Argentina and Chile have disputed the ownership of the small islands of Picton, Lennox and Nueva at the eastern entrance to the Beagle channel (off Tierra del Fuego and north of Cape Horn). The territory has long been under Chilean control but Argentina formally claimed the territory in 1967. Argentina was concerned with both the prestige and principle of its nationalist claim, and with the strategic and economic value of the sea that would be controlled by the extension of a 200-mile limit around the islands. In addition, with the islands under Chilean control, Argentina argued that access to its key naval base at Ushuaia would be severely restricted. In 1971 both sides accepted international arbitration and the International Court of Justice ruled in favour of Chile in 1977. Argentina rejected the ruling and both sides then made war-like gestures. Talks in 1978 reached only partial agreement and in December both sides accepted mediation by the Vatican. Two years later Chile accepted the Papal proposals but once again Argentina rejected them. Further border tension in April and September 1981 resulted in yet another round of talks and threats in 1982.

Chile and Argentina

Argentina's sudden occupation of Britain's Falkland islands in 1982 raised Chilean fears that it would also resort to force to support its claim in the Beagle channel. But the British victory (with apparently tacit, Chilean support) and above all the end of

A deal is struck

military rule and the return to democracy in Argentina, led to moderation in Buenos Aires. After yet another round of Vatican mediation, on 5 October 1984 both sides accepted a deal that (1) confirmed Chile's possession of the islands, (2) gave Argentina some oil and mineral rights, and (3) confirmed existing claims to Antarctic territory. Despite all the noisy threats, this had been a relatively painless conflict.

Bolivia, Peru and Chile

Farther up the continent, a more complicated conflict simmers away. Bolivia has been a landlocked country ever since the war of 1879–84 when Chile seized the port of Antofagasta and the surrounding area. Luckless Peru joined the war to support Bolivia, but instead lost its southern provinces of Tacna and Arica to Chile. Tacna was regained in the 1929 treaty of Ancon.

A failed compromise

Bolivia's relations with Chile have barely improved. Diplomatic relations were severed in 1962 when Chile was accused of reducing the flow of the Lauca river. Relations were resumed in 1975 and Chile offered Bolivia a narrow corridor to the sea in exchange for territory in Bolivia's Southwest. Needless to say, Peru complained that this was a violation of the Ancon treaty, which prevents the transfer of mineral-rich former Peruvian territory to a third party without Peru's consent. The deal also collapsed because of Chile's unreasonable demands, and in March 1978, relations between Bolivia and Chile were once again severed. Not quite a stunning success for compromise but at least the hot-heads remain under control.

Peru and Ecuador

Further to the north, 125,000 square miles of the Amazon basin in north Peru is claimed by Ecuador. Spanish manipulation of the natural frontier had left Ecuador without access to the Amazon or any other major waterway. After a brief war in July 1941, the Rio Protocol (January 1942) delimited the frontier in Peru's favour. Argentina, Brazil, Chile and the United States were established as guarantors of the settlement, but Ecuador remained dissatisfied and in 1960, declared the 1942 accord null and void. Peru, having already been defeated in wars to its south and having already lost territory to Bolivia and Chile, was unwilling to compromise with its weaker neighbour, Ecuador. In any case, the guarantors were reluctant to reopen the matter and rejected Ecuador's claim.

Impotent Ecuador

In subsequent years Peru claimed that Ecuador had illegally seized some border posts and in January 1981 fighting broke out in the Condor mountains. In the five-day war, Ecuadorean troops were driven back and a ceasefire, arranged by the Organization of American States (OAS) came into effect on 1 February. The OAS commission responsible for the ceasefire (United States), Argentina, Brazil and Chile) agreed to supervize the border area. Periodic reports of oil finds in the contested territory have raised the stakes but Ecuador simply lacks the power or the external support to change the status quo. Sporadic clashes continue and may yet develop in a more dangerous fashion as Brazil extends further west in its conquest of Amazonia.

Nevertheless, it remains rare for South American countries to resort to force to settle disputes. Indeed, there were signs in 1991 that some of them might even be getting the habit of economic cooperation. Although the idea of a Latin American Free Trade Association petered out, in March 1991 Brazil, Argentina, Paraguay and Uruguay agreed to set up a Southern Cone Common Market by the end of 1994. With a market of 190 million people and more than half the GDP of Latin America and the Caribbean, the region has decent prospects if it can overcome the traditions of economic and political incompetence.

Getting together

Reading

P. Calvert, *Boundary Disputes in Latin America* (London: Institute for the Study of Conflict, 1983).

V. Gamba-Stonehouse, *Strategy in the Southern Oceans* (London: Frances Pinter, 1989).

M. Morris and V. Millan, *Controlling Latin American Conflicts* (Boulder, Colorado: Westview, 1983).

H. Munoz and J. Tulchon (eds), *Latin American Nations in World Politics* (Boulder, Colorado: Westview, 1984).

The Falklands – or the Malvinas

As conflicts over decolonization fade away, peculiar accidents of history remain to be resolved. One of the most bizarre anomalies must be the contest between Britain and Argentina over the Falkland islands and their dependent territories. The rival claims rest on a confusing historical background.

The forsaken islands
The Falkland islands lie 300 miles off the coast of Argentina and have a population of barely 2,000 (not counting the far more numerous sheep). The islands were 'discovered' by Britain in 1592 but France built the first settlements on the islands in 1764 and called them 'les Malouines', after St Malo in France. In 1765 the British established a settlement and a year later France relinquished its rights to Spain, which in turn established a settlement in 1767. Britain withdrew in 1774 but maintained its claim to the islands. Spain retained a garrison on the Falklands until 1810 when the islands were abandoned. Argentina became independent of Spain in 1816 and asserted its claim to the Falklands in the 1820s. Argentine settlers were then expelled by the American navy in 1832 and Britain reasserted its sovereignty in 1833.

Subsistence sheep farming
The island of South Georgia lies 800 miles east of the Falklands and the South Sandwich Islands are a further 470 miles east. They were discovered by Britain in 1775; Argentina only claimed sovereignty over these islands in 1948. Various other tiny, uninhabited islands became part of Britain's Antarctic territory on 3 March 1962. Argentina insists that Britain is acting as a colonial power and that its claim to the islands is invalid. But the people of the islands have repeatedly chosen to maintain the link with Britain and have refused to accept arrangements which would lead to the transfer of sovereignty over the islands to Argentina. Their lives are focused on subsistence sheep farming and the often feudal demands of a controlling British company.

Lease-back
In 1955 Britain submitted the dispute over sovereignty to the International Court of Justice but the Court declined to hear the case because Argentina and Chile refused to agree to submit to its jurisdiction. Talks between Britain and Argentina in 1965 were inconclusive and the following year a small detachment of Royal Marines was placed on the Falklands, after the Right wing Argentine dictatorship staged a symbolic invasion. Talks in 1977 included discussion of sovereignty but Britain pledged to consider the wishes of the islanders, thereby giving them a veto over Anglo-Argentine negotiations. Some reports in 1980, however, suggested

Britain was prepared to transfer formal sovereignty to Argentina but to 'lease back' the islands so they would remain under British or local administration. In January 1981 the Falklands Legislative Council opposed the lease-back plan but supported the continuation of talks. By early 1982 negotiations had run into the ground and Argentina's military dictatorship, already facing serious domestic problems, warned it would use 'other means' to settle the issue.

As if this obscure dispute was not peculiar enough, on 19 March 1982 Argentine scrap-metal merchants landed illegally on South Georgia and raised the Argentine flag. On 2 April, Argentine armed forces invaded the Falklands and Britain immediately raised a naval task force to retake the islands. While British forces steamed 8,000 miles south to demonstrate that Britain was not entirely powerless, negotiations conducted under American auspices failed to remove the 10,000 Argentine troops. On 25 April Britain recaptured South Georgia and further mediation by Peru also failed. Britain regained the islands in fierce fighting between 21 May and 14 June. *Argentina invades*

Britain lost 255 dead for the sake of pride, principle and penguins, while Argentina lost over 700 dead for the defence of its nationalist principles and the survival of a fading military dictatorship. The islands have not quite returned to normal near-subsistence sheep farming and coastal fishing. Hundreds of British troops were based there, distorting the local economy and enhancing the doubts about defending so few, so far, for so little. Despite speculation about the potential for valuable offshore resources (such as oil) nothing substantial has yet been found. In fact, the need to defend the island's fishing resources from being depleted by foreign trawlers, caused even more headaches for London. In November 1986, a 150-mile zone of restricted fishing was proclaimed by Britain, and rejected by Argentina and its supporters. *The cost*

The passage of time, the election of a democratic government in Argentina, and the rethinking of British military deployments after the European revolutions of 1989 all led to an easing of tensions. With the Argentine economy in dire straits, the desire for aid from the EC was great enough to allow both Britain and Argentina to begin informal talks in August 1989. Talks in Madrid in October led to the restoration of full diplomatic relations without Britain or Argentina having made any substantial changes to their positions. It seems that a final settlement will have to wait even longer, and certainly for a new party in power in London. *Easing tension*

Reading

P. Calvert, *The Falklands Crisis* (London: Frances Pinter, 1982).

L. Freedman and V. Gamba-Stonehouse, *Signals of War* (London: Faber, 1990).

J. Goebel, *The Struggle for the Falklands Islands* (New Haven: Yale University Press, 1982).

Organization of American States

Outside Europe and some parts of Asia, the states of the Americas have the longest tradition of independence and sovereignty. They also have the oldest international regional organization and one of the best records of resolving international disputes without resort to war. These three trends are no doubt inter-related. But this relative regional stability also owes something to the predominance of one power, the United States, both throughout the region and within the Organization of American States (OAS).

The OAS is officially devoted to strengthening the security of the Western hemisphere, to the settlement of inter-American disputes and to the promotion of economic and social cooperation. Most of these purposes have their origins in the early attempts at Pan-American union. The United States' Monroe Doctrine of 1823 was primarily intended to keep outside powers out of the region and to enhance United States hegemony. The first real attempt at Pan-Americanism, apart from United States' imperialism, was the first Congress of American States convened in Panama in 1826 by Simon Bolivar. But because of Latin American divisions and Washington's power, it was the United States-inspired Union of American Republics in 1889–90 which created the Pan-American Union as its permanent organ in 1923 and the forerunner of the OAS. *The Pan-American Union*

The Pan-American Union convened a conference in 1945 which proclaimed the Act of Chapultepec, a treaty of mutual assistance. On 2 September 1947 in Rio, a regional mutual defence pact was signed by nineteen of the twenty-one American republics (Ecuador and Nicaragua refused and Cuba withdrew in March 1960). After 1950, the United States also signed bilateral defence pacts with a number of states. *The Rio Pact*

The OAS itself resulted from the desire to give permanent legal form to the hitherto loosely-organized Pan-American Union. The Charter was signed at Bogota by twenty-one American republics in April 1948 and reflected both the principle of non-intervention in domestic politics and the concept of collective defence. The OAS was recorded as a regional alliance under the United Nations, but its headquarters in Washington remained a symbol of American dominance. In 1970, a General Assembly was created as the supreme organ of the OAS. *The OAS Charter*

The relative peace of the Americas can, in part, be attributed to the OAS' moderate success in regional peacekeeping. In 1965 it *Peacekeeping*

243

sent an inter-American peace force to the Dominican Republic to replace American troops, after the latter had intervened to forestall a Left-wing takeover. In 1969, El Salvador and Honduras agreed to allow a 7-man OAS committee to investigate the human rights of Salvadoreans in Honduras. The OAS arranged a ceasefire and supervized an exchange of prisoners. In 1981 it called on Ecuador and Peru to cease military operations, arranged a ceasefire and sent in a monitoring team. OAS services were also called upon in disputes between the Dominican Republic and Haiti (1949–50, 1962–5), Cuba and Guatemala (1950), and Costa Rica and Nicaragua (1955–6, 1977).

The Cuba problem

The OAS has also had some notable failures. The United States has been particularly irked that what it saw as Soviet influence, for example in the Communist take-over of Cuba, was not halted. The OAS was racked by debate in 1960–2 over Cuba. Havana was suspended because adherence to Marxist Leninism was deemed contrary to the inter-American system. Mexico refused to implement the ensuing sanctions and by 1975 the boycott of Cuba was in such disarray that members were officially allowed to restore normal diplomatic relations with Cuba. A meeting of 8 democratic members of the OAS in November 1987 agreed to support the restoration of full Cuban membership. Latin Americans have rarely been seriously worried about the impact of Marxism or the Soviet threat but have often seen fit to mouth anti-Communist slogans to ensure United States support and cash. These states were usually more concerned about problems of development, while Washington viewed the region in East–West terms.

The OAS restrained

The OAS has also been unable to resolve any of the region's boundary disputes and was impotent during the Falklands war in 1982 and in the series of Central American conflicts of the 1980s. It has obtained its relatively good reputation among regional organizations in large part because it operates in a mostly peaceful environment, not because it has achieved any conspicuous successes.

Economic cooperation

In the wider politics of the region, the OAS has had a similarly mixed record. In 1959 the Inter-American Development Bank was established, but early hopes for the formation of a common market similar to the EC proved exaggerated. Over 80% of Latin American trade still goes by sea, suggesting that states still look outside, rather than inward to fellow members of the continent. Certainly local leaders often look to the United States for guidance far more quickly than they consult their neighbours.

A new concern for human rights

In 1961 the OAS launched the Alliance for Progress to further social and economic development but that program only worked so long as the United States was providing the funds and was satisfied with its political orientation. In 1979 the Inter-American Court of Human Rights was established and concern was expressed over the situation in Argentina, Chile, El Salvador, Haiti, Paraguay and Uruguay. But the states of the region were willing to take little concrete action.

Latin American states have taken a leading role in calling for a New International Economic Order and have sought to persuade the United States to implement these ideas on a regional basis through the OAS. But the United States' objections were the same as for the broader NIEO proposal, and Washington insisted that these issues were best dealt with by such global institutions as the World Bank and the IMF. The United States has gradually reduced its proportion of OAS funding from two-thirds to half. In fact, in the 1980s, the OAS returned to its original concern with smaller scale, regional issues. Most of the major issues affecting the region were handled outside the OAS. Whether it was the Contadora group's attempts to reach a Central American settlement or the discussion of international debt in the World Bank and the IMF, the OAS was seen as too cumbersome to confront these pressing problems.

Latin America and the NIEO

The problems of debt and unrest are of course linked. The large debtor nations of the OAS (Brazil, Mexico and Argentina) believe that the United States was too obsessed with the exaggerated Soviet–Cuban–Nicaraguan threat and so failed to tackle the regional instability that often resulted from its own stringent measures to reduce Latin America's massive debt. The OAS is obviously hampered by its domination by the United States, but the members are mostly unwilling (or not allowed by the United States) to take the radical steps to sever the links with Washington. With the decline in concern in the USA with Left-wing threats in Latin America after the revolutions of 1989–90, and the growing concern over the drug problem in the region, perhaps far more attention will now be paid to the roots of unrest in local politics.

Debt and unrest

Reading

G.P. Atkins, *Latin America in the International Political System* (New York: Free Press, 1977).

G. Connell-Smith, *The Inter-American System* (London: 1966).

H.E. Davis and L.C. Wilson (eds), *Latin American Foreign Policies* (London: The John Hopkins University Press, 1975).

H. Han, *Problems and Prospects of the OAS* (New York: Peter Lang, 1987).

E. Milensky, *The Politics of Regional Organizations in Latin America* (New York: Praeger, 1973).

8

THE MIDDLE EAST

Israel and Palestine

The conflict between Arabs and Israelis has been one of the most continuous and complex in the post-war world. Although casualties have not been as high as one might expect for such a prolonged dispute, the risks of great power involvement have been high. The Superpowers have pursued strategic, economic and ideological interests in the region and, as a result, have regularly found themselves entangled in dangerous confrontation. The local conflict has involved a number of states but it is made even more byzantine by the fact that the core and crux of the problem pits a fragile Israeli state against an unrepresented, politically fragmented and militarily weak Palestinian people. The conflict is essentially rooted in the strong and ancient claims of two peoples to a single tiny slice of Mediterranean coastline at the crossroads of the Middle East.

Israel's roots
Israeli claims hark back to Biblical times when a Jewish kingdom dominated the area and Jews were the majority population in the 1,600 years before the Roman occupation. Rome conquered the territory it called Palestine (after the Philistines who lived along the coast) and expelled the Jews. By the 9th century the vast majority of the remaining population had become Islamic and, with the odd interlude such as the Christian Crusaders, the area remained firmly under Muslim control.

Zionism
In the 19th century, when nationalist movements were helping shape European states and Jews were persecuted in Europe, many Jews were attracted to the notion of Zionism – the creation of a Jewish homeland in Zion (a Hebrew word for Israel). For centuries, Israel had remained the focus of prayers and cultural identification of Jews scattered around the globe. Jewish settlers began returning to Israel, a land then held by the crumbling Turkish Ottoman Empire. Although initially the local Palestinian population was content to live side-by-side with the new Jewish settlers, as their numbers swelled Palestinian nationalism began to emerge.

Britain's predicament
The British took over Palestine from the Turks in 1917 and successive British governments managed to promise some form of home rule to both Jews and Arabs. In 1920, British control was codified in a League of Nations Mandate from which Britain soon split an eastern section which was later to form the Kingdom of Jordan. Jewish immigration into the western section, Palestine, increased and Palestinians feared that their majority would soon be eroded. While riots in Palestine led Britain to restrict Jewish

immigration, anti-Semitism in Europe, especially in Hitler's Germany, increased the pressure for Jews to find refuge in Israel. In 1937 Britain proposed partition of the territory, a move which most Jews supported but the Arabs rejected. During the Second World War the Jews suspended their attacks on British rule to aid the war effort in Europe. The Palestinian leadership supported the Axis powers in the hope of seeing the British removed from the Middle East.

With the end of the Second World War and the knowledge that 6 million Jews had died in the Nazi holocaust, pressure grew for massive settlement in Israel. Britain, already weakened by the war, handed the Palestine problem to the United Nations. The General Assembly (with both Soviet and American support) voted on 29 November 1947 to partition the territory. Jews accepted the plan, which gave them 56% of the land but most of the rich agricultural areas to the Palestinians. Neighbouring Arab states rejected the plan – the Palestinians were not asked – and when the state of Israel was proclaimed on 14 May 1948, 6 Arab states invaded. Although the Jewish state was not expected to survive such an onslaught, by January 1949 ceasefires established Israel's *de facto* frontiers as 20% larger than provided for in the partition resolution (yet this was still only 17% of the original Palestine Mandate). Most of the remaining 80% of Palestine was occupied by the Kingdom of Jordan. Neither Jordan, nor Egypt which occupied the Gaza Strip, sought to establish a Palestinian state, preferring to keep the spoils.

Britain quits Palestine

Some 600,000–720,000 Arab Palestinian people fled Israeli control as a result of fear and Jewish intimidation. According to some estimates, about half that total were recent Arab immigrants to Palestine. Sixty-four per cent of the refugees fled to territory earmarked for Palestine (the West Bank of the Jordan river and the Gaza Strip), 10% to Jordan (east of the river), 10% to Syria and 14% to Lebanon. Although Arab states did not integrate their brethren into their states, Israel took in a larger number of Jews from Arab countries and beyond. Between 1948 and 1972, Israel took 580,000 Jews from Arab countries (including 260,000 from Morocco and 129,000 from Iraq), 600,000 from Europe, 60,000 from Iran, 20,000 from India and a further 100,000 from the Soviet Union in the early 1970s. In 1984–5 yet another 10,000 Ethiopian Jews were air-lifted to Israel, and in 1990 hundreds of thousands began arriving from a reforming Russia.

Exchanging populations

This massive shift was not uncommon in the immediate postwar world, but Arab states refused to recognize the existence of Israel. With its territory only twelve miles across at its narrowest point and Arab leaders promising to drive the Jews into the sea, Arab states could reasonably hope for victory in a second round.

Israeli security problems

Israel's parliamentary democracy (the only one in the Middle East) included a 10% Arab population (Hebrew and Arabic were the official languages) but was under regular threat from guerrilla raids from its Arab neighbours. In 1955, 250 Israelis died in such raids and the Israeli army launched counter-attacks.

The Suez débacle

Israel had become closely identified with Western interests as the Cold War forced states to choose sides. Soviet diplomacy became more active in the Middle East when a military coup in Egypt brought to power a radical régime led by President Nasser. Egypt antagonized British and French interests by nationalizing the Suez Canal and by receiving modern Soviet arms. In 1955 Nasser closed access to Israel's southern port of Eilat on the Gulf of Akaba and, in October 1956, Israel, Britain and France colluded in an attack on Egypt. The United States and the Soviet Union forced all three to quit by March 1957 and the United Nations agreed to send 3,000 men to patrol the Israel–Egypt frontier and keep the Gulf of Akaba open.

Growing radicalism

Sporadic raids into Israel continued and Israeli shipping was denied the use of the Suez Canal. Arab states became increasingly aware that a military defeat of Israel would be difficult and, in part as a symbol of this frustration, in 1964 a group of Palestinian liberation movements joined together to form the Palestine Liberation Organization (PLO). But the conflict continued to be primarily between Israel and established Arab states. In 1966, a radical régime emerged in Syria led by the Ba'ath Party and raids were launched on Israel. Although this régime was shaky, Nasser viewed it as a challenge to his leadership of the Pan-Arab movement. In May 1967, Nasser demanded that UN forces leave the frontier, imposed a blockade on the Gulf of Akaba and mobilized his forces. Western attempts to form a flotilla to break the blockade failed and Israel faced a ring of hostile states when Jordan put its troops under a unified command with Egypt.

The Six-Day War

Israeli forces struck a pre-emptive blow on 5 June 1967 and in six days took the Sinai peninsula from Egypt, the West bank from Jordan and the Golan Heights from Syria. Superpower forces had been put on alert as the Soviet Union sought to deter Israel from totally humiliating Moscow's Arab allies (Jordan, however, was armed by the West). This time the United States was not prepared to force an Israeli withdrawal and Israel was convinced that its victory was so devastating that Arab states would give up their hope of eliminating the Jewish state. In November 1967 the United Nations Security Council passed Resolution 242, which called for recognition of all states in the area and evacuation of territory occupied in the 1967 war (but not the 1948 one). Israel accepted the Resolution (as did the Great Powers) but the Arab states were more equivocal.

The Arab states refused to abandon their hope of a military solution. Egypt's war of attrition (1969–70) along the Suez Canal led to devastating, deep-penetration Israeli raids which, in turn, led the Soviet Union to provide air cover. But it was the emergence of Palestinian resistance that was the most striking change after the 1967 war. Following the failure of the established Arab states to defeat Israel with conventional military power and Israeli occupation of all Palestine, the PLO and its splinter allies sought to take their fate into their own hands. PLO forces fought King Hussein of Jordan for power in 1970 and, despite a campaign of international terror (notably aircraft hijacking), the PLO under Yasser Arafat was forced to set up headquarters in Lebanon. Beirut became the springboard for such raids as the killing of eleven Israeli athletes at the 1972 Munich Olympics. Israeli counter-attacks against Lebanon were fierce, often resulting in far more casualties as the PLO bases were situated in crowded refugee camps. Palestinian resistance in Israeli-occupied territory was militarily insignificant.

The PLO challenge

Although the Palestinian movement was making the headlines, it was unable to shake Israeli military supremacy. The new Egyptian leader, Anwar Sadat, sought to obtain Superpower, and then American, aid in arranging an Israeli withdrawal. But the United States was preoccupied with the Vietnam War. Sadat, in conjunction with Syria, launched a surprise attack on Israel on 6 October 1973 (the Jews' holiest day, Yom Kippur). Despite early Arab military gains, Israeli forces eventually took even more territory than they had held after 1967. Once again, Superpower involvement ran the risk of getting out of hand, this time because both were closely engaged in rearming their allies. At the height of the crisis both Superpowers placed troops on high alert in order to deter each other's intervention and force their allies to cease firing.

The Yom Kippur War

But this time, the United States was prepared to extend its influence in the Arab world (and at the Soviet Union's expense) by pressing Israel to surrender some occupied territory. In a series of disengagement accords (1974–5) with Syria and Egypt, Israel gave up all territory taken in 1973 and some of that acquired in 1967. However, no progress was made on the Palestinian issue. The PLO terror attacks continued (e.g. 20 children were killed in an attack on a school in May 1974) and Israeli counter-attacks in Lebanon became a deadly, predictable response. But, despite the violence, the PLO gradually gained wider international recognition. It was granted United Nations observer status in 1974 and in 1975 the General Assembly condemned Zionism as racism.

The PLO strikes again

The dramatic breakthrough in obtaining Arab recognition of Israel came in the courageous visit by President Sadat to the Israeli Knesset (Parliament) in November 1977. In protracted negotiations

Camp David Peace

under American auspices at Camp David in September 1978, an Israel–Egypt peace treaty was signed in March 1979. In exchange for Israeli evacuation of Sinai, Egypt recognized the Jewish state; Israel also pledged to begin negotiations for Palestinian autonomy and in the meantime still held the Gaza Strip pending a settlement of the Palestinian issue. Thus the people of Gaza, living in the squalor of refugee camps, were unwanted by Egypt and Israel but unable to obtain autonomy until a general settlement was reached. But no other Arab state or movement was prepared to talk to Israel. For a time, Egypt was isolated in the Arab world because of this peace treaty, and a 'rejectionist front' led by Syria (with Soviet support) was established.

'Peace for Galilee'

With Egypt removed from the military equation, Israeli security was vastly enhanced. In June 1982 it turned to a 'solution' of the Palestinian problem and terrorist attacks. In 'Operation Peace for Galilee' Israel swept into Lebanon to eliminate PLO forces and remove the controls of the radical Palestinian leadership that opposed Israeli rule on the West Bank. Military success was swift, the Israelis trouncing Syrian troops in the way and forcing 15,000 PLO fighters to leave in August. But the Lebanese quagmire trapped Israeli troops in a debilitating anti-guerrilla war and it was unable to impose a new order or peace treaty on Lebanon. As a result of attacks on Israeli forces, mounting Israeli domestic economic problems and a change of government in mid-1984, Israel decided to quit Lebanon. This was a divisive war that for the first time was not perceived in Israel as a 'war of necessity'. By June 1985, when Israeli troops left Lebanon, many also saw this as the first war Israel had lost.

Israeli objectives

If the Israeli objective was merely to deal a military blow to the PLO, they were successful. There was also no question in Syrian minds that Israel was dominant on the battlefield, especially with Egypt sitting on the sidelines. But neither Syria nor the PLO was prepared to recognize Israel and so the political conflict remained embedded in concrete.

The intifada

The international environment for a settlement seemed to be improving when Egypt was gradually readmitted to the Arab fold (it rejoined the Arab League in 1987) and a reforming Soviet Union began re-establishing diplomatic links with Israel. The revolutions in Eastern Europe in 1989 put pressure on Arab radicals to come to the negotiating table because their former sources of aid were drying up and Israel was being reinforced by the influx of tens of thousands of Russian Jews. But a hardline, albeit fragile, Israeli government was in no mood for compromise, especially as the Palestinians in the occupied territories had finally found their voice. The Palestinian uprising, or *intifada*, may merely have been a 'war of stones', but like any good guerrilla war it proved impossible to suppress by traditional military means. After three years of skirmishes starting in December 1987 when Arabs threw stones and Israeli soldiers fired back with rifles, more than 750 Palestinians had been killed by Israelis and 300 by fellow Palestinians. Only 55 Israelis had been killed.

While foreign television crews grew bored and moved on to the more dramatic scenes in Eastern Europe, the regular blood-letting continued, despite Israeli arrests of more than 40,000 Palestinians. Although the PLO was cajoled by the Americans into renouncing the use of terrorism and accepting the existence of Israel, elections in the occupied territories were delayed by Israeli intransigence and PLO haggling about terms. When Iraq invaded Kuwait in August 1990 the PLO came out as one of the few supporters of Iraq. Israel, as a key, if quiet member of the anti-Iraq coalition, hoped that the United States would no longer press Israel for concessions to the Palestinians. However, President Saddam Hussein of Iraq put the pressure back on by insisting on a linkage between his withdrawal from Kuwait and an Israeli withdrawal from Palestinian land. While both Israel and the United States rejected any such linkage, in practice the United States found that after the defeat of Iraq, it was under pressure to move quickly to a settlement of the Arab–Israeli dispute.

Palestine and the Gulf crisis

In many senses, the issues remain unchanged from 1948. On the one hand Arab states need to come to terms with a Jewish state in their midst. Egypt, and to a certain extent Jordan, have already agreed to do so. Syria holds out as long as it sees benefits from leading the revolutionary, 'rejectionist' forces. On the other hand, recognition of Israel is only half of the problem that the UN partition resolution set out to solve. While there are increasing signs that the Palestinians are prepared to settle for a state on the West Bank and Gaza Strip, they are unwilling to recognize Israel until the Israelis accept such an independent Palestinian state. The close involvement of Jordan in any solution, perhaps as part of a federation with a Palestinian state, might ease the problem. But for the time being the issues appear far from solved. As long as the crux of the problem – the sharing of a small territory by rival claimants – is not faced, this long-running conflict will run and run.

The Jordanian option

Reading

S. Bailey, *Four Arab-Israeli Wars and the Peace Process* (London: Macmillan, 1990).

T. Freedman, *From Beirut to Jerusalem* (New York: Farrar, Straus, and Giroux, 1989).

A. Kleinman, *Israel and the World After 40 Years* (New York: Macmillan, 1990).

B. Morris, *The Birth of the Palestinian Refugee Problem* (Cambridge: Cambridge University Press, 1988).

D. Peretz, *Intifada* (Boulder: Westview, 1990).

Z. Schiff and E. Ya'ari, *Intifada* (New York: Simon and Schuster, 1990).

Disappearing Lebanon

The confusion that is Lebanon has defied the best meddling efforts of Lebanon's neighbours and the great powers alike. For all intents and purposes, a single Lebanese state has ceased to exist. Great powers have, at times, become directly entangled in local rivalries but have increasingly become resigned to the fact that the rewards are not worth the risks. Even local powers, like Syria or Israel, find it next to impossible to control the myriad factions in the chaos that is their neighbour Lebanon. The ruin of what once was the 'playground' of the Middle East can be explained in part by the deep religious divisions in the Lebanon, but the roots of the conflict are more rotten still.

The origins of the dispute in the Lebanon can be traced far back into history but the intense conflict has been a feature only of the past decade. Lebanon, or ancient Phoenecia, became part of the Byzantine Empire but the spread of Islam in the 9th century created a mixed Christian–Muslim population. The brief presence of Christian Crusaders helped split some of the Christian sects, as the Ottoman Turk rule (1516–1918) did the Muslims. In the dying days of the Ottoman Empire (from about 1860) France became the 'protector' of the Christian population that lived mostly along the coastal strip. *Mixing Christiâns and Muslims*

France administered Lebanon from 1920 under a League of Nations mandate and helped expand Christian influence. Lebanon declared independence in 1941 under guidance from the Free French forces and a republic was established in 1943. All foreign troops left in 1946, even though neighbouring Syria coveted Lebanon as its own. Even in its earliest days, modern Lebanon was a delicate balance of Christian and Muslim groups. France had declared that there was a slight Christian majority and so an unofficial but firm agreement was established that the President would be a Maronite Christian, the Prime Minister a Sunni Muslim and the speaker of the parliament a Shia Muslim. The seats in the Chamber of deputies were allocated on a communal basis – 13 Maronites, 9 Sunni, 8 Shia, 5 Greek Orthodox Christian, 3 Druze (a Muslim sect), 3 Greek Catholics, 2 Armenian Catholics and one other. *The French mandate*

Even if this delicate communal balance was at one time accurate, it was soon overtaken by the influx of Palestinian refugees in 1948 (mostly Sunni Muslims) and the higher Muslim birth rate. Needless to say, Christian groups were unwilling to change the *The Palestinian influx* system that gave them power and with Western, and tacit Israeli, support (another non-Muslim entity in the Middle East) the country remained barely stable. Despite brief interludes of unrest, for example 1958 when American troops were called in to help keep order, Lebanon prospered as the business and commercial centre of the Middle East.

PLO gunmen rule   Not surprisingly, this fragile prosperity was not nearly robust enough to cope with the major dislocation caused when the Palestine Liberation Organization, driven out of its headquarters in Jordan in 1970, set up in Lebanon. With Palestinian refugee camps in Beirut and south Lebanon serving as bases, raids were launched against Israel and Western interests around the world. Israeli counter-attacks were fierce and helped undermine Lebanese sovereignty and the government's ability to keep order. Palestinians looked to their own protection and Palestinian gunmen ruled large areas of south Lebanon and Beirut. The Christians fought back against the erosion of their independence, which in turn helped create a Palestinian–Muslim Leftist alliance. In April 1975 serious fighting broke out, forcing the Christians to concentrate on defending their traditional territory on the coast north of Beirut.

Syria steps in   Outside powers stayed out of this messy conflict but Syria, which saw Lebanon as part of its natural sphere of influence, intervened in April 1976 to protect the faltering Christians. Syria was not particularly interested in protecting the rights of Christians in the Middle East but it did see an advantage in a weak but controllable Lebanon. Israel also provided secret support for the Christians in their struggle to control the Palestinians. After a ceasefire in October 1976, Syrian forces were used as the bulk of the Arab Deterrent Force (ADF) of 30,000. An uneasy truce was punctuated by PLO raids on Israel and by Israeli counter-strikes. The writ of the Lebanese government ceased to run in the south and in March 1978 Israeli troops invaded the southern area to sweep out PLO bases. In June, a United Nations force (UNIFIL) of 4,000 was put in place to monitor the frontier, but Israel also supported a Christian militia (the South Lebanon Army, SLA) to provide a buffer along Israel's northern frontier.

Israel steps in   The border was not completely calm but by mid-1981 the problem seemed to be under control. Nevertheless, in June 1982, Israel launched Operation Peace for Galilee in an attempt to clear PLO forces out of Lebanon. By August, south Lebanon was cleared and PLO fighters were evacuated from Beirut. The Syrian troops in the ADF were easily swept aside but Israel soon found itself incapable of controlling Lebanon any better than the Syrians. Israel's military operation only stimulated the growth of the cancer of communalism, as was evident in the Christian massacre of Palestinians in camps at Sabra and Chatilla, nominally under Israeli protection.

Israeli troops soon withdrew from Beirut as a Western peacekeeping force of 5,800 (including French, British, Italian and US troops) tried to keep a semblance of order. But Western attempts to give the Lebanese government a breathing space to create a unified state (and above all a unified army) foundered on the rocks of entrenched communalism and because the rival militia were better armed and trained than the Lebanese army. Radical Shia Muslims launched devastating suicide raids on Western troops, for example, killing 241 American soldiers in a single raid on 23 October 1983. In February–March 1984 the Western troops withdrew and Israeli forces began pulling back.

Anarchy in Lebanon was nearly complete. Sporadic mediation efforts failed and gunmen (including children armed with rockets) ruled the streets and countryside. Outside powers had been forced out, the Syrians and Israelis were bloodied and less ambitious for control and local militia ran wild. The nominal President of Lebanon, a Maronite Christian, was barely able to control even his beleagured Christians (some wanted to declare an independent Christian Lebanon). The Druze militia, once a tacit ally of the Christians (Druze in Israel serve in the Israeli army) now turned on the weakened Christians in order to consolidate their strongholds in Lebanon's central mountains. Shia Muslims, once the weaker Muslim group, took advantage of the defeat of the PLO to take over much of southern Lebanon as Israeli troops departed. *The anarchy of rockets*

By June 1985 Israeli troops had pulled out of Lebanon (though some 'observers' were left to assist the SLA), having suffered some 600 dead and having inflicted some 12,000 casualties among the Lebanese. Jerusalem had little to show for its pains except the replacement of PLO extremism with a more radical Shia domination. Israel left the SLA in charge of the frontier but attacks from Lebanon on Israel's northern settlements continued. Shia militia began taking over former PLO strongholds in the south. They attacked both Israeli targets and Palestinian camps in Beirut where previously Christians had massacred Palestinians. Syria, although nominally in control of a rump of the PLO and supporting the Shia militia re-took its major role in parts of Lebanon in February 1987, but found it was incapable of restoring order and became increasingly worried by independent-minded Shia leaders. *Twelve thousand casualties*

Fifteen years of fighting had eliminated virtually all ground for compromise. The Christian leader who agreed to a 1985 pact was swiftly overthrown. Gangs of gunmen ran wild in Beirut and the countryside, some kidnapping foreigners and capturing the fleeting attention of the international media. All was anarchy. The gunmen governed, while the notional President Elias Hrawi tried to find some way to gain control. He had been installed by a conference in Taif (Saudi Arabia) in October 1989, but his powers *Aborted peace* were purely on paper for the first year of his tenure. It was not until the Iraqi invasion of Kuwait in August 1990 that there was some real movement towards peace.

Syria sweeps through

Syria, once high on the hate-list of Western powers concerned about support for terrorism, joined the anti-Saddam Hussein coalition. His reward was a free hand in Beirut to sweep away the powerful Christian General Michel Aoun which made it possible for Syria to arrange a clear out of all militias from Beirut in November 1990. Pesident Hrawi's writ, at least with a Syrian counter-signature, could now run in Beirut, and was gradually extended out to the countryside. Syria was certainly unable to extend its power much further before it ran into Israeli forces.

The partition solution

Although the mess in Beirut has been tidied, Lebanon still seems ripe for partition. A revised constitution that gave more power to the majority Muslims might satisfy some, but it certainly would be unacceptable to most Christians. Yet partition also would not be easy. Christians in the north were divided from those in the south under Israeli protection. Furthermore, divisions within the Muslim camp had already reached lethal proportions. In fact, Lebanon had virtually ceased to exist as a sovereign state and it was difficult to see it ever being re-created.

Reading

H. Cobban, *The Making of Modern Lebanon* (London: Hutchinson, 1985).

A. Dawisha, *Syria and the Lebanese Crisis* (London: Macmillan, 1980).

R. Fisk, *Pity the Nation* (New York: Atheneum, 1990).

T. Freedman, *From Beirut to Jerusalem* (New York: Farrar, Straus, and Giroux, 1989).

Iran and Iraq

The Middle East's most deadly conflict since 1945 has taken place where two great ancient empires once fought for regional dominance. But war between oil-rich Iran and Iraq has not been the trigger for the Third World War, as many feared. Remarkably, local neighbours and the Superpowers were content to sit on the sidelines while the two bully boys of the Gulf bled each other dry. As an example of cynicism in world politics it was hard to beat, but then Iran and Iraq themselves set the tone by waging what must rank as one of the most senseless conflicts since the First World War.

Both sides maintain valuable oil facilities in the Gulf area but this did not keep either from pursuing their broader political aims by war. Following the Muslim revolution in Iran in 1979 and the resulting instability, Iraq saw an opportunity to reassert its insignificant territorial claim and assert its political aspirations to leadership in the Gulf. The war was ostensibly about the southern border between modern-day Iran and Iraq which runs along the Shatt al-Arab waterway (the Arvand river, according to Iran). Iraq claimed the frontier to be on the eastern (Iranian) bank but in March 1975 had signed an agreement with Iran that recognized the principle of a frontier down the middle of the river. In return, Iran agreed to cease aid to Kurdish rebels in Iraq. *The causes of war*

On 22 September 1980 Iraq attacked Iran along a 300-mile front. Iraqi President Hussein claimed his objectives to be sovereignty of the Shatt al-Arab waterway and the withdrawal of Iran from Abu, Musa and Tumb islands in the Gulf. However, Hussein's objectives also apparently included the overthrow of the new Islamic Republic of Iran and recognition of Iraq as the leader of the Arab world. *The outbreak of war*

Iraq gained control of most of the desired territory within the first month of the war, although a quick victory was denied by fierce Iranian resistance. A military deadlock ensued for the next eighteen months. Sporadic combat continued despite various international peace missions. A turning point came early in 1982 when Iran launched two successful counter-offensives: at Deshful in March and along a sixty-mile front between Susangered and Khoramshar in April. Khoramshar was recaptured in May. By July, Iraqi troops had withdrawn to the pre-war boundary and beyond. However, Iran also met fierce opposition as it crossed the *Iraq's short-lived gains*

Iraqi frontier and the war once again settled into a deadly slog in the Gulf marshes.

Widening the war In February 1986 and January 1987 Iran made some gains near the frontier with Kuwait, which it threatened to drag into the conflict. In an effort to end the war, Iraq attacked Iranian oil terminals and exports in the Gulf. Iran, which unlike Iraq was dependent on oil exports in the Gulf to fund the war, retaliated by attacking the oil exports of other Gulf states supporting Iraq. In December 1986 Kuwait had asked for international protection and in mid-1987, the great powers, which included first the Soviet Union, responded with oil tankers, reflagging of Kuwaiti tankers and naval protection for the convoys. Iran responded with mine-laying and the tension increased. Initially, Europeans were reluctant to join in the protection of convoys but the Iranian refusal to accept a UN Security Council call for a ceasefire in July 1987 tipped the scale in favour of concerted action by Western powers. American ships sunk Iranian vessels and even accidentally shot down an Iranian civilian aircraft, so killing 290 passengers.

Towards a ceasefire As Iranian troops lost territory in the ground war and Iraq seemed increasingly prepared to use chemical weapons, in 1988 Iran realized it had lost the initiative. The Western intervention had clearly upped the stakes and forced Iran to recalculate the cost it was prepared to pay, especially at a time when the domestic economy was in dire straits. On 18 July 1988 Iran accepted the UN Security Council ceasefire which eventually came into force on 20 August under the supervision of a specially created UN Iran–Iraq Military Observer Group. Peace talks began at the foreign ministerial level in Geneva on 25 August.

These talks immediately became deadlocked over the status of the 1975 Algiers agreement, which reflected the generally-held deep suspicion of the real motives for a cease-fire. Both sides held a total of 200,000 prisoners of war, maintained major forces in the region and acquired new weapons for their arsenals. Iran wanted Iraq to withdraw from 2,600 square kilometres of occupied territory and Iraq wanted priority placed on clearing the Shatt al-Arab waterway. It was not until Iraq invaded Kuwait in August 1990 that a solution could be found. In order to ensure he was not facing a war on several fronts, Iraq's President Saddam Hussein capitulated to all Iranian demands, essentially leaving Iraq back where it was when it started the war. In contemplating a conflict that cost close to 2 million casualties and a decade of lost development, neither side can feel it was worth it.

Reading

J.M. Abdulghani, *Iraq–Iran War* (London: Croom Helm, 1984).

A. Cordesman, *The Iran–Iraq War* (London: Janes, 1987).

S. Grumman, *The Iraq–Iran War* (New York: Praeger, 1982).

A. Hourani, *A History of the Arab Peoples* (Cambridge, Mass.: Harvard University Press, 1991).

E. Karsh and I. Rautsi, *Saddam Hussein* (New York: The Free Press, 1991).

S. Tahir-Kheli and S. Ayubi (eds), *The Iraq–Iran War* (New York: Praeger, 1983).

Where are the Kurds?

There are some 19 million people of Kurdish origin, constituting the world's largest ethnic minority without a land of their own. Unlike many manufactured nations of the Middle East, the Kurds have a language and culture of their own, but as one of their leaders noted, they are the 'orphans of the universe'. Since the collapse of the Turkish Ottoman Empire, they have been divided between modern Turkey, Syria, Iraq and Iran. The Treaty of Sèvres in 1920 provided for separate countries for both Kurds and Armenians, but the Turkish nationalist leader Attaturk refused to implement the pact; after a brief war, the 1923 Treaty of Lausanne offered Turkey better terms. Although there was a brief uprising following the abolition of the Turkish Caliphate in 1925, Turkey has offered no hope of independence. Iranian Kurds (5 million) have been in dispute with all manner of rulers, to no avail.

The KDP   The most powerful Kurdish group, the Iraq-based Kurdistan Democratic Front, was allied to Iran in the early 1970s in an effort to take on the Iraqi régime. But in 1975 the Shah of Iran was given territorial concessions by Iraq in exchange for abandoning the Kurdish cause. During the Iran–Iraq War, the KDP helped Iranian troops, and Iraq organized its own anti-Khomeini force (the Patriotic Union of Kurdistan). The sight of Kurds dying on both sides of the war for their subjugators was yet another irony in this brutally complex conflict. In March 1988 Iraq used chemical weapons in Halabja against its own Kurds.

Iraq on the   Iraqi Kurds (4 million) have rebelled at various times (1922–3,
attack   1944–5, 1950–2, 1991) and since 1970 they have had a degree of local autonomy that is regularly ignored. The ending of the Iran–Iraq War allowed both countries to deal ruthlessly with their Kurdish minorities and Iraqi forces were again in action with chemical weapons. The main battles took place in 1989 on Iraqi territory with Iran once again playing an important role as a support-base for the rebels. Yet Kurds know only too well the unreliability of Iran in such matters, especially when Iran has no interest in supporting an independent Kurdistan.

Following the defeat of Iraq by allied forces in 1991, the Kurds tried and failed again to win independence although allied forces did create a safe-haven in northern Iraq which might yet help win more real autonomy for Iraqi Kurds. The best hopes for Kurdish autonomy lie with Turkey, the most developed of the three main host countries. If Turkey seriously expects to join in European integration then it will have to improve its record of treatment of Kurds. Yet the importance of Turkey in the anti-Iraq coalition following the Iraqi invasion of Kuwait in August 1990 has meant that the West had to tread carefully in helping the Kurds when they tried again to gain independence from Iraq in the spring of 1991. Despite the relief effort in 1991, no great power seems interested in redrawing the maps of the region and the only local power that has such aspirations – Iraq – is hardly sympathetic to the Kurdish case. The Kurdish Workers Party (KPP) in Turkey (but based in Syria) is nationalist and unfashionably Marxist in orientation, and its guerrillas have been hunted in southeast Turkey. Some 2,000 Kurds were reported to have died in this conflict in the five years up to 1990.

To make matters more complex, Kurds live around the head-waters of the Euphrates river in Turkey and the Turks have begun damming the river in order to fill their own reservoirs. The down-stream states, Syria and Iraq, grew particularly concerned in December 1989 and threatened to support the KPP. The KPP leader lives in Syria, as do various anti-Turkish Armenian groups. Syria is certainly concerned that the plan to reduce the flow of water from 32 to 20 billion cubic metres of water will also reduce its quality, although the water held back will go some way to satisfying Turkey's desire to become a breadbasket for the region. Iran has the Tigris waters to make up its expected shortfall and is constructing dams of its own. There is a trilateral commission designed to cope with such complex problems, but Turkey is reluctant to submit its case to outside judgement, even though Syria threatens to use military force to resolve the problem. So what else is new in the Middle East?

Add water to the wars

Reading

H. Arfa, *The Kurds* (Oxford: Oxford University Press, 1966).

G. Chailand (ed), *People Without a Country* (London: Zed Press, 1980).

E. Ghareeb, *The Kurdish Question in Iraq* (Syracuse: Syracuse University Press, 1981).

The Minority Rights Group, *The Kurds*, Report Bo.23, 1989.

Iraq and Kuwait

Just when the world was thinking that the collapse of Communism would bring a 'peace dividend' and a new world order could be shaped, old-style power politics returned with the Iraqi invasion of Kuwait on 2 August 1990. And yet this crisis *was* very different from those of the Cold War era. As great power alignments shifted, the United Nations was mobilized into constructive action, and world leaders contemplated whether, and how, they should use force in the late 20th century. The stakes were certainly well beyond the fate of the 2 million inhabitants of the tiny oil-rich monarchy of Kuwait.

Ancient Iraqi claims

Iraq, with its 16 million people, is more than twenty times the size of Kuwait. But as the inheritor of the great Mesopotamian empires, its sense of self-importance has deep roots. Kuwait, by contrast, is a relatively recent invention with a less weighty sense of history. Iraq claims that 8th-century maps show modern-day Kuwait as ruled from the Iraqi city of Basra. Certainly the Kuwaiti ruling family, the Sabahs, were part of the Utub clan which migrated from central Arabia in search of water in the early 18th century. They came to what is now Kuwait City and built a fort – the name Kuwait is the diminutive of *kut*, the common word in the Gulf for fort.

Until the First World War, Kuwait was under the nominal control of the Ottoman Empire, although it was in fact part of the administrative district of Basra. The Sabahs, who had ruled Kuwait since 1756, had secured a degree of independence for themselves by playing off the Turks, the British and the future Saudi rulers, but they always recognized the need for foreign protectors. After 1899, Britain essentially ran foreign policy for the Sabahs and in 1913, as war loomed in Europe, Britain and Turkey agreed that Kuwait was an autonomous district of the Ottoman Empire and the borders were formally demarcated. When Turkey declined to ratify the deal because of its alliance with Germany, Britain recognized an independent Kuwait.

Imperial cartography

But the Sabahs continued their own independent diplomacy and after the war Britain decided to redraw the frontiers. In order to compensate the Saudis for the territory they gave up to Iraq, Kuwait's rights to the coastal hinterland south of the 1913 frontier were dissolved and this area became the 'neutral zone' which both countries could use. Iraq's border with Kuwait was also set by the British and as a result Iraq was left virtually landlocked. With a

26-mile coastline and the only passage to the sea via the easily closed Shatt-al-Arab waterway, Iraq looked on greedily at Kuwait's 120-mile Gulf coast with a superb port.

These frontiers were confirmed when Iraq obtained its independence in 1932, but it was not long before Baghdad began pressing for the leasing of rights to Kuwaiti islands which it claimed as its own. In the 1930s Iraqi rulers claimed control of all Kuwait and railed against the machinations of British imperialism, but Britain kept the Sabahs in power.

On 19 June 1961 Britain granted Kuwait full independence but six days later the radical leader of Iraq, Abdul Karim Qassim (who came to power in 1958), claimed Kuwait belonged to Iraq. Following unfounded rumours of Iraqi troops movements, Kuwait sought support from the Arab world. But none was forthcoming and so Britain was beseeched for protection, and troops arrived in July. The Arab League troops arrived in September but were gone by 1963 as the crisis soon passed.

The 1961 crisis

With a new leader in 1963, Iraq moderated its foreign policy and recognized Kuwait in October 1963. The border was accepted in exchange for substantial payments and in November an economic agreement virtually abolished customs duties on trade. But yet another change of leader in Iraq led to the Iraqi seizure of a border post in northeast Kuwait in March 1973. The action was part of an Iraqi claim to the islands of Bubiyan and Warbah which control access to the Iraqi port of Umn Qasr. It was not until 1977 that forces were stood down along the frontier. With the outbreak of the Iran–Iraq War in 1980, Kuwait felt Iraq was otherwise distracted and indeed Iraq came to rely on Kuwaiti aid.

Iraqi conciliation and conflict

As a supporter of Iraq, and a state run by a Sunni-emirate, Kuwait felt concerned about Shiite agitation (a quarter of the Kuwaiti population). The once-moderate politics of Kuwait were silenced by a government crackdown and a dissolution of parliament. The indigenous Kuwaiti population, a minority in its own country, depended on foreigners to sustain the menial part of the economy, and yet they refused to grant the foreigners rights and privileges of the oil-created prosperity. Kuwait, with its population of some 400,000 Palestinians, also took a more sharply anti-Israeli and anti-American line on the Palestinian question. In 1984, when Kuwait was refused permission to buy sophisticated American weapons, Kuwait turned to the Soviet Union. When Kuwaiti tankers came under fire in the Gulf War in 1987, and the United States at first was reluctant to offer protection, Kuwait turned once again to the Soviet Union. But when the United States did reflag and protect Kuwaiti ships, the Kuwaitis refused to allow the United States basing rights. This was hardly likely to encourage Americans to make major sacrifices for Kuwait in the future.

The impact of the Iran–Iraq War

Facing Iraq
again

The cease-fire in the Iran–Iraq War in 1988 gradually revealed the still-unsettled Iraq–Kuwait dispute and the precariousness of the Kuwaiti position. As a war-devastated state governed by a supposedly radical socialist régime, Iraq looked across at the tiny 'air-conditioned Eden' which looked like the world's largest shopping mall and complained that this was not the proper order of things. Kuwait, which by virtue of its invested oil revenue had a stake in the stability of the international market economy, was opposed by a poor Iraq that wanted higher oil prices in order to rebuild its country and repay its debts of $40 billion.

The short road
to invasion

On 17 July 1990 Iraq turned to Kuwait as a solution to its need for more money and its desire for access to the Gulf, both denied by the failure to defeat Iran in the recent war. Iraq saw Kuwait as an opponent of higher oil prices and so revived claims to the Kuwaiti portion of oil fields that straddled their mutual border. Iraqi claims on Bubiyan and Warbah were also raised again. When Iraq moved troops to the frontier, most observers saw this as sabre-rattling but few believed Iraq would really invade. Kuwait rebuffed Iraqi demands (apart from agreeing to an oil price rise), believing that Iraq would never invade a country that had given it $10 billion in recent years. Yet it was precisely the allure of such easy wealth, and the lack of clear signals of deterrence from anyone else (including the Gulf Cooperation Council), that encouraged Iraq to sweep into Kuwait on 2 August in a predictably simple military operation. As Iraqi troops, the strongest in the Arab world, edged up to the Saudi border, the United States and many Western states shuddered. Was Iraq about to seize a major portion of the world oil supply by invading Saudi Arabia – the linchpin of American interests in the Gulf?

The United
States responds

In a rapidly escalating crisis, the United States pledged support for Saudi Arabia. After years of having supported Iraq against Iran, and turning a mostly blind eye to Iraqi atrocities at home, the United States was now talking of Saddam Hussein as a new Hitler. Under American leadership, an anti-Iraqi coalition was built on NATO states, comprising such friendly Arabs as Saudi Arabia, Egypt and the smaller Gulf states, uneasy bedfellows like Syria, and friends further afield in Asia and the South Pacific. In a dozen resolutions of the United Nations Security Council between August and November, Iraq was told to leave Kuwait. A full blockade and a régime of sanctions was imposed, but seemed unlikely to quickly force an Iraqi withdrawal from Kuwait. With support from the Soviet Union (a former close ally of Iraq), the Security Council then sanctioned the use of force after 15 January 1991 and the United States deployed nearly a half a million men at the head of an international coalition.

Operation 'Desert Shield' became operation 'Desert Storm' on 16 January when a devastating air attack was launched against Iraq. The sometimes uneasy coalition felt worried about waiting too long and in any case the Western members were particularly anxious to demonstrate that in the new, post-Cold War order, local bullies would be contained. While the allies had a strong military hand and a weak political one, Iraq felt it had a strong political card in its appeal to Arab unity (especially regarding the Palestinians) while it knew it was militarily vulnerable. Israel was hit by Iraqi Scud missiles in an attempt to widen the war and weaken the resolve of Arab members of the coalition, but as the Israeli casualties were low and American pressure high, Israel stayed out of the war on Iraq.

Desert Shield, Desert Storm

After last-minute peacemaking, especially by the Soviet Union, failed to win an Iraqi capitulation, the ground war began on 23 February. In a remarkably swift campaign, allied forces soon liberated Kuwait and occupied 15% of southern Iraq. With an air war that had already devastated Iraq's nuclear and chemical weapons capability, not to mention the majority of its ground forces, the ground war was more a rout than the 'mother of all battles' threatened by Saddam Hussein. After a mere one hundred hours of ground combat, Iraq accepted a ceasefire. Iraqi casualties were estimated at 100,000, as opposed to less than 400 Americans, 60 British, 35 French and 300 in the forces of the Arab coalition. But Iraqi forces had torched hundreds of oil wells before departing, leaving a legacy of pollution that would endure for years to come.

The mother of all battles

On 3 April the UN Security Council passed resolution 687 arranging a permanent ceasefire, Iraqi acceptance of the 1963 frontier, a full inspection of Iraqi demilitarisation, compensation for war damages, and the placement of a peacekeeping force on both sides of the Iraq–Kuwait border. The essential allied objectives of demonstrating that aggression would not succeed and the humiliation of Iraq was achieved. But Saddam Hussein remained in power, and with sufficient military punch to subdue uprisings in the south and in the Kurdish areas of the north. As Western troops went home, Iraq was left mostly to its own murderous devices and Iraq's neighbours were left with a humbled and badly wounded enemy. This latest war in a volatile region was over, but it was unlikely to be the last we would hear of conflict in the Gulf.

Fighting the peace

Reading

M. Farouk-Sluglett and P. Sluglett, *Iraq Since 1958* (London: I.B. Tauris, 1990).

E. Karsh and I. Rautsi, *Saddam Hussein* (New York: The Free Press, 1991).

J. Miller and L. Mylroie, *Saddam Hussein and the Crisis in the Gulf* (New York: Times Books, 1990).

D. Pryce-Jones, *The Closed Circle* (London: Weidenfeld and Nicolson, 1989).

A. Rush, *Al Sabah* (London: Ithaca Press, 1987).

R. Schofield, *Kuwait and Iraq* (London: Royal Institute of International Affairs, 1991).

How Many Yemens?

As two Yemeni states merge into one, is the conflict that involved local powers and the Superpowers about to end? While the great powers from far afield certainly seem keen to see the rivals sink their differences, their neighbours may not be so pleased. Either way, this oil-poor state in an oil-rich region, sits astride strategic waterways for the passage of other people's wealth.

The formation of two Yemeni states was yet another irrational spin-off from the disintegrating Ottoman Empire. The Shia Muslim kingdom in North Yemen was established after the demise of the Ottoman Turkish Empire in 1918. It emerged from isolation in 1958 by forming an alliance with Egypt in an attempt to force the British to leave their Crown Colony in nearby Aden. But contact with the outside world, and especially revolutionary Egypt, sparked a republican movement and, in 1962, the Yemen Arab Republic (YAR) was proclaimed after a military coup. *Carving out North Yemen*

In the bloody civil war of 1962–9, royalist forces were funded by neighbouring Saudi Arabia. The United States supported the Saudis who were concerned about Gulf stability. The republicans were aided by Egypt, which soon found 50,000 of its soldiers bogged down in a vicious guerrilla war. In 1967, Nasser withdrew his troops in a compromise agreement with the Saudis. The Soviet Union stepped in with large scale aid to republican forces. But the peculiar compromise resulted in much reduced combat and a republican administration but with royalists in the main positions of power. Hardly a recipe for stability. *Civil war*

While the North Yemeni civil war was winding down, the neighbouring ancient kingdom of Sheba, then known as the People's Republic of Southern Yemen, obtained independence from Britain in 1967. British forces held the capital of Aden as a strategic base but local rebellion and London's changed foreign policy priorities made it too costly. The radical successors to Britain established the only Marxist régime in the Arab world, renamed the People's Democratic Republic of Yemen (PDRY) and obtained large amounts of Soviet aid in exchange for use of the Aden base. The repressive measures of the PDRY forced 300,000 refugees to flee to the YAR. As a result, an unholy coalition of Saudi Arabia, Libya and the predominantly Soviet-armed YAR, emerged to support the refugees in attacking the PDRY. Moscow was certainly getting a good test for its weapons. In the warfare that broke out from October 1972, both sides were predominantly Soviet-armed. The *Revolution in Sheba*

Arab League arranged a ceasefire but proposals for a union of the two Yemens never developed because of the basic incompatibilities of the régimes.

Illusions of Yemeni union

The idea of union, even between these two states with common cultural characteristics, seemed far-fetched. While the YAR was a mixed Shia/Sunni régime of indiscriminate politics, the PDRY was a Marxist régime with a nearly uniform Sunni Muslim population. While the YAR was a non-aligned state, supported by Saudi Arabia and the United States financially and the Soviet Union and Saudi Arabia militarily, the PDRY signed a friendship pact with the Soviet Union in October 1979 and had close relations with the Eastern bloc states. The National Democratic Front supported by the PDRY against the YAR was reined in since 1983, but it was still a source of friction between the two states.

The Oman frontier

As if this inter-Yemeni Cold War was not complicated enough, the PDRY has also stirred up, and then sought to control, conflict with its eastern neighbour. Oman obtained independence from Britain in 1970 but continued to receive crucial British aid in a successful campaign to suppress a PDRY-backed rebel movement in Dhofar province. In 1981 Oman helped form the Saudi-dominated Gulf Cooperation Council, a grouping of moderate states intended to provide stability and a counter-weight to radical influences in the Gulf, such as the PDRY. The PDRY responded by forming alliances with radical Libya and Ethiopia. Libya had once backed anti-PDRY rebels but five years is a long time in Middle East politics. Therefore it was not surprising that, in the light of the high costs of the war, high risks of Superpower intervention in the sensitive Gulf region and meagre returns, both the PDRY and Oman sought to reduce tension. The Saudis, Western interests, and the Soviet Union supported these moves. In October 1982 the PDRY and Oman signed a treaty normalizing relations and although sporadic border incidents continued for a while, both sides soon sought to control the conflict.

Broader coalitions

The American Rapid Deployment Force exercised along with Omani forces, thereby raising acute concern that the Yemeni states would become embroiled in a Superpower conflict. The local states did not allow matters to get out of hand and in January 1985 both Oman and the PDRY held talks on border disputes; in April it was agreed to exchange ambassadors. In 1985, Oman announced it was willing to establish diplomatic relations with the Soviet Union. The PDRY also resumed diplomatic relations with Saudi Arabia in 1983 but even here border clashes continued.

Towards a Yemeni union

Against a background of clearly unstable local politics (there was a coup in the PDRY in January 1986), the two Superpowers began to patch up their differences about conflict around the world. Yemen was not high on the agenda, but the Yemenis themselves could read the writing on the cracking Berlin Wall. The Superpowers would no longer support regional conflict. What is more, hardline Marxists found no support from the Soviet Union, and East European friends disappeared overnight in 1989.

Thus the South Yemenis virtually capitulated to the North and in an agreement in November 1989, agreed on complete union which was enacted in May 1990. The North Yemen leader became President and the South Yemen leader took the lesser job of Prime Minister. Both work in the former capital of North Yemen, Sana. With some 13 million people (10 million in the North), the new Republic of Yemen is the most populous in the Arabian peninsula, but also the poorest. Some 2 million of its people work abroad. When Iraq invaded Kuwait in August 1990, Yemen effectively took Iraq's side, much to the annoyance of Saudi Arabia. Scores would have undoubtedly been settled after the main battle with Iraq was complete.

As the Yemenis learned from the new détente in Europe, they also absorbed the new vogue for market economies and political pluralism. The new Yemen is supposed to have both, but certainly the notion of democracy seems hard to imagine in practice. Yet it is precisely such reforms that worry Yemen's neighbours, especially autocratic Saudi Arabia. Once upon a time the Saudis saw the threat from Marxism, but now it looks like democracy has them worried.

Democratic diseases

Reading

R. Bidwell, *The Two Yemens* (Boulder, Colorado: Westview, 1983).

L. Graz, *The Turbulent Gulf* (London: I. B. Tauris, 1990).

F. Halliday, *Revolution and Foreign Policy* (Cambridge: Cambridge University Press, 1990).

T. Mostyn, *Iran, Iraq and the Arabian Peninsula* (New York: Facts on File, 1991).

R. Stookey, *South Yemen* (Boulder, Colorado: Westview, 1982).

9

AFRICA

Revolution in South Africa

The struggle of a black majority against a dominant white minority is the last major racial conflict and provokes a clamour of international indignation that such a blatant evil can still exist. Until 1989, the year of revolutions, it seemed as if South Africa was stuck in its racist mode for decades to come. And yet, just as Eastern Europe suddenly found freedom, black South Africans began to think they too would benefit from the new democratic wind. The struggle is now no longer so much about whether to dismantle racist white rule, but whether it can be done without too much bloodshed.

Boers and the British   The origins of this virulent conflict lie with the foundation of a Dutch colony in 1652 and the annexation by Britain in 1814 of Cape Province. As white settlers expanded into the hinterland and the people prospered, numerous black tribes were drawn to the area. Conflicts emerged between the English and Dutch settlers (Boers) and between the whites and the indigenous black population. The discovery of valuable natural resources (gold and diamonds to name but two) in the mid-19th century increased the value of the prize. The Union of South Africa was created by the British parliament in 1909 and the Status of the Union Act of 1934 emphasized that South Africa was an independent sovereign state. However, the democracy that developed was for whites only. The radical Nationalist Party came to power in 1948 and imposed a system of apartheid – separate development for the races. Despite increasing international condemnation of racist rule and opposition at home, the rule of the Afrikaaner (Dutch descendants) majority of the white population was not under immediate threat.

Apartheid and Africa's white tribe   The problem of South Africa is twofold: local and international. The domestic policy of apartheid has evolved over thirty years. Unlike other colonial or post-colonial countries, South Africa has a substantial (4.8 million) white minority within a total population of 31 million (22.8 million blacks). Seventy per cent of the whites live in the north eastern third of the country. Many whites have family ties in Africa extending back centuries and have evolved their own distinctive political culture. Thus the English and Afrikaaner population can claim to be a 'white tribe of Africa'. Unlike other groups of whites in Africa who arrived only recently, South Africa's whites have nowhere to go. However, instead of simply living as another tribe in Africa, the whites have dominated life in South Africa, denying fundamental rights to the black majority. Separate development has not been equal development.

The South African authorities have tried to deal with their minority status by setting aside reserved areas for blacks as 'homelands'. According to government plans, some 14% of the area of South Africa has been allocated for the 72% of the population that is black. The most valuable resources and fertile land are outside the homelands. Some of these homelands have moved to 'independence', including the Transkei (1976), Boputhatswana (1977), Venda (1979), and the Ciskei (1981). They are based largely on tribal lines but are home to about half of South Africa's black population. Those blacks living in white South Africa are considered legally to be citizens of their language-group homeland, even if they were born in white South Africa. They are thus aliens in white areas, subject to deportation. The population density of the homelands is inevitably higher than in most other African states. Relocation of blacks often unconnected to homelands continues on a large scale.

Homelands

The most explosive problem in South Africa is that of the urban blacks who live near white areas. Widespread poverty is the dry tinder that flares with the spark of rebellion, often over seemingly minor issues. The Sharpeville massacre in 1960 claimed 67 dead, the Soweto uprising in 1976 included 600 dead and unrest since September 1984 led to over 3,000 dead in the first three years. Most of the deaths were caused by inter-black struggles between radical 'comrades' and more establishment elders who cooperate with white rule. So far, white supremacy has survived in large measure because it can play off one black force against the other.

Rising uprisings

The leading black opposition movement, the African National Congress, was banned until the reforms of 1990 when it was brought in as the major black negotiating voice. Its *de facto* leader, Nelson Mandela had been jailed for over two decades and was released along with other ANC figures in 1989–90. A spin-off of the ANC, the Pan-African Congress, supports a more black only policy and has a military wing called Poqo (we alone). The United Democratic Front remained legal when the ANC was not, and was a moderate collection of civic associations. Finally, Chief Gatsha Buthelezi of the 6 million plus Zulu tribe leads his Inkhatha movement which has long been willing to consider a solution along tribal lines instead of one-adult-one-vote. The hundreds of dead in inter-black conflict in 1990 and 1991 were mainly among supporters of Inkhatha and the ANC.

Black groups

Although universally condemned, and especially in black Africa, South Africa has been able to deflect any serious pressure from outside. As the economic powerhouse of southern Africa, it could naturally be expected to be a magnet for trade. Although

The Front line states

the states of the Southern Africa Development Coordinating Committee (SADCC comprises Angola, Zambia, Botswana, Zimbabwe, Mozambique, Malawi, Tanzania, Lesotho, Swaziland) oppose South Africa's racial policies, they have been drawn into a web of economic interdependence. South African goods are often cheaper and of better quality than local or foreign items; South Africa's harbours work and therefore can be used to transport goods; and South African expertise is often useful in running key industries such as the railways. To be sure, South Africa nurtures such dependence. By sabotaging alternative supply routes (e.g. the Benguela railway in Angola) South Africa helps make its aid an offer the SADCC states cannot refuse. Not surprisingly, the 'front line states' find it economically advantageous to take a back seat in the struggle, for example about imposing economic sanctions on South Africa.

Thump and talk   During the mid-1970s, as South Africa's ring of buffer states (Angola, Rhodesia and Mozambique) fell into black African hands, Pretoria feared that it might no longer be able to buy off its opponents in the region. But as these states struggled to be more economically viable their dependence on South Africa became even more acute. Coupled with by far the most powerful armed forces in sub-Saharan Africa (and probably even with a nuclear bomb in the basement), South Africa was able to impose its will. In March 1984, South Africa forced Mozambique into a non-aggression pact that would curb ANC activity from bases in Mozambique. Devastating South African raids and economic pressure had brought the Mozambique economy near to collapse. However, despite overwhelming military and economic predominance, South Africa is only able to turn its neighbours from effective hostility to open impotence. Hostility from outside is therefore controlled but not eliminated.

Soggy sanctions   South Africa's other main worry is the possibility that sanctions will be imposed by the richer Western powers. So far, sanctions have not had conspicuous success. Bans on sporting contacts have hit South African pride but not morale. An arms embargo has mostly been well observed but key parts have made their way through various back doors and, in conjunction with other pariah states (e.g. Israel or Taiwan). Indigenous arms production has produced sophisticated weapons. Certainly South Africa's military punch has been as deadly as ever in the years since the embargo.

South Africa's clout   Economic sanctions have so far been mostly ineffective because of South Africa's importance in supplying key raw materials (especially uranium) and the existing heavy foreign investment in the South African economy. Ten per cent of all South African investment comes from abroad as does a further 20% of capital stock. Just 5 states account for 90% of all foreign investment in

South Africa. Britain accounts for about half the total outside investment, with some 150,000 United Kingdom jobs estimated to be dependent on South African trade. The United States accounts for some 20% of foreign investment in South Africa or 1% of total United States investments abroad. Germany, France and Switzerland account for the bulk of the rest of foreign investment. The United States is South Africa's largest trading partner. The top four exporters to South Africa (US, UK, Japan) account for more than 50% of total exports. Yet by 1986 Western firms began pulling out: fifty-five US companies left in the eighteen months from January 1985, including General Motors and IBM. The loss of confidence was turning into the most effective international sanction as South Africa's economy staggered through recession.

The combination of economic problems at home, some effects of sanctions (notably in finance and other parts of the service sector) and a squeezing of the white government between the extremes of white radicals and black activists, led to the first major breakthrough towards black majority rule. At first the steps were cautious. In 1983–4 the white rulers began undoing some of the worst examples of 'petty apartheid'. They enfranchised some of the coloured and Indian population and in April 1986 the much hated 'pass laws' were abandoned. As each concession to black rights was made, a powerful Afrikaaner blacklash hit the white government that attempted to negotiate a middle course. *Undoing petty apartheid*

In the second half of 1989, with revolutions in Eastern Europe, a new white government in South Africa under F. W. de Klerk promised major reforms. He released ANC leaders and unbanned the organization. The violence in the black townships continued and as the government calculated the prestige of the ANC was tarnished as it got its hands dirty trying to sort out the mess of inter-black politics that resulted in 3,000 deaths in 1990 alone. But in the short-run the ANC had sufficient credibility to help undermine the homelands, several of which suffered major unrest in 1989–90. The ANC then opened direct talks with the white government about the next steps for reform. *Quickening pace of reform*

The hard bargaining was still to come. The official act under which the population is registered by race lies at the heart of apartheid and is set to be removed; the Group Areas Act segregates residential areas and the Land Act limits black ownership of land to barely 13% of South Africa. The fate of the homelands is up for debate as the citizenship laws assigning blacks to specific homelands have only been partially abolished. Ultimately, the whites will have to decide if they wish to surrender power in favour of black majority rule. Given the size of the white population and the strength of its Afrikaaner extreme, it still seems some way from this, the toughest of choices. *The bargaining to come*

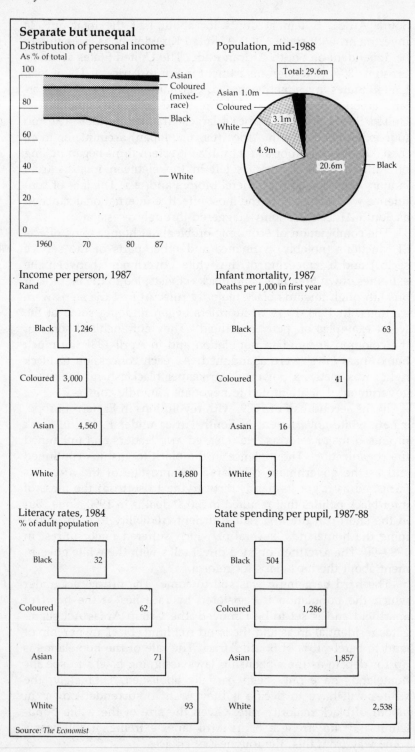

Separate but unequal

Distribution of personal income
As % of total

Population, mid-1988
Total: 29.6m

Income per person, 1987
Rand

Black	1,246
Coloured	3,000
Asian	4,560
White	14,880

Infant mortality, 1987
Deaths per 1,000 in first year

Black	63
Coloured	41
Asian	16
White	9

Literacy rates, 1984
% of adult population

Black	32
Coloured	62
Asian	71
White	93

State spending per pupil, 1987-88
Rand

Black	504
Coloured	1,286
Asian	1,857
White	2,538

Source: *The Economist*

Reading

G. Carter and P. O'Meara, *International Politics in Southern Africa* (Indiana University Press, 1982).

'South Africa', *The Economist*, 3 November, 1990.

G. Leach, *The Afrikaaners* (London: Macmillan, 1988).

S. R. Lewis, *The Economics of Apartheid* (New York: Council on Foreign Relations, 1990).

S. Nolutshungu, *South Africa in Africa* (Manchester: Manchester University Press, 1975).

R. Omond, *The Apartheid Handbook* (London: Penguin, 1985).

Western Sahara

Some Third World conflicts have deceptively simple origins but can quickly degenerate into complex, confusing and apparently irreconcilable disputes. The conflict over the Western Sahara is now a bewildering maze of shifting alliances focused on the states of the Maghreb (Morocco, Algeria, Tunisia, Libya and Mauritania). Although the ostensible conflict concerns self-determination and control of phosphate resources, this combustible material burns in the dangerous atmosphere of regional rivalries.

A botched colonial legacy
The Western Sahara problem is based on Morocco's claim to territory disputed with its neighbours and an indigenous population desiring independence. But nothing is so simple when Third World states manipulate a botched colonial legacy for their own current conflicts. Although France was the dominant colonial power in Morocco, in 1884 Spain successfully claimed the 1,000-kilometre Saharan coast between Morocco and Mauritania as its sphere of influence. As Spain's basic interest was the protection of its vital Canary Islands off the Saharan coast, it was hardly intrinsically interested in the Saharan desert territory, and certainly not in its hinterland. The Western Saharan population of some 200,000 nomadic herdsmen (according to UN estimates) paid little heed to the artificial colonial boundary drawn for the territory.

A 400-year-old claim
On the other hand, Morocco *was* acutely concerned about the frontier. Following independence in 1956, it reasserted a 400-year-old claim to the territory of Spanish Sahara and parts of Algeria and Mauritania. In 1957 a Moroccan invasion of the Sahara was defeated by Spanish troops and in 1963, following Algerian independence, a brief Moroccan invasion of the iron-rich Tindouf region of Algeria was also repulsed. But Moroccan attention became more firmly fixed on the Spanish Sahara in 1965 when large phosphate resources were confirmed at Bu Craa and a refinery and road to El Aiun were built.

Moroccan moderation
Over the next five years Morocco adopted a more conciliatory approach which seemed to enhance its position. In 1968 Spain gave up its enclave of Ifni on Moroccan territory. Morocco and Algeria signed a friendship pact the following year. Morocco also recognized Mauritania and abandoned its claim to Mauritanian territory. However, under pressure of the growing international call for decolonization, in 1967 Spain set up the Yema'a (a council of elders and elected officials) to assist with local administration

in the Sahara. In 1973 the Yema'a also asked for self-determination, while a more radical nationalist group, the Polisario Front, was formed to give diplomacy a push by more direct action. In 1974, Spain agreed, in principle, to self-determination for Western Sahara.

The local states, and especially Mauritania and Morocco, were jolted into action and in 1974 the two agreed to partition the Western Sahara when the opportunity arose. At the same time, Morocco persuaded the United Nations to take the Saharan issue to the International Court of Justice. In October 1975, the UN and ICJ ruled ambiguously that there were important pre-colonial ties between the Western Sahara and Mauritania and Morocco but they also noted there was no reason why the fate of the territory should not be decided in accordance with the wishes of the local population. Following the death of Franco, Spain procrastinated, but on 14 November agreed with Morocco and Mauritania to partition the territory. Spanish withdrawal in early 1976 left Morocco holding two-thirds of the territory including the phosphate resources. *Partition*

In February 1976, Polisario declared the establishment of the Saharan Arab Democratic Republic (SADR) and launched a guerrilla campaign, supported by Algeria, against the weaker Mauritanian position. There were also direct Morocco–Algeria clashes but most of the fighting took place further south. Although France provided air support for Mauritania, it had difficulty defending the iron ore mines at Zouerate and the railway to Nouadhibou. In 1978 a military coup deposed the Ould Daddah régime in Mauritania and the new junta concluded a peace treaty with SADR in 1979. *Mauritania defeated*

Morocco, on the other hand, was able to fend off Polisario. While the rebels (armed by Algeria and Libya) held much of the empty desert, Morocco held the vital towns and phosphate resources. With United States aid (there was a relatively small American base at Kenitra) Morocco made the best of superior military equipment and constructed an 'electronic defensive wall'. *Morocco holds the phosphates*

Morocco was far less successful in the diplomatic battle with Polisario. With support from Algeria, SADR gained increasing recognition in the Organization of African Unity (OAU). In February 1982, SADR was finally admitted to the OAU but could not take its seat because Morocco mobilized its supporters to keep it out. Ironically, the OAU and the Third World were split by the issue of whether self-determination should take precedence over pre-colonial claims. Radical and conservative voices in the Third World squabbled openly, while the Superpowers watched quietly on the sidelines. In 1984, the OAU agreed to admit the Polisario delegation and Morocco withdrew. By 1985 Polisario was recognized by sixty-four states. *Recognizing Polisario*

*Uncomfortable
allies*

In 1984, in one of the most peculiar twists of the war, Libya and Morocco signed an agreement on 'union'. From Libya's point of view this was an attempt, following its partial withdrawal from Chad, to pursue new foreign policy adventures and outflank Algeria. Morocco was obviously overjoyed to undermine Polisario's support and to build bridges to the radical African and Arab camps. Even if the 'union' proved abortive, it did Polisario no good at all. But paradoxically, it also put Algeria and the United States (who both opposed Libya) on the same side of an issue. As the war dragged on, the natural confusion of regional politics emerged in all its bewildering variety.

The wall of sand

But the political and military stalemate remains. While both Morocco and Polisario want a referendum in the Western Sahara, Morocco refuses Polisario's demand for a withdrawal prior to any vote. Meanwhile, on the battlefield, the Moroccan 'wall' – a 2,500–kilometre-long barrier of sand 2.75 metres high, with modern electronic surveillance devices – had been gradually moved forward. By 1985 it included almost all the disputed area's population. Polisario troop strength had been cut by more than half and its attacks were losing their punch. But the Moroccan economy is also strained by the war effort and the régime needs to rely on the enhanced national solidarity that it earns from the conflict. Morocco is also backed up by conservative African and Arab states, low-key American support, and even tacit Soviet support as a result of an important phosphate contract.

*Saharan
stand-off*

In March 1985, King Hassan of Morocco appealed to the United Nations to arrange a referendum, declaring that he no longer trusted the OAU. Confidential Morocco–Algeria negotiations in 1985 (there had been earlier talks in 1978 and 1983) did not necessarily herald Algeria's abandonment of Polisario but seemed to indicate that the stand off might hold for quite some time. The Algeria–Morocco frontier was opened in 1983 and Algeria was enticed by the possibility that it might be able to develop its iron ore resources at Tindouf if Morocco were to allow access to the sea. Algeria had become less radical than in its early years and, as a major local power, was beginning to see the advantages of playing the leading role in establishing the unity of the Grand Maghreb.

*Squeezing
Polisario*

Algeria continued to provide the only real support for Polisario, but by the late 1980s it had clearly decided that its own internal economic problems required better relations with Morocco. In 1988 Algeria–Morocco talks led to Morocco and Polisario accepting a UN plan for a ceasefire and a referendum for Western Sahara. But the parties failed to agree on how to hold the vote and in the autumn of 1989 the fighting flared again. In the spring of 1991 there were new signs of a compromise, but on the shifting sands of the Maghreb no one could be sure any deal would be stable.

Reading

S. Amin, *The Maghreb in the Modern World* (London: Penguin, 1970).

T. Hodges, *Western Sahara* (Westport, Conn.: Lawrence Hill, 1983).

W. Knapp, *North West Africa* (London: Oxford University Press, 1977).

W. Zartman (ed), *Man, State and Society in the Contemporary Maghreb* (London: Pall Mall, 1973).

Chad and its neighbours

Chad is cursed with a devastating combination of poverty, a debilitating colonial legacy, rapacious neighbours and corrupt leaders. No single curse fully explains its agonizing civil war. To be sure, the absurd boundaries drawn by France played a major part in shaping the modern conflict. But since the end of colonial days non-Africans have been mostly reluctant to become entangled in the vicious vendettas of local leaders. Only when neighbouring Libya – one of the Third World's unguided missile (albeit only medium range) – looked like increasing its influence did the great powers take a more active interest. On balance, the most important causes of what is essentially a civil war in Chad are to be found in the labyrinthine local politics.

Divided Chad
Half of Chad's 4.5 million people are nomadic Arab Muslims, living mostly in the north desert bordering on Libya. Southern Chad, below the 14th parallel that divides Africa's nomadic Arabs from the blacks, is a richer agricultural area producing the country's key export crop, cotton, most of which is owned by French interests. Chad's population is primarily black and with a mix of Christian and animistic beliefs. In pre-colonial days the Northerners dominated the south, often selling Southern blacks into slavery. Now it is one of the world's poorest countries.

Rebellion breaks out
French colonial rule ended in August 1960 and Chad became a one-party state in 1962. Because north Chadians feared the richer south, France stayed in control of Northern Chad until 1965 to ease the transition. Full-scale rebellion broke out in the North in 1965, led by the banned National Liberation Front (FROLINAT). In 1968 France helped the régime to crush the rebellion.

Libya looms
Neighbouring Libya, under the radical leadership of Colonel Qadafy (who came to power in 1969) began to take a more active interest in Chad's affairs. In 1973, Libya assumed control over the disputed Aouzou strip in Northern Chad, a 70,000-square-kilometre region thought to be rich in uranium. In 1975 a military coup in Chad brought to power a new government calling for national reconciliation but, with Libyan support, FROLINAT spurned the peace offer.

Back to the strongholds
In early 1978 FROLINAT established a unified command under General Goukouni Oueddei and seized territory from government forces. With French military aid, the rebels were contained but President Malloum appointed a new Prime Minister, Hissein Habré (a former FROLINAT leader) in order to reach a peaceful

agreement. However, fighting continued and Habré seized control in January 1979. This time French troops were sent to help restore order and enforce a ceasefire. For a short while the opposing factions retreated to their strongholds.

Neighbouring Nigeria, concerned with growing Libyan influence in Chad, tried its own hand at friendly meddling by attempting to organize a settlement. In April 1979 a transitional government, including both Habré and Goukouni, was formed but it excluded southern factions, some of which now also had Libyan support. The northern-dominated régime was denounced both by its domestic rivals and 'concerned' neighbours.

Nigeria niggles

A further agreement in August put Goukouni in power but the fragile ceasefire broke down in March 1980. In May, French troops were withdrawn and the régime signed a friendship pact with Libya. Habré's forces were causing serious concern for the régime and in October Libyan troops were called for by Goukouni Oueddei. Soon 15,000 Libyan troops were in place and in January 1981 plans were made for a union between the two countries.

Union with Libya

Opposition to the Chad–Libya union came from both inside and outside Chad. Goukouni backtracked and in September 1981 he asked for and obtained the withdrawal of Libyan troops. Nigeria attempted to lead an inter-African, OAU-supported, peace-keeping force in Chad in November. However, an OAU-arranged ceasefire and election did not materialize and in June 1982 Habré took control.

Habré takes charge

A brief lull was broken in May 1983; following the distraction of a Nigeria–Chad frontier fracas, Goukouni's forces in the north took the opportunity to expand their influence. Although the OAU recognized the Habré regime in June, rebel strength increased. The northern town of Faya Largeau was taken by the Libyan-backed Goukouni forces, retaken by Habré in July 1983 and taken again by the rebels in August. While Libya was actively supporting the rebels (and former state leader Goukouni) Habré received active American support. The United States was anxious to control Libyan power in what was viewed by the more paranoid sections of the Reagan administration as a surrogate East–West conflict. France, on the other hand, was now more cautious, having been caught several times in the sticky and complicated web of Chad politics. Under pressure from Francophone Africa and the United States, France eventually did deploy some 2,000 troops in an attempt to impose a ceasefire. The result was *de facto* partition of Chad at the 16th parallel.

The powers pay attention

Talks in January 1984 collapsed as Habré seemed content to procrastinate behind his French screen. Goukouni upset this complacency with military operations below the 16th parallel and French forces were killed and aircraft lost in the ensuing skir-

France dragged in

mishes. Although Habré was not stirred to act, France was. On 17 September 1984, France and Libya negotiated a hasty mutual withdrawal agreement (not including the Aouzou strip). In the absence of proper international observation and in the light of French haste, it is not surprising that the withdrawal was one-sided. French troops were pulled back to the Central African Republic while Libya made only a token withdrawal.

Further factionalism

In the atmosphere of stalemate, the natural fierce factionalism in Chad politics re-emerged in 1986. Goukouni Oueddei's supporters drifted off to join Habré's government and in October even Libya began to look at new options. But the ensuing period of quiet was short-lived. In December 1990, Mr Habré's former commander-in-chief of the armed forces, Idriss Deby, seized power after having fled because of an abortive coup in 1988 and a brief period of resistance in the countryside near Sudan. French forces did not intervene, having grown exasperated with Habré's variable moods and confident that Deby was not backed by the Libyans.

Controlled risks

It seems clear that the root of the conflict was primarily the local rivalries between political factions, personalities and ethnic groups. Outside intervention, even of a Libyan kind, only fed on the fertile soil of factionalism. While Libya, and to a certain extent Nigeria, sought to extend their spheres of influence in Chad, neither was willing to take large risks for small material rewards. Libya's control of the Aouzou strip is still opposed by France, among others, but by and large Libyan control of this strategic area was tacitly accepted. Until the politics of Chad are stabilized, and that seems unlikely in the short-term, the embers of regional and possibly even great power conflict will regularly flare up.

Reading

I. Griffiths, *An Atlas of African Affairs* (London: Methuen, 1984).

R.W. Hull, *Modern Africa* (Englewood Cliffs, New York: Prentice Hall, 1980).

A.A. Mazrui and M. Tidy, *Nationalism and New States in Africa* (London: Heinemann, 1984).

J. Wright, *Libya, Chad and the Central Sahara* (Towota, New York: Barnes and Noble, 1989).

On the Horn of Africa

Somalia is draped along the African coast of the Indian Ocean and the Gulf of Aden, forming the Horn of Africa. Politics on the horn are dominated by conflict between two states, Somalia and Ethiopia, and secessionist movements within Ethiopia in Eritrea and the Ogaden. This complex pattern of local warfare has been further aggravated by cynical manoeuvring on the part of other neighbours and great power supporters. More recently, both Superpowers have been content to neglect the local wars and let combatants get on with the inconclusive killing.

Ethiopia has been mostly independent since Biblical times and remained so even during the Western imperial scramble for Africa. The modernization programs launched by Emperor Haile Selassie in the 1930s were threatened by imperial pressures from the Italian territories of Eritrea and Somalia. In the ensuing Abyssinian War and Italian occupation of Ethiopia (1936–41), Ethiopia's future became closely entwined with neighbouring Eritrea. In fact, Eritrea is not a coherent area and was the creation of Italian colonial rule. It is a predominantly Muslim area (whereas Ethiopia is largely Christian) along the coast. Its northern plateau is inhabited by mainly Christian Tigrinya speakers who share a language and religion with the Tigre province of Ethiopia. However, although it has some ethnic links with Ethiopia, Addis Ababa's rule did not extend that far for any length of time. But possession of Eritrea would provide Ethiopia with its only access to the coast. *Ethiopia hangs on to independence*

Italian control of Eritrea was surrendered to Britain in 1941 and UN-organized discussions were held in the late 1940s to decide the fate of the territory. Despite Ethiopia's claim to Eritrea, the local people desired independence. In December 1950 the UNGA decided that Eritrea should be an autonomous region of Ethiopia and Addis Ababa's rule began in 1952. Although opinions within the United Nations were divided, Haile Selassie had become a close ally of British and American interests and therefore his Western friends were anxious to help obtain access to the sea. However, in 1962 Ethiopia unilaterally imposed direct control of Eritrea from Addis Ababa and began eliminating opposition. In 1963 the Eritrean Liberation Front began seriously to challenge Ethiopian control and it, in turn, was soon superceded in the struggle by the more radical Eritrean People's Liberation Front (EPLF). *Eritrea and the EPLF*

Ethiopian control was firmly, if ruthlessly, maintained until a major famine in 1973 and deepening unrest in Addis Ababa over *A coup and the Cubans* the pace of reform within Ethiopia. As a result of the breakdown in order, a military coup on 12 September 1974 brought a Marxist régime to power. Ethiopia abandoned its close alignment with Western powers and instead became closely aligned with the Eastern bloc. At the same time, Eritrean rebels (previously supported by the Soviet Union and trained by the Cubans) stepped up guerrilla action against the new Ethiopian régime. Ethiopia launched a major attack on the rebels in 1976 but halted operations in June at the request of fellow revolutionary Arab states. But continuing guerrilla successes forced Ethiopia to strike back in 1978, this time supported by heavy Soviet supplies and 15,000 Cuban troops. The government was able to recapture most rebel-controlled territory. Casualties numbered thousands, and hundreds of thousands of refugees fled north into Sudan.

Keeping Sudan sweet   Intermittent talks have been held and inconclusive fighting continues, mostly during the cooler seasons. In 1980, conservative Sudan and radical Ethiopia signed a friendship treaty, largely because Ethiopia wanted the Sudanese border closed to the EPLF. However, fighting continued and led to a major Ethiopian drive in 1983 against EPLF forces, as well as rebels supporting an independent Tigre.

By 1989, with Soviet and East European aid sharply cut back, Ethiopian forces fell back on the capital. Some 500,000 Eritreans had died in the war so far (out of a population of 4 million), but they finally seemed to have the Ethiopians on the run. Eritrean and Tigrean rebels then surged forward, although many of their people within 'liberated' territory were starving – Ethiopian government policy was to encourage the starvation as it ran out of more orthodox weapons of war. Perhaps not surprising in this, the poorest country on earth.

Somalia and the Ogaden   Clearly, the Ethiopian régime has its hands full with rebel movements, and not only in the north. In the southeastern Ogaden desert, it has faced Somali-backed insurgents. Somalia was formed in 1960 by joining British and Italian Somaliland, but one-third of all Somali people lived outside the borders of the state. The British, who had controlled Somali territory after the war, wanted to create a Greater Somalia including the Ogaden desert (occupied by Britain after the Italians were removed from Ethiopia). But, because of Superpower objections, a smaller Somalia was created and in 1955 the Ogaden was handed back to Ethiopia. A radical Left-wing military coup in Somalia in 1969 brought to power a régime that soon sought assistance from the Soviet Union. Expensive, modern Soviet naval facilities were built on the Horn of Africa, and were viewed in the West at the time as a major strategic setback.

As a result of the anarchy in Ethiopia following the 1974 coup, Somalia began to take advantage of the power vacuum and supported the rebel Western Somali Liberation Front. Fighting in the summer of 1977 resulted in large gains in the Ogaden. The Soviet Union opposed its ally's actions and in November 1977 the Somalis ejected the Soviets from their fancy new naval facilities and requested, and quickly obtained, American support instead. The United States was only too pleased to supplant the Soviet Union on the Horn of Africa, especially as at the other end of the see-saw on the Horn, they had recently lost influence in Ethiopia. By then, Moscow was satisfied to transfer its allegiances to the more powerful Ethiopia and, with the aid of Cuban troops, in March 1978 Ethiopia inflicted a heavy defeat on Somali forces and their rebel allies. The war coincided with a massive drought in the Ogaden, forcing 800,000 people to flee to refugee camps.

Superpowers switch sides

Although Somalia then ceased any serious attempts to take the Ogaden, in 1982 the Ethiopians supported a Somali force opposed to the Siad Barre régime in the capital, Mogadishu. The attempt to destabilize the Somali regime was half-hearted and, with rapid American aid, Somalia was able to fend off the threat. In the meantime, Ethiopia extended a hand of friendship to pro-Western Kenya – a neighbour of Somalia with a large Somali minority population living in areas along the frontier. Kenya tried to serve as an honest broker in the dispute over the Ogaden (on the strength of its common pro-Western ties with Somalia) and although no significant progress has been made, the overall level of tension in the region has been reduced. A civil war in Somalia in 1990–91 led to large numbers of refugees crossing into Ethiopia, only to die along with the millions starving as a result of the Ethiopian conflicts.

Rumbling tension

These conflicts on the Horn of Africa must rank as some of the most cynical and complex. Yes, the famine in Ethiopia is horrific, but so much of it seems due to war and irrational policies of various warring factions. Even the Superpowers have been at their most cynical, switching sides in mid-war. The Horn of Africa is an uncomfortable place on which to be perched.

Famine and cynicism

Reading

M. Bell, *Contemporary Africa* (London: Longman, 1986).

C. Clapham, *Transformation and Continuity in Revolutionary Ethiopia* (Cambridge: Cambridge University Press, 1988).

F. Halliday, *Threat From the East?* (London: Penguin, 1982).

A. Mazrui and M. Tidy, *Nationalism and New States in Africa* (London: Heinemann, 1984).

B. H. Selassi, *Conflict and Intervention in the Horn of Africa* (New York: Monthly Review Press, 1980).

Angola and Namibia

Portugal was the last European power to relinquish its colonial holdings in Africa. As a result of the overthrow of the Portuguese dictatorship in April 1974, independence was granted to a number of African peoples. There followed, in swift succession, a series of explosions of pent-up unrest, with many jagged pieces still causing pain to millions of Africans. The Superpowers were also hit by the shrapnel as they scrambled for 'advantage'. Nowhere was the scramble more undignified or dangerous than in Angola.

From 1655 to 1951, Angola was a Portuguese colony, best known for its slave trade. Between 1951 and 1955, Angola was a Portuguese Overseas Territory and from 1955 to 1975 it was a province of metropolitan Portugal. While their African neighbours almost all obtained independence, three main Angolan Liberation movements developed. *Portugal and the slave trade*

The FNLA (*Frente Nacional de Libertacao de Angola*) was founded in 1962 and based overwhelmingly on the Bakongo tribe (12% of the population) in northwest Angola. By 1975 this group had the largest military force but many of its members were more concerned with establishing an independent Bakongo state than an independent Angola. FNLA support and training came from neighbouring Zaire. *FNLA, MPLA, UNITA*

The MPLA (*Movimento Popular de Libertacao de Angola*), founded in 1956, was a radical Left-wing party which appealed across tribal lines and was the favourite of the Soviet Union. The third movement UNITA (*Uniao Nacional para a Independencia Total de Angola*) was founded in 1966 by Jonas Savimbi, who had left the MPLA in 1964. It was based on the largest tribal group, the Ovimbundu (about 31% of the population) and operated from neighbouring Zambia until 1967 and then from Namibia. In 1974 UNITA was the weakest group militarily and relied on Maoist, guerrilla tactics.

Following the Portuguese revolution, all three movements declared a ceasefire and opened offices in the capital, Luanda. President Kenyatta of Kenya attempted to head off a war between the movements by arranging the Alvor agreement of 15 January 1975, which called for a transitional government to be set up by 31 January and for independence by 11 November. This tripartite government was also to control an integrated armed force. However, the agreement never stood a serious chance of working and open fighting in March made a civil war inevitable. *The Portuguese revolution*

291

The initial gains by the FNLA led the Soviet Union to increase supplies to the MPLA, although Moscow had originally supported the Alvor agreement. In August, the United States sent supplies to the FNLA and large quantities of Soviet arms went to the MPLA in September and October. China had also been involved as a supporter of the FNLA but abandoned competition with the Superpowers when the level and pace of aid went beyond its meagre resources. In October 1975, South African troops invaded in force in support of UNITA, making rapid advances towards Luanda. Soviet arms and Cuban troops were then airlifted to the MPLA. The FNLA was virtually eliminated and the South African/UNITA threat in the south was contained. The MPLA, which controlled Luanda, declared independence on 10 November and received still more Soviet aid to defeat its opponents. The presence of South African troops on Angolan territory helped galvanize African states' support for the MPLA and the OAU also recognized the MPLA régime. South African troops withdrew to form a cordon sanitaire on Angola's southern frontier with Namibia.

Events in Angola also had an important impact on Superpower relations. For critics of East–West détente in the mid-1970s, it was a symbol of Moscow's perfidy and Western weakness in the face of a relentless Soviet drive to expand its influence around the globe. For others, Angola was a symbol of a misguided attempt to extend East–West rules of détente to a messy civil war, the outcome of which was basically irrelevant to the overall Superpower balance. In the end, the Angolan events dealt a serious blow to détente. Only during the Carter administration (1976–80) did American policy towards Angola soften and American oil interests in Cabinda province were expanded. Soviet influence remained but the primary Communist ally was Cuba which maintained 25,000 troops in Angola. It was ironic that Cuban troops should guard American oil workers in Cabinda but pragmatism rather than the clash of ideologies was clearly a more reliable guide to the causes of events in Angola.

Cuban troops remained in Angola for a variety of reasons. Militarily, they helped ensure the stability of the régime and protect it against South African raids on SWAPO camps in Angola. The most serious military threat continued to come from UNITA rebels operating in strength in southern Angola.

In 1989, as the Superpowers retreated from direct engagement in such conflicts, they also nudged their friends to the negotiating table. In June 1989 a cease-fire was negotiated but it quickly collapsed when UNITA refused to have its forces integrated with the government's. But on 1 May 1991, a peace agreement was reached as a result of Portuguese mediation and Superpower pressure. It provided for a merger into a national army and multiparty elections to choose a new parliament and president in late 1992. The UN would supervise the ceasefire, much as it did in nearby Namibia.

Namibia (Southwest Africa) had been ruled by South Africa, despite the lapsing of its League of Nations Mandate. After decades of fighting the Southwest African Peoples Organization (SWAPO), South Africa finally accepted UN involvement in organizing genuinely free elections in November 1989. SWAPO won a slight majority but would clearly have to work with the South African-backed Democratic Turnhalle Alliance in managing the transition to a new constitution and government without South African troops.

To an independent Namibia

The progress in Namibia, as in Angola, had much to do with the new wave of great power détente in 1989–90. Without major supporters that can be played off, the local actors have to get down to the tougher business of finding a local settlement. If conflict continues, it is now far harder to blame anyone except the locals.

Reading

C. W. Freeman, 'The Angola/Namibia Accords' *Foreign Affairs*, Summer 1989.

A.J. Klinghoffer, *The Angolan War* (Boulder, Colorado: Westview, 1980).

J.A. Marcum, *The Angolan Revolution II* (Chicago: University of Chicago Press, 1978).

R. Green, *Namibia* (London: Longman, 1982).

I. Griffiths, *An Atlas of African Affairs* (London: Methuen, 1983).

A. Mazrui and M. Tidy, *Nationalism and New States in Africa* (London: Heinemann, 1984).

K. Sommerville, *Angola* (Boulder: Westview, 1986).

The Organization of African Unity

The idea of Pan-Africanism is only a creation of the early-20th century. Not surprisingly the idea has been ruined in a continent divided along tribal, cultural and linguistic lines. Unfortunately, there is more that divides than unites Africa and the divisions seem to be growing ever deadlier.

Founding the OAU   Various competing attempts were made in the late 1950s and early 1960s to overcome the legacy of colonial conflict and illogical boundaries. But with rapidly accelerating decolonization, the need for a regional organization became more urgent. The Organization of African Unity (OAU) Charter was signed by thirty-two heads of state in Addis Ababa on 25 May 1963. At its inception, the OAU was a compromise between those, such as Ethiopia, Liberia, Nigeria and Somalia, who wanted a loose association of states, and the supporters of a more integrated, federal Africa, such as Ghana, Guinea and Morocco.

Agreed objectives   The agreed objectives of the OAU were to promote African unity, coordinate efforts to improve living standards, defend the sovereignty of states and eliminate colonialism. Unlike other regional groupings such as NATO or the EC, the OAU was given no role in collective security or economic integration. Its working languages are African but also the old colonial English and French. The heads of state are supposed to meet annually and the Council of Ministers every six months. However, getting together round one table has proved difficult; at the 1976 summit, for example, a mere seven of the forty-seven heads of state turned up. When they do meet, fist fights in the debating chamber are regular events. But OAU members do take the organization seriously. In 1979, Liberia spent half the government budget on holding the annual conference and in 1980, even poorer Sierra Leone spent two-thirds of its budget.

No real unity   Unity and common sense have so far largely eluded the OAU. While it was fairly easy to agree on the need for decolonization, it has proven far more difficult to manage disputes that have since arisen among dissatisfied sovereign neighbours. Most troublesome and bloody of all have been the effects of conflicts within individual member states which spill over into international conflict.

OAU success   Of course, the OAU has had some success. One of its main tasks was the support of anti-colonial struggles and that process is virtually complete. Although the struggle was mainly waged inside individual states, the OAU served as a persistent advocate of the cause. Its Liberation Committee, although chronically short of funds, coordinated external aid to a number of liberation struggles. The OAU has also succeeded in playing 'honest broker' in relatively simple conflicts. It played a useful role in the Algeria–Morocco frontier dispute, setting up a mediation committee in November 1963, which arranged a ceasefire in 1964 and a border settlement in 1968. In the Gabon–Equatorial Guinea dispute over islands, the OAU commission defined the maritime frontier in 1972. Above all, the OAU has been useful in upholding the principle that despite unjust colonial frontiers, existing borders in Africa are to be maintained.

Civil war and OAU unity

However, it was this very principle of the sanctity of frontiers that hurt the OAU in the Nigerian Civil War in 1967–70. Although some OAU members supported the secessionist state of Biafra, secession was rejected in principle by the OAU. It therefore could not be a broker in this cruel conflict. Similarly, the OAU sat on the sidelines during the Angolan Civil War in 1975–6 and when Tanzania and Uganda went to war in 1978. It did help arrange several truces between Ethiopia and Somalia in their dispute over the Ogaden but it lacked the power to see that the truces were enforced.

At a standstill

While sitting on the sidelines has caused embarrassment to the OAU, more recent African conflicts have brought the organization virtually to a standstill. The question of seating SADR over Moroccan objections in the early 1980s eventually culminated in Morocco's withdrawal in November 1984. Earlier summits had already been abandoned or crippled by the deadlock. In 1983 Libya opposed the Chad delegation led by Hissein Habré and ended the already unlikely prospect of Pan-African efforts resolving the Chad issue. In December 1985 the OAU-arranged uneasy ceasefire between Mali and Burkina Faso (formerly Upper Volta) broke down. Five days of fighting between two of the world's poorest states was ended by pressure from local states and the pathetic performance of what passes for the armed forces of the protagonists. The civil war in Liberia in 1990–91 pushed 750,000 refugees into Sierra Leone and the Ivory Coast, but the peacekeeping force that came to help was from the sixteen-member Organisation of West African States.

Concentrating on development

In part because of such debilitating disputes, the 1984 and 1985 OAU summits agreed to concentrate on problems of development rather than politics. Certainly Africa had every reason to develop real cooperation. In a continent where it is often easier to fly to neighbouring states via Europe and merely 5% of trade is between African states there is plenty of scope.

Coming of age

The OAU's attempt to ignore political disputes and concentrate on basic cooperation may well mark its coming-of-age. Clearly there can be no return to the early, heady days of the OAU when the issues seemed sharper (anti-colonialism) and its leaders, (Nasser, Nkrumah, Haile Selassie) had a clearer vision of the future. Now not even the Superpowers are much interested in Africa, and they are especially not interested in becoming embroiled in local conflicts. Aid is being cut and the failure of Africans to help themselves with sensible economic policies and greater democracy only strengthens 'compassion fatigue'. With growing instability, endemic coups, serious environmental problems, and an inclination on the part of much of the developed world to concentrate on their own 'developing world' in Eastern Europe or Southeast Asia, the OAU seems likely to remain a mirror of the problems and disunity of the continent.

Reading

M. Bell, *Contemporary Africa* (London: Longman, 1986).

P. Calvocoressi, *Independent Africa and the World* (London: Longman, 1985).

L. Cockcroft, *Africa's Way* (London: I.B. Tauris, 1990).

D. Lamb, *The Africans* (London: Methuen, 1985).

A. Mazrui and M. Tidy, *Nationalism and New States in Africa* (London: Heinemann, 1984).

G. Naldi, *The Organization of African Unity* (New York: Mansell, 1989).

C. Young, *Ideology and Development in Africa* (New Haven: Yale University Press, 1982).

Index